A SHORT HISTORY OF
AFRICAN
AMERICAN
LITERATURE

Other Books in the Series

A Short History of American Literature

A Short History of Australian Literature

A SHORT HISTORY OF

AFRICAN AMERICAN LITERATURE

Nandana Dutta

Orient BlackSwan

All rights reserved. No part of this book may be modified, reproduced or utilised in any form, or by any means, electronic or mechanical, including photocopying, recording or by any information storage and retrieval system, in any form of binding or cover other than in which it is published, without permission in writing from the publisher.

A SHORT HISTORY OF AFRICAN AMERICAN LITERATURE
ORIENT BLACKSWAN PRIVATE LIMITED

Registered Office
3-6-752 Himayatnagar, Hyderabad 500 029, Telangana, India
E-mail: centraloffice@orientblackswan.com

Other Offices
Bengaluru, Chennai, Guwahati, Hyderabad,
Kolkata, Mumbai, New Delhi, Noida, Patna

© Orient Blackswan Private Limited 2024
First published 2024

ISBN 978 93 5442 433 5

Typeset in Simoncini Garamond Std. 10.5/13 by
Akhil Offset Printers, Hyderabad 500 020

Printed at
Shree Maitrey Printech Pvt. Ltd., Noida

Published by
Orient Blackswan Private Limited
3-6-752 Himayatnagar, Hyderabad 500 029, Telangana, India
E-mail: info@orientblackswan.com

The publisher has endeavoured to ensure that the URLs for external websites referred to in this book are correct and active at the time of going to press. However, the publisher has no responsibility for the websites and can make no guarantee that a site will remain live or that the content is or will remain appropriate.

Contents

Map of the United States of America	*vii*
Acknowledgements	*ix*
Introduction	*xi*
1. Sustaining Culture *The Oral Tradition*	1
2. Struggling for Literacy and Literate Identities *Slavery and Freedom: 1619–1865*	22
3. Up from Slavery *Reconstruction to the New Negro Renaissance: 1865–1919*	67
4. Cultural Awakening *The New Negro or Harlem Renaissance: 1919–40*	101
5. Modernism *1940–65*	142
6. Pride and Anger *The Black Arts Era: 1965–75*	173
7. New Directions *The Contemporary Period: 1975 to the Present*	199
8. Conclusion	260
Index	271

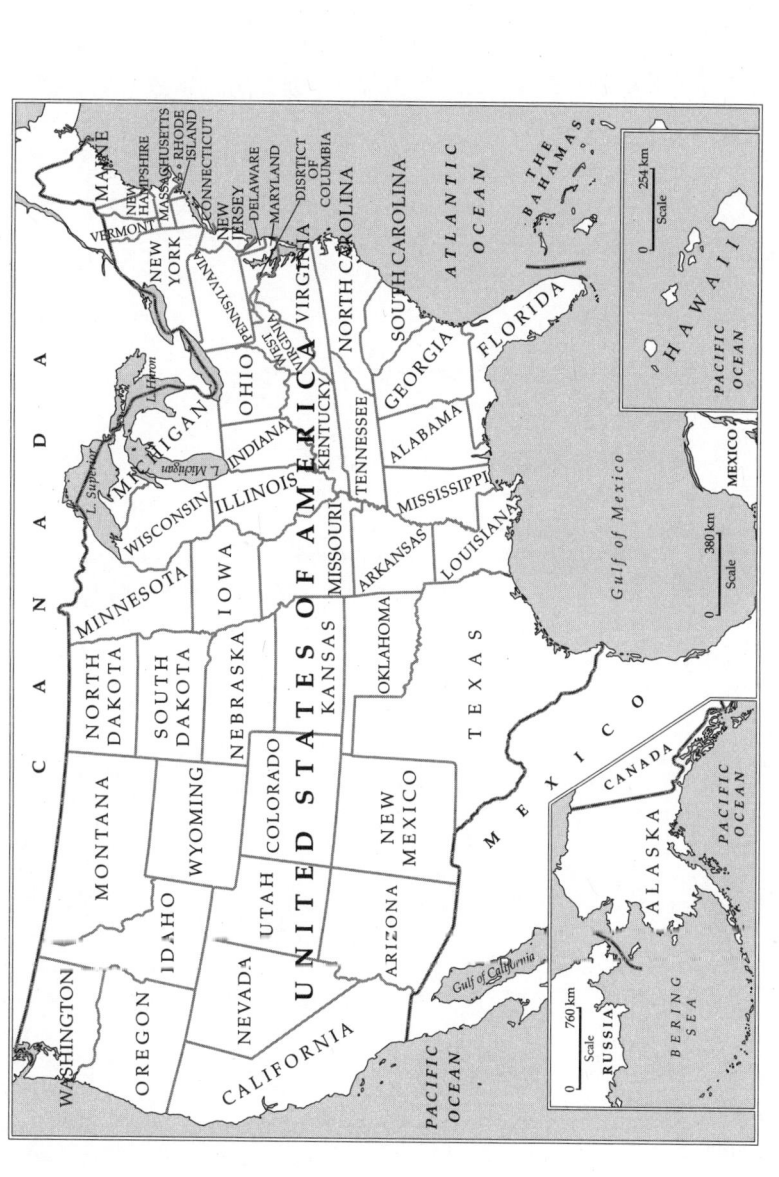

Acknowledgements

I would like to thank Sreenath and Orient Blackswan for continuing to ask me to write on American literature. This book owes its existence to their belief in this project. I am grateful to Mahalakshmi who meticulously copy-edited the manuscript.

My interest in African American literature has its beginnings in the works of Richard Wright that I borrowed from my teacher, friend and now retired colleague Aparna Bhattacharyya, who was then completing her PhD on Wright. Subsequently I read from her great collection of African American neo-slave narratives. I thank her for this and for her support of every project I have embarked on.

I thank my friends and colleagues in the Department of English at Gauhati University for their often unknowing contribution to the work.

My final thank you is to my brother Utpal, for sharing in the many ideas, pedagogical issues and unexpected childhood memories that the process of writing threw up.

Introduction

African American literature has been written against many kinds of challenges. The primary one, of displacement, has occupied considerable space in the imagination because of its scale, organisation and thoroughness. It is documented that "[d]uring the 350-year history of the transatlantic slave trade, Europeans made more than 54,000 voyages to and from Africa to send by force at least ten to twelve million Africans to the Americas. Scholars estimate that close to 400,000 Africans were sold into slavery in North America, the large majority ending up in the American South" (Andrews, Web n.p.).

But the compelling factors for the developing trajectory of the literature were not always only slavery and race issues, but also the more general developmental and economic challenges faced by a growing nation. While the early experiences were those of slavery and racism, as we enter the twentieth century, other, more complicated issues arise. Growing militancy, the leadership of Malcolm X, the alternative tantalisingly offered by the Nation of Islam, the radicalism of the Black Panthers, and above all the opening up into international intellectual circuits – of Modernism, of political awareness, the affiliations to Marxism, travel, especially to France and Russia and the Caribbean, the labour movement worldwide – all of these produced responses that shaped literary representations. The participation of African Americans in these processes brought them under the surveillance of the FBI – headed at the time by J. Edgar Hoover – a surveillance that determined what came to be published and read (See for instance, Maxwell). Writers from the time of the Harlem Renaissance to the era of the Black Arts Movement came under the scanner, and their writings were minutely studied by Hoover's spies who looked for signs of sedition and threats to the idea and entity of the US. These were unexpected difficulties, way beyond the known oppressions of slavery and the discriminations of racism. If the earlier literature emerged against those overtly violent processes, changing conditions of life and relationships, and the growing complexity of the impulses to resist and counter as new modes of discrimination cropped up, saw engagements that were intensely political. The political became a position, a critical mode and a literary sensibility, revealing hidden aspects of the conditions of African American lives.

Dickson Bruce Jr. finds "the origins of African American literature to be in a process in which black and white writers collaborated" (ix), and speaks of "webs of interaction among African Americans and between black and white Americans that encouraged literary endeavor" (x) in the emergence of an authoritative African American voice. Bruce Jr. highlights "interaction" as crucial to this emergence, claiming that "traditions for an African American voice were shaped during the colonial era by English literary conventions, African and African American oral traditions, religious developments involving blacks and whites alike, and ambiguities in race relations, all interacting to create new literary forms and possibilities" (x). In a very different and newer work, Gene Andrew Jarrett (2011) too looks at interactions and exchanges between key figures, ideas and positions. A central idea that runs through most histories is the way in which African American literary work became an integral part of the American nation-building project through interpretations, representations and critiques of racism and slavery, even as it shaped an African American voice and identity. Bruce Jr. notices "the development of an authoritative black persona and the emergence of a distinctive black perspective on events" (xi). Others have looked at (1) the autobiographical impulse and mode as a way of organising African American literature (for example, Olney 1974, Andrews 1993), (2) the ideology of resistance and the blues (Baker Jr. 1985), (3) signifying as a critical and creative practice, (4) engaging with the past through indirection and humour (Gates 1989). Still others have studied the African American male Other through neglected authors in order to present a much greater diversity than usually acknowledged (Hogue 2003), and used feminist lenses for a gendered reading of the literature.

Slavery, racism and the idea of racial difference are engaged with in unique and different ways by writers of each period that is demarcated by historical events or by significant cultural movements. Forms of negotiation with the past, and with folk and oral culture are incorporated into writing. The representation of the black body makes the sheer physical/sexual brutality of slavery palpable while use of black speech in poetry, drama and fiction lends style and distinction. Toni Morrison captures the way oral folk elements that formed the cultural and emotional bases of the community, would be integrated into the writing: "If my work is faithfully to reflect the aesthetic tradition of Afro-American culture, it must make conscious use of the characteristics of its art forms and translate them into print: antiphony, the group nature of art, its functionality, its improvisational nature, its relationship to audience performance..." (in Sale 41).

Beginning in the memories of stories and songs in lost spaces, that music remained in the literature. The dialect evolved in a process of engagement of African languages with English and became a unique and distinctive thing. The stories of animals in clever and humorous narratives were an aspect of the resistance that an enslaved people put up – to keep themselves whole and to find a space that they could own. Orality, music, writing – these were a progression but also a composite, a simultaneity of effects that marked everything they wrote and said and felt. In one impressive gesture, through the painful medium of the slave narratives, evolved two of the major forms of this literature – the slave narrative and the autobiography.

Worth noting further is the basic performative element of this culture – the use of bodies and voices as critical, creative impulses. Against these foundational conditions and forms, poetry, fiction, autobiographies and drama developed. The circumstances available for writing also meant that other forms like the speeches delivered in the lecture circuit, sermons, pamphlets, and journalistic pieces also came to be composed. And perhaps among the most important of nonfictional, ideological writings were the literary manifestoes about race and creativity, like the statements of Du Bois and Angus Wilson on black theatre and its central role in the life of the community, or of Langston Hughes on the obstacles that the fact of race placed before the black writer. The cultural-activist approach saw the setting up of organisations and sites like publishing houses, newspapers and magazines, and playhouses that enabled different forms of racial uplift – all serving to distinguish African American cultural experience and free it from the stereotypes fashioned by whites as mechanisms of control.

The sense of community and shared suffering, collective memory and trauma, resistance and resolve, and the formation of identities as the race moved into different phases of experience are fundamental themes in this literature, as are themes of mobility, transnationalism and identity.

The *idea of community* has remained a constant in the history of the race. It has been both theme and condition, enabling and enriching writers. From the time individuals were captured and held in transit spaces on the African coast and then loaded into the holds of ships for transport to the American (and Caribbean) slave markets, the experiences of physical and mental suffering, dehumanisation, uncertainty about the future, and longing for the homes and lives of an African past, were similar. Community is first evident during the Middle Passage when people from several African tribes and groups who had been captured or sold to slave traders, were thrown together on ships that took them across the Atlantic Ocean to the Americas and the West Indies: "European captors often forced the African captive to sing and dance on the decks of slave ships in order to preserve the health – and therefore the value – of their human cargo" (Jones, Jr. 16). Jones, Jr.'s essay cites Alexander Falconbridge, a surgeon, who worked on the late eighteenth century slave trade, on this practice. This eyewitness account of the slave trade and slave suffering is available at https://www.pbs.org/wgbh/aia/part1/1h281.html with details of suffering that only a doctor would notice and understand. The site offers unexpected riches including a song on the loss of a young boy Equiano – apparently on the disappearance of Olaudah Equiano from his home and village in West Africa. The forced performances as also the compulsions of having to live together from the time of their capture until they were separated and sold in the slave markets forged bonds "across clan and tribal lines". Jones, Jr. insists that it was the coerced performances that "fostered racial solidarity" (17) and also that "the on-deck performance constituted one of the 'simple but cooperative efforts . . . [that] may be viewed as the true beginnings of African-American culture and society'" (Mintz and Price [*The Birth of African-American Culture: An Anthropological Perspective*] in Jones, Jr. 16).

Over the years such collectives and communities transformed in the details, taking on new ideological emphases and projects, but by and large the cultural history of the race can be seen as one of people working together – not just in the precarious togetherness of the plantations, but equally in the efforts to escape where community is about collaboration and support (the Underground Railroad is a symbol of such collaboration in the pre-Civil War years). Subsequently, the fellow feeling, and awareness of the importance of collaboration as well as the imagination of freedom and what it would mean, saw them working towards this goal through publishing houses, magazines and journals, anthologies, educational institutions, and cultural and political organisations, all contributing towards the formation of a narrative of racial uplift and enlightenment, directed at the formation of agency and identity. Even where the individual leader or intellectual articulates the effort, it is always towards the betterment of the race. Much of the literature is expressive of this sentiment. Setting, the ubiquitous feature of the novel form, here becomes the setting of slavery and racism, and the individual story hardly ever remains that. It is almost always the collective experience that is exemplified in stories like the one told in *Beloved* and this aspect is clearly pointed to by the author either within the text itself or through innumerable historical paratexts. The shared circumstances bound the people together even as they constituted collective memories, and after they had moved out of the era of slavery, the persistence of racism and discrimination kept the memory of past horrors alive.

Community ensured feelings of brotherhood/sisterhood, enabled acts of helping each other to escape (as seen in the accounts of Douglass, Jacobs and many others), the setting up and conduct of the Underground Railroad and solidarity during work and punishment. It marked celebrations, and songs and dances on the plantation, and especially in the slave quarters, while forcing recognition of the shared *precarity* of such moments. As a fundamental feature of life and work and moments of joy, it became an obvious and important theme in literature, a nuanced idea that is visible in the way literature came into being, in the forms that came to be shaped, and in the particular way memory works as 'rememory' – Toni Morrison's innovative concept of a collective remembering. It is evident, therefore, in the content of the literature as well as in its formal innovations that are often drawn from community cultural practices. The slave narrative – the history of which is marked by different kinds of collaborative efforts to bring it to a reading public, not least of which was its place within the abolitionist cause – represents a particularly good example. It is an idea that is sought, as in a community of and with readers; it is what is depended on for support and strength and well-being; and it appears in the collective forms of the oral that constitute a perennial source of inspiration – in the blues and jazz, folk tales, gospel music, the spirituals and sermons – forms that originate in collective life and have been infused into the body and soul of this literature. So the great literary genius is one who has best embodied the collective experience in highly individualised stories and emotions. And the best representations of the collective experience have also explored the ways in which community has been shadowed by the penal practices within the institution of slavery – punishment of those who have aided escapes or have in some way stood with another – practices that have tried to prevent community and solidarity.

Community awareness is artistically expressed through the blend of individual stories with collective history and experience, and in the shared intonations of black speech. The personal is a powerful perspective on the community's collective life and this is seen running through all of the literature. Community feeling and a sense of the need for empowerment and upliftment for the entire race were compulsions in the discrete educational programmes set out by Washington and DuBois, one determined to make his people technically skilled and employable, the other speaking of 'soul' as the necessary goal of education.

A second broad theme is that of *mobility*, with corresponding mobility effects. It begins from the displacement of a people from their homes to an alien land. The sea journey to America is the primary movement for the race, followed by the stasis of life on the plantations. Capture, adventures among the Native Americans, and journeys to England and Europe with or without their masters are all seen. There is the special case of Olaudah Equiano whose journey and subsequent life in Europe was driven by exceptional individual resolve. Up to the Civil War, mobility for the African American was mostly in bids (often, but not always, successful) to escape from plantations and move to the North. Escape and its recounting in the form of the slave narrative became the preeminent form of this period. Subsequently, movement was to the northern cities, and for many, to the West. In the early twentieth century, Harlem emerged as an urban refuge and site of cultural efflorescence for free and newly freed African Americans, and as a destination for new immigrants from the Caribbean, becoming a fertile ground for the mix of cultures. Physical mobility was accompanied by other forms of liberation. Education freed many from the stasis of the dark early years. Freedom was both of body and of the mind. And as the twentieth century progressed, the transnational became a major element of this basic theme as the traffic in people between and amongst countries and continents increased.

Meanwhile, at the heart of the pre-Civil War stage of slave history was the Underground Railroad – constituted to aid escape, and made up of disguised travel routes, safe houses and aid along the way, and stealthy movement till the successful escapee arrived in the cities and towns of the free states. Water, as in rivers to be crossed or to be used as a route, swamps to hide in, or to throw off the scent of pursuers with dogs, finds representation throughout the literature and especially in the slave narratives, as an element of mobility. Eventually the theme expands to include marches associated with political and cultural programmes. Mobility is also the circulation of art and ideas. Amiri Baraka's poem "Black Art" moved around magazines and anthologies, becoming one of the most widely travelled poems during the Black Arts era. Howard Rambsy II uses two terms, transmission and socialisation, to denote the processes through which poems and other art reached readers and audiences – "*transmission* refers to the material production and circulation of writers' compositions. *Socialization* connotes how writers interact with fellow writers, audiences, and various discourses" (4, original emphases).

A third overarching theme that is evident from almost the start of this literature is that of *identity,* as slaves and free men and women of the community sought ways to represent themselves – as Africans (through changing terms like coloured, Negro, Black and African American), as Americans, as educated and cultured, as transnational individuals, and as preachers, teachers, and professionals – to counter the 'single' identity as slave. And yet the past as a collective experience and collective memory is an integral aspect of many of these self-constructions. In a sociological study of slavery and its collective remembering as cultural trauma, Ron Eyerman has written:

> The trauma of forced servitude and of nearly complete subordination to the will and whims of another was [thus] not necessarily something directly experienced . . . but came to be central to their attempts to forge a collective identity out of its remembrance. . . slavery was traumatic in retrospect, and formed a 'primal scene' which could, potentially, unite all 'African Americans' . . . whether or not they had themselves been slaves or had any knowledge of or feeling for Africa. (1)

The history of the race inflected the thinking and writing of even those who had not directly suffered slavery. Shared remembrance across generations and spaces functioned as a bond for the community that is most vividly illustrated in literary works of different periods.

The idea of a collective trauma that is a constant in African American history would account for the unforgettability of the past and its repeated return in literature. Even when, during the Harlem Renaissance, Modernism, the Black Arts Movement, and other cultural phases we find writers who prefer to analyse the present or look towards redemptive experiences that include transnational engagements or the formal and thematic concerns of Anglo-European literary Modernism, there is a running element of trauma. And in the 1970s and after there is a concerted effort to recall the past in the powerful form of the neo-slave narrative. Collective memory and collective emotion therefore add fresh dimensions to the theme.

The identity of the African American individual is a stitching together of many fragmented selves. The self, shattered by years of racist perception and treatment, psychologically scarred and physically brutalised, has to remake painfully and slowly, a new self out of these materials. The healing is always incomplete, and the rupture caused by the traumatic past remains, as in the branching 'chokecherry' tree left as a remnant of whipping on the back of Sethe in Morrison's novel, *Beloved,* where the wound may have healed but the flesh carries this visible trace. It is both metaphor and embodied reality, as the self that was fragmented by shame and debasement and physical torture, tries to re-make itself against its ever present reality.

Alongside these themes and preoccupations that mark the literature and provide it with subject matter is one important feature that is common to all genres – the *performative*. Having its deep foundations in orality, in songs and tales and dances remembered in mind and body, the performance aspect of the oral in devices like call-and-response, and in the tone and rhythm of music and dance, was always available to draw on for developing distinctive styles of writing. The insertion of performative elements in writing became a common practice. The emergence of theatre as an instrument of public expression, but also as a mode of conversation amongst playwrights, directors, actors, and the audience, saw the performative become a crucial part of exercises in racial upliftment and consciousness raising, even as it served as a site for innovation and creative interpretation of race history and contemporary race issues.

While *community, mobility* and *identity* are overarching themes, resistance to oppression and tyranny, and the struggle for dignity and voice are important features that derive from and are closely enmeshed in them. Each theme develops through aspects of victimhood and the transcendence of this state, and each of the periods we look at has key institutions and effects, like religion and the black church, the printing presses, educational institutions, cultural organisations that conducted writing programmes, and theatre groups and workshops that enabled overcoming and transformation as well as cultural development and articulation. There is, therefore, growing diversity and complexity as the literature moves through various periods and historical changes.

The literature that came out of pain, suffering and efforts to mitigate these was bound to be *political*, containing resistance and critique. Politics was practice and cultural strategy. The first use of politics is subversive – in the making of an image of the self that is grateful and submissive and mostly speaks of black suffering tangentially. The style of response known as *masking*, often seen in the slave narratives, is one form of this subversive politics and it grows in sophistication as we move towards the Civil War. Following the war, the banning of slavery, the years of reconstruction, and the gradual access to education and employment, politics is in the adaptation to new conditions. Booker T. Washington's programme of clever manouevering is an example, where the African American is urged to improve himself/herself without giving offence, acquiring skills in certain professions and taking jobs at the lower levels of the economic scale. The more overt and oppositional politics emerges in the critiques by Ida Barnett and others who responded angrily to the violence against free blacks in cities like Memphis. Then there is the philosophically robust resistance exemplified in the works of Du Bois that counters Washington and provides another model for the next generation. With the turn of the century and greater opportunities, protest becomes more systematic and intellectually ambitious, and ideas of separate nation, back to Africa and other militant positions replace the earlier more accommodative ones.

Slave revolts (there were many of these right from the start, and from the eighteenth century onwards they were often the subject of plays), collective protest, and increasingly gathering groundswell of action that would result in the efforts at upliftment and reconstruction after the Civil War, especially in programmes for education of the newly freed slaves, were represented in writing but were also aspects of the conditions of textual production. The slave narratives – written or dictated 'after' escaping or being freed, for instance, were in equal measure accounts of slave experience and examples for the community. They addressed white and black alike with different but equally compelling agendas. In their headnote to Du Bois in the *Norton Anthology*, Gates Jr. and McKay claim that Du Bois was able to neatly bring together individual and community experience: "It was Du Bois's genius to realize that to protest the color line most effectively and originally in a new century, he had to find ways to personalize it, to make its reality not merely a social and legal fact but a profound psychological factor in the African American's sense of self and relationship to society" (607). Such an agenda represents the ways in which the history of the race and especially the sufferings of slavery were incorporated into literature, as the direct experience of slavery receded and became part of individual and collective memory.

Literary historians Abby Arthur Johnson and Ronald Maberry Johnson have noted the contending pulls of literature written for individual satisfaction and literature written in support of the race. Both these impulses persist, because the collective goal of uplifting the race is fundamental and remains as a political understructure in all of the literature. The individual artist who reflects on the practice of literary art is in fact articulating the politics of presenting the African American race as capable of producing great art that is on par with art produced by whites.

Through these processes of engaging with the circumstances in which they found themselves at different stages in the history of America, and with the collective memory of the near and distant past, African Americans fashioned themselves and their literature.

1

What is it then that distinguishes African American literature? Even as the story will vary in the periodisation generally accepted today (and represented in this book), if we take as a point of origin the oral forms and storytelling traditions that tell of the trickster who always triumphs by using his wits against stronger adversaries, and note the circumstances of life for slaves on the plantations – we find distinctive modes of narration that incorporate elements of the oral (particularly, call-and-response, the assumption of a shared tradition and performances), and a certain mood or overall feeling that is in equal parts tragic and comic, and that eventually found expression in the blues. Twenty-first-century African American studies, which acknowledges melancholy as its defining feature (see Crawford), is in this tradition, the mood defining the conviction that forms of racism still stalk the African American community and find reflection in the literature. These two modes are crucial to the kind of story that African American literature tells, *has* to tell, which involves suffering, endurance, overcoming, keeping the spirit alive and the important role of laughter, the ironic and the comic emerging from the tragic depths of slave experience. Storytelling is crucial for a people who were denied writing – storytelling that preserved memories of lives left behind in Africa, but that was also necessary to bear witness, and record the present life of the race. Such narrative desire is evident in the transition from the oral to the written and the simultaneous existence of the oral and the written in the forms of literature. It is Toni Morrison who once again eloquently expresses this simultaneity and illustrates its use in her novels. African American writing, she says, has "to be both print and oral literature: to combine those two aspects so that the stories can be read in silence, of course, but one should be able to hear them as well" (Morrison, "Rootedness" 199).

These dynamics might be said to account for the nature of this literature, the styles adopted but also what was said and how these were conceived and reached final expression.

Related aspects are the importance of religion/Christianity, the complicated gender and race relations, especially sexual relations between the master and the female slave, and the resulting mixed children that would eventually lead to other kinds of phenomena – like "passing" seen in Nella Larsen's novel of that name, but also in many other texts presenting racial mixture and miscegenation; in the emergence of the "mulatto" in Langston Hughes's poem and play of that name; and a more complicated issue of intraracial attitudes – an example of which can be seen in Dorothy West's sharply ironic novel *The Living is Easy*.

Since this book is organised by period and chronology we will also note how each period, broadly classified by historical or historical-cultural events, has its own set of characteristic features that resulted in unique literary efforts – unique in style, subject matter and overall intention, and in the way all of these elements came to be balanced by authors in each phase of development.

2

Since this is a literary history written from the outside, without the passion of 'authentic', felt, experiential, physical and emotional engagement, and written for a readership that may be coming to the literature for the first time, it is necessary to look for other points of connection. The India connection of African American literature is not extensive but there are interesting points of contact.

A letter that was written by B. R. Ambedkar to Du Bois (the letter and Du Bois' response are reproduced in an article on the website of the South Asian American Digital Archive or SAADA), refers to the similarity between the condition of "the Untouchables in India" and the "Negroes in America" and makes a request for a copy of the petition made by the National Negro Congress to the UN. Du Bois replies with sympathy, showing awareness of the untouchable problem, and promises to send the detailed petition to be prepared and presented before the UN by the NAACP. According to the author of the SAADA article, Manan Desai, there is no record in this archive of further exchange between the two men. Du Bois also solicited a piece from Mahatma Gandhi (and later from Rabindranath Tagore) that he reproduced in his magazine, *Crisis,* with accompanying commentary. Following the assassination of Mahatma Gandhi in 1948, Du Bois wrote a longish piece as an obituary and tribute, that was published in *Unity,* calling Gandhi "a leader in the peace movement and also a leader in the rise of the colored peoples" (2).

In another article, Manan Desai analyses the Marathi critic Manohar Namdeo Wankhade who did a PhD in American literature from the US and then wrote extensively on the Dalit literary movement in Maharashtra, drawing parallels between the trauma of the Dalits and the African Americans, and using one to understand and articulate the other (Desai, "Caste in Black and White").

Some of this work grows out of a fascinating dissertation that Desai wrote on the US and South Asia connections in the twentieth century when many Indians were visiting the US and/or studying at US universities. He maps the trajectory of these associations: from engaging with the African American subject as a way to reflect on the "Untouchable *problem*" in early observers, to the search for a *solution* to it in Wankhade and writers like Namdeo Dhasal influenced by his powerful writings (Desai, "The United States of India" 151, emphases in original). These cultural encounters perceived the African American oppressed figure as a companion and fellow traveller in the efforts to process, understand and articulate Dalit experience.

The parallels between the Dalit and African American experience have continued to be of interest in studies of oppression. One of the recent works representing this trend is Isabel Wilkerson's *Caste*. And Namdeo Dhasal, Dalit poet and activist, and Raja Dhale, writer and activist, founded the Dalit Panthers in 1972, clearly modelling the movement on the Black Panthers.

The expansion of the literary and the range of its circulation way beyond the conventional definitions of literature and the changing nature of readership or audience are factors that influence reception. If such changes appear to be a twenty-first-century phenomenon, their beginnings are traceable to the last years of the twentieth century with challenges to the printed book, changes in understanding of the literary canon and of what constitutes good or bad literature (mainly through a postmodernist rethinking of hierarchies and binaries), changes in reading habits and taste and in the nature of the readership. At the same time the twenty-first century has been a critical time for people around the world, with terrorist attacks, natural disasters, poverty, discrimination and distress graphically brought into our homes and lives by television channels and even more intimately by social media. The meanings of literature in this climate are no longer the old and expected. And the audience or readership of literature is unexpected to say the least. Who reads what, and where? To what end? And have forms of reading also changed? Do we read in the same ways any more? The availability of the audio book, of excerpts from literary texts online, the summaries and notes provided in Google and the proliferating industry in lessons on YouTube, have stretched the limits of what constitutes reading.

Even if a literature (of a people or a country) is read as part of an academic course, the character of the location determines reception and interest. The prescribed text generates enthusiasm only if it also speaks to the reader, appeals to her emotions, and helps engagement with and understanding of the contemporary. In this view how does African American literature come to us now, at this point in our national life and in this state of our discipline?

Racism as an element in the life of the African American people is regularly reinforced. Episodes of racist violence and prejudicial treatment are reported frequently and also find place in social media. Barack Obama tweeted after the police murder of George Floyd in Minneapolis: "we have to remember that for millions of Americans, being treated differently on account of race is tragically, painfully, maddeningly 'normal' – whether it's dealing with the health care system, or interacting with the criminal justice system, or jogging down the street, or just watching birds in a park" (@BarackObama. . . 29 May "My statement on the death of George Floyd").

The history of racism is not of the past, not over and done with. It is still there and it returns every once in a while to remind us of the sleeping monster at the heart of civilisation. The knowledge of it and the constant reminder and power of its effects decides, colours, shapes, and gives muscle and rhythm to this magnificent literary culture. The lessons of interracial relations, and power relations amongst unevenly positioned entities, are there for all races and cultures of the world. Emotional intelligence, the lesson we learn from the study of literature, gives us glimpses of the possibility of a sympathy that cuts through differences. The history of the African American people and their culture speaks to us particularly as we rue the endemic disparities of India, the lynching of vulnerable individuals by groups or mobs, the misery and distress of the poor, the unemployed, the dispossessed and the displaced. As every new incident of racial violence (institutionalised or directed by individuals) involving African Americans as targets is reported, for us in India a corresponding incident and image is likely to swim up before our eyes. The reason and the politics behind these are not the subject of this book. But as readers we are attuned to find both similarity and difference – the similarities are our route into the unfamiliar and strange, and our sympathy and interest in this literature is whetted by such correspondences.

As we read with interest the literary representation of experience, the literary working out of pain and suffering and the evolution of new forms and styles and strategies – as exercises in coping, and surmounting and emerging triumphant – it is simultaneously an exercise in understanding of ourselves and the situations that we engage in. It is this transformative process that the reading of a literature of this kind promises

For Indians, the early exposure to African American life and culture did not always come from the literature. It was the sporting icon, the musician, the charismatic leader who first captured our imagination, often in the pages of the magazine *SPAN*. Or we discovered them in stray references and characters in books by white authors. In *Uncle Tom's Cabin*, we had the experience of what is called the kind master who was equally caught up in the system as were the slave traders, drivers and catchers. Through Mark Twain's *The Adventures of Huckleberry Finn* we met Jim whose fatherly presence gives the young Huck the sense of love and protection that he never received from his own father. In Harper Lee's *To Kill a Mockingbird* we encountered slavery and racism in its harshest form, even as we met the character of Mammy (as well as the notion of stereotypes with which one race made sense of another) in the monumental and hugely popular *Gone with the Wind*. Much of this also had to do with the libraries we had access to and what these stocked. The rich children's library that I grew up with in Shillong had one of Joel Chandler Harris's collections of folktales, and Brer Rabbit and his gang, the trickster (so familiar from our own folktales) and other figures never appeared to us as coming from a different culture. They were all stories – seen on the same plane as other folk and fairy tale collections that sat side by side on the library shelves.

Then there were films like *Color Purple* and *Sister Act* and fan moments for the fantastic Whoopi Goldberg; or the feel-good movie *Hidden Figures* (2016; dir. Theodore Melfi) where three black women who work at NASA find grudging acceptance for their exceptional talents. The permission to use the white washrooms is a concession that echoes the ironic twist at the end of Mari Evans' poem "Status Symbol": "They" give the "Negro" the status symbol: "the key to the White Locked John" (Norton 1808).

Our notion of the literary in the departments of English in higher education institutions in India is often somewhat nebulous. Because of this perhaps we have had a fascination for the sociological and historical as an engine of development and change in literary history, demonstrated by the PhD dissertations on authors and their times, by the way we teach in context-heavy mode, and by the comfort felt by our students when they can move from the literary or formal and aesthetic to the contextual, historical and biographical. Given the nature of syllabi in English departments in India, African American Literature has featured only as a few texts in American Literature courses and has sat alongside courses on Indian English Literature (including translations from Indian regional literatures), postcolonial literature, North-East Indian English literature (in the Universities of India's northeastern states), Dalit literatures and so on. Unconsciously (but frequently with some deliberation on the part of syllabus makers) this has set up comparisons and connections, one literature often seen in the light of the others.

Besides some distinct connections like those between Du Bois and Gandhi, and Du Bois and Ambedkar mentioned above, and the example of the Black Panthers in the formation of the Dalit Panthers, there are other, lesser known similarities of experience. One of these is the instance of the transport, by steamer of indentured labour from places in Central India to the tea plantations in Assam. These men and women, who were virtually captives, were transported in conditions reminiscent of the Middle Passage and the bodies of those who died during the journey were cavalierly thrown overboard into the waters.

This kind of evidence and suggestions of affinity and connections (admittedly not always substantiated by concrete documentation), is part of the challenge of writing a literary history that will be of use to new readers.

Recent works like *The Other Slavery* by Andres Resendez on the enslavement of Native Americans raises questions about how slaves felt about other slaves and dispossessed peoples. The horrific tortures that many of the literary texts reveal would possibly account for the fact that this and other literatures that have emerged out of oppression experiences are marked by considerable self-obsession. This is true of Dalit literature and much of the writing emerging out of India's North East. The comparative strain is more apparent once the transnational element becomes part of African American life, as many travel abroad, are exposed to other literatures and encounter others who have also suffered. The extension of African American identity in the twentieth century to a wider black identity with the inclusion of other and newer kinds of discrimination from different parts of the world has inflected and helped develop ambitious new interpretations of the traumatic race history in the US.

The evidence of research done in books like *The Other Slavery*, representing scholarship that throws unexpected light on the race question, makes it necessary to ask: how does this surrounding, sometimes tangential work show up the core issues of this literature anew? These perspectives also suggest the need for an approach that extends comparison to other fields of traumatic experience that would lessen the singularity of pain that this literature often seeks to project. Community as an idea and a condition that sustained the race is also exclusive. Excessive trauma turns the individual inward to the self, and the injustices directed at it perhaps inures one to another's pain. Something like this, an ambivalent, confusing response, might also account for the open-eyed reporting of violent and disturbing moments in the slave narratives – beatings and burnings and tortures on the human body, one's own and those of others.

Textbooks have their limitations and are particularly expected to be responsible in offering information, acquainting readers with the basics of a field and, in the case of a literary history, a chronology that recognises beginnings, developments and shifts. They are bound by such pressures and are often compelled to go with the most well established pattern even while recognising the cutting edge work that might destabilise and introduce more complex ways of reading.

Perhaps what is needed is a politically inflected writing of literary history. Jarrett, who is clearly writing a political history, uses the now increasingly acknowledged notion of "emergence" – identifying "flashpoints", "the process by which someone or something emerges or bursts into action or being, not out of nothing but transformed from one form to another; and it refers to the powerful effects of that emergence or transformation" (Kazanjian 27, cited in Jarrett *Representing the Race* 17). This method is demonstrated in his building of chapters around the dialogue/exchange/conversation between major figures in each period – Jefferson and David Walker for instance in the first chapter, but also in interaction with political and cultural organisations and societies as in the case of Douglass with several such sources of discourse. Jarrett shows how this is not simply a progressive story of protests, resistance and empowerment but, as he declares of the plan of his book, "racial representation has long succeeded as an intellectual and cultural genre of political action in African American history". So Jarrett's literary history is also significantly an intellectual history that embodies politics and is the domain of both the elite and the popular (*Representing the Race* 11). It is aware of the point raised by Eddie S. Glaude that what is needed (in a tangent from the Black Studies Movement) is "'a form of political engagement that steps out of the shadows of the black freedom struggles of the 1960s and 1970s, which would recognize the diversity of African American political interests'" (Glaude, *In a Shade of Blue: Pragmatism and the Politics of Black America*, in Jarrett 14). However, while recognising the significance and rationale for such histories, this book stays with its brief – that of providing a short introduction.

3

The understanding of literature against a rich and complex background is a growing trend in the writing of literary history today. Recent studies in the field show literature as a product of its milieu and this includes the market, the reading habits of a time and the many other socio-historical and cultural pressures that prevail in a period. One of the significant theoretical developments that has contributed to this multifaceted understanding of literature has been New Historicism which "reinstated the cultural field to which the text had originally referred" (Kaes 150). It "expands the terrain normally covered by literary history", enables literary studies to "deal with representations which have a social as well as a textual dimension" and encourages an "associative way of presentation" (Kaes 156).

Mario J. Valdes and Linda Hutcheon sum up what goes into the writing of literary histories: "The 'history' of literature is, in fact, the multiple and complex histories of its production, but also of its reception" (2). They also speak of "the move from the more traditional *national* model of literary history to a 'comparative' one" (2; original emphasis) which is "literary history . . . both made possible by and even demanded of our age of international information access and electronic technology" (4). The transition from national to comparative models is seen in the expansion of the category of race as it was understood up to the early years of the twentieth century, to include all those who arrived from other non-white spaces and the changing character and extent of the race as their writings were included as part of a much expanded category of black writing. This expansion has been an ongoing process and the infusion of fresh insights from people who have experienced racism under colonialism, or under neo-colonial processes, but have had no experience of slavery and its specific experience of oppression, continues to enrich the literature.

Valdes and Hutcheon suggest that this new perspective must take account of "economic, political, and broader cultural and social perspectives on issues like race or gender. . . . Newly theorised by post-colonial and gender theorists, these perspectives help make conscious the ideological underpinnings of the experience of producing and responding to literature – and of writing literary histories" (2).

For instance, Bruce Jr. locates the origins of African American literature in a historical context that includes, among other things, African and American oral traditions, European conventions, American race relations, and political activism and he speaks of "interactions and exchanges" (x). The backdrop for the emergence of this literature is now no longer just the site in which slavery prevailed but includes the African locations from which slaves (who were often from prosperous and powerful tribes and families) were brought, as well as Britain where many Africans ended up and where the publication industry and the travel accounts by those who had either worked in or had business interests in Africa contributed to discourses about Africans, establishing their distinctive appearance, their colour and their 'inferiority'. It is also the story of the continuing arrival of Africans who are captured and brought forcibly much after the actual period of slave holding is over. Zora Neale Hurston recounts the story of Cudjo Lewis or Kossola-O-Lo-Loo-Ay (alive at the time she did her research) who she interviewed over a period of three months in 1927. He was "the last known surviving African of the last African slaver – the *Clotilda*" as Deborah G. Plant says in her Introduction to *Barracoon*. He tells Hurston the story of the slave trade that tribes found so profitable and engaged in late into the nineteenth century, often for settling inter-tribal disputes – in his case between the powerful Dahomey and the Takkoi – declaring that it was his own people who had sold him into slavery (Hurston).

The primary challenges in literary history writing are the organisation of the literature and accounting for its development. How does the literature come about and how should it be written about? In a classic study of the field, *Is Literary History Possible?* David Perkins states his version of this problem that underlines the argument of his book: "The aspects it concentrates on are two: the aporias of form or, in simpler terms, the insurmountable contradictions in organizing, structuring, and presenting the subject; and the always unsuccessful attempt of every literary history to explain the development of literature that it describes" (ix).

What should literary histories of other literatures be like when written by outsiders? Issues of access, empathy, interpretative cultures and a constant comparative impulse are likely to arise as also a consciousness of the target readership that might encourage an over-enthusiastic attempt to make the literature familiar and ordinary. The question of who reads and why is also rendered crucial when it is so easy to appropriate, and frame within an institutional, scholarly apparatus which can familiarise, explain, and explain away too much. Keeping this literature unfamiliar, keeping it perhaps 'uncomfortable' so that it appears fresh and interesting at every reading might be what is needed.

A 2017 special issue of the journal *American Literary History* on new black literature points to "audience engagements, including efforts, often bodily efforts, to translate and make meaning" (Crawford 780). Besides, there are issues of periodisation, of which author goes into which period, especially when many authors straddle two periods, beginning in one and writing well into the next.

Above all, of course, is the issue of selection. How much is enough, given that an entire literature must be taken account of? Why are some authors included and not others? What really is a 'representative selection'?

A Note on the Volume

As literary history writing has transformed, the form of narrativisation (or letting the history speak for itself) has given way to a more self-conscious narrative. One of the features of writing that is discernible in newer histories is the citation of sources for the information presented – something that students who have learnt their literary histories from traditional works might not be familiar with. There is reference to works of scholars without which this history would not be possible.

Online sources are listed wherever these are available so that readers may use this volume as a step towards more detailed readings. In case of the oral and performative forms, websites where they can actually listen to the recitation of oral forms are given since the flavour of the oral is difficult to capture in the written.

Black English – an area of distinctive and independent research – is only touched upon (as information). We all recognise it, realise its distinctiveness and see it in the styles of contemporary speech even as we note how internal this is to the community – a community of speech to which others do not always have access, something that is especially true for readers in India. Its representation in written literature is evident and the recognition and appreciation of it is very much part of the pleasure that this body of writing offers. "Black America, Black English, Black Dialect, Black Idiom, Ebonics", called "'the language of soul'" by Geneva Smitherman (1, in Stoudamire n.p.), is defined by her as "'a language mixture, adapted to the conditions of slavery and discrimination, a combination of language and style interwoven with and inextricable from Afro-American culture'" (3, cited by Stoudamire n.p.). According to Stoudamire:

> [I]n order to communicate with other Africans from various areas in Africa and with their enslavers, the Africans created their own speech community by inventing a language. The pidgin language that the Africans produced combined syntactic and grammatical features of various West African languages with English words and grammar. Africans substituted English words for West African words but retained many of the phonetic and grammatical structures of West African languages. (n.p.)

This suggests a degree of complexity that would require a very different kind of linguistic-cultural research and is beyond the scope of this volume.

One particular use of terminology in the volume calls for some explanation. The term African American, while most widely employed now, is also often accompanied by another term, black. In order to get some clarity into this usage and my own recourse to both terms, we might go back to a comment made by the Reverend Jesse Jackson in a December 1988 news conference: "To be called African-American has cultural integrity," Jackson said. "It puts us in our proper historical context." He refers to other examples of hyphenated Americans, and how "they connect their heritage to their mother country and where they are now" (cited by Martin 83). This is useful. The historical shift from 'colored' to 'Negro' to 'Black' to 'African American' as well as 'people of colour' (to refer to other racial origins) marks the changing nature of identity. But this book has generally gone with the popular usage of African American for people born in the US and descendants of the original Africans brought from Africa, whereas Black is a term that has also had specific cultural importance (see for example terms like "Black Arts Era" or "Black Studies") while also indicating later arrivals who have not had the same historical experiences as the African American. The terms change with the chronological-historical development of this book. 'Black' has also been used in terms like 'black body', 'black speech' as well as in the black-white binary. Noting how these terms appear in extant scholarship, I have tried to use them as naturally as possible, in the manner of the critics cited throughout the book.

One other area that has not featured as a separate category is that of the popular. Some of the popular writing like romances, detective fiction, science fiction, and children's fiction are occasionally referred to, but given the volume of such work it has only been possible to register their presence.

While the intention of this book is certainly to establish the uniqueness of African American literature for Indian readers, the fact of its setting, for us, within the wider field of American literature is unavoidable. We need to see it in this setting to appreciate its difference and understand its urgencies and its character. The developments in American Studies – especially what has been called a "transnational turn" that "effected the most significant reimagining of the field of American studies since its inception" (Pease 1) – have facilitated rethinking in ways that have made the field more hospitable to those of us who do English on its margins. Within this turn, the theme and fact of mobility (Kunow) is particularly useful, connecting us as it does to a similar transnational mobility that recent histories of African American literature have established as a key element of how it evolved. The two related themes of transnationality and mobility are therefore kept in mind while writing this history, besides questions of identity, freedom and agency, as well as the continuous assessment of slavery and its oppressive effects on the body and soul. Since these do not appear in the same way for all texts or authors, chapters will refer to them as and when they become relevant.

Further, as this is a chronological account, genres are attended to in different periods, though a particular genre may dominate a period or alternatively may be a minor practice alongside other genres, and this may have to do with both the period and individual authors. Therefore, as an author is discussed there would be mention of all the genres in which s/he wrote.

Chapters have generally followed the periodisations now commonly accepted and found in authoritative anthologies of African American literature like the *Norton* (the single volume first edition and the two-volume one that followed) and the two-volume *Wiley Blackwell* anthology. Each chapter covering a given period is written around crises – which is sometimes in the form of an event or often that of a condition or state – like slavery, Civil War, life on the plantations, the abolishing of slavery, Reconstruction and the disillusionment following its failure, struggles for uplift, the rise of militant protest, and finally the Black Lives Matter movement, the women's renaissance and the role of diasporic writers originally from the West Indies and subsequently from various African countries.

The chapter divisions are chronologically set, but within each age the chapters break across the chronological, allowing themes and ideas to determine their shape. In a way, therefore, the chapters are both continuous and linked as well as self-contained. In writing about each of the selected authors, a brief biography is usually provided while giving a sense of the corpus of a writer's works.

One important point that has decided the amount of biographical information or the discussion of literary works, is the easy availability of such information. A minimum is given, keeping in mind that in the process of reading some of this information might be relevant and the text may be read without frequent interruptions for searches. But a literary history in the era of the Internet is by definition more indicative, pointing out what can be found and studied on one's own.

With regard to in-text citations, shorter texts are cited from the Norton and Wiley anthologies and text citations appear with the anthology name and page number. Where the introductory material from these volumes is cited, the editors' names are used. So (Norton 10) and (Wiley 1, 17) appear for texts but (Gates Jr. and McKay 10) and (Jarrett 10) would mean that it is editorial material that is cited. Further, these books are listed in Works Cited against the editors' names. There are multiple Jarrett books for which shortened titles are used. Kevin Young's Library of America anthology of African American poetry has been the source for many poems and these are cited from Young. Most of the fiction and drama discussed has been either from print copies or from e-texts available online. For the *Cambridge History of African American Literature (CHAAL)*, the paginated Kindle text is used and is indicated as such.

Finally, African American literature is usually a miniscule component in a small portion of the English Literature syllabus – American Literature – at BA (Honours or Major) and MA levels in English Departments across the country. Students might occasionally discover it through stray texts that make an appearance in the Indian book market, feature in book reviews, or because a particular book suddenly becomes a bestseller and points the way to others. This book is written for such a reader, the information given on life and texts determined primarily by the need to make available a basic introductory text that will give a sense of what this body of writing is like, expecting the interested reader to follow up on texts and areas that are mentioned or only briefly discussed.

Works Cited

Andrews, William L. "An Introduction to the Slave Narrative". *Documenting the American South: North American Slave Narratives.* At (DocSouth), a digital publishing initiative sponsored by the University Library at the University of North Carolina at Chapel Hill; it also provides access to digitised primary materials that offer Southern perspectives on American history and culture.

———. *African American Autobiography: A Collection of Critical Essays.* Englewood Cliffs, NJ: Prentice Hall, 1993.

Baker Jr., Houston A. *Blues, Ideology, and Afro-American Literature: A Vernacular Theory*. Chicago: Chicago UP, 1985.

Bruce Jr., Dickson D. *The Origins of African American Literature, 1680–1865*. Charlottesville and London: UP of Virginia, 2001.

Crawford, Margo Natalie. "The Twenty-First-Century Black Studies Turn to Melancholy". *American Literary History*, Vol. 29, No. 4 (2017). 799–807. doi:10.1093/alh/ajx032. Advance Access publication October 16, 2017.

Desai, Manan R. "The United States of India: South Asian Translations of America, 1905–1974" (Diss. 2011. now available as a book).

———. "What B. R. Ambedkar Wrote to W. E. B. Du Bois". (April 22, 2014). N.p. https://www.saada.org/tides/article/ambedkar-du-bois.

———. "Caste in Black and White: Dalit Identity and the Translation of African American Literature". *Comparative Literature* (2015) Vol. 67, No. 1. 94–113. https://doi.org/10.1215/00104124-2862043 .

———. *The United States of India: Anticolonial Literature and Transnational Refraction*. Philadelphia: Temple UP, 2020.

Du Bois, W. E. B. "Gandhi". *Unity* (1948). Du Bois Papers>Series 3. Articles>Gandhi. credo.library.umass.edu/view/full/mums312-b210-i001. Also at digitalcommons.org

Eyerman, Ron. "Cultural Trauma and Collective Memory". *Cultural Trauma: Slavery and the Formation of African American Identity*. New York: Cambridge UP, 2002. 1–10. (Chapter available at www.cambridge.org).

Gates Jr, Henry Louis. *The Signifying Monkey: Towards a Theory of Afro-American Literary Criticism*. New York: Oxford UP, 1989 (25th edition, 2014).

Gates Jr, Henry Louis and Nellie Y McKay. Eds. *The Norton Anthology of African American Literature*. New York and London: W.W. Norton & Company, 1997.

Hogue, Lawrence W. *The African American Male, Writing and Difference: A Polycentric Approach to African American Literature, Criticism, and History*. Albany: SUNY Press, 2003.

Hurston, Zora Neale. *Barracoon: The Story of the Last Slave*. Foreword Alice Walker. Ed. Deborah G. Plant. London: Harper Collins, 2018.

Jarrett, Gene Andrew. *Representing the Race: A New Political History of African American Literature*. New York and London: New York UP, 2011.

Johnson, Abby Arthur, and Ronald Maberry Johnson. *Propaganda and Aesthetics: The Literary Politics of Afro American Magazines in the Twentieth Century.* Amherst: U of Massachusetts P, 1979.

Jones, Jr. Douglas A. "Slavery, Performance, and the Design of African American Theatre". *The Cambridge Companion to African American Theatre.* Ed. Harvey Young. Cambridge: Cambridge UP, 2013.

Kaes, Anton. "New Historicism: Writing Literary History in the Postmodern Era". *Monatshefte.* Vol. 84, No. 2, New Historicism (Summer 1992). 148–58.

Kazanjian David. *The Colonizing Trick: National Culture and Imperial Citizenship in Early America.* Minneapolis: U of Minnesota P, 2003.

Kunow, Rudiger. "American Studies as Mobility Studies: Some Terms and Constellations". *Re-Framing the Transnational Turn in American Studies.* Eds. Winifred Fluck, Donald E. Pease and John Carlos Rowe. Hanover, New Hampshire: Dartmouth College Press, 2011. 245–64.

Martin, Ben L. "From Negro to Black to African American: The Power of Names and Naming". *Political Science Quarterly.* Vol. 106, No. 1 (Spring 1991). 83–107. https://doi.org/10.2307/2152175

Maxwell, William J. "African American Modernism and State Surveillance". In *A Companion to African American Literature.* Ed. Gene Andrew Jarrett. Oxford and Malden: Wiley-Blackwell, 2013. 254–68.

Mintz, Sidney and Richard Price. *The Birth of African American Culture: An Anthropological Perspective.* Boston, MA: Beacon Press, 1992 [1976].

Morrison, Toni. "Memory, Creation and Writing". *Thought: Fordham University Quarterly.* Vol. 59, No. 4 (December 1984). 385–90.

———. "Rootedness: The Ancestor as Foundation". *African American Literary Criticism, 1773 to 2000.* Ed. Hazell Arnett Ervin. New York, NY: Twayne, 1999. 198–202.

Olney, James. *Tell Me Africa: An Approach to African Literature.* Princeton: Princeton UP, 1974.

Pease, Donald. "Introduction". *Reframing the Transnational Turn in American Studies.* Eds. Winifred Fluck, Donald E. Pease and John Carlos Rowe. Hanover, New Hampshire: Dartmouth College Press, 2011.

Perkins, David. *Is Literary History Possible?* Baltimore and London: The Johns Hopkins UP, 1992.

Rambsy II, Howard. *The Black Arts Enterprise and the Production of African American Poetry.* Ann Arbor, Michigan: U of Michigan P, 2016 [2011].

Sale, Maggie. "Call and Response as Critical Method: African-American Oral Traditions and Beloved". *African American Review.* Vol. 26, No. 1, Women Writers Issue (Spring 1992). 41–50. https://www.jstor.org/stable/3042075.

Smitherman, Geneva. *Talkin and Testifyin.* Boston: Houghton Mifflin Company, 1977.

Stoudamire, Shawnkeisha. "From the African American Oral Tradition to Slam Poetry: Rhetoric and Stylistics". *McNair Scholars Journal.* Vol. 16 Issue 1, Article 10 (2012). http://scholarworks.gvsu.edu/mcnair/vol16/iss1/10 Accessed 5 May 2020. n.p.

Valdes, Mario J. and Linda Hutcheon. "Rethinking Literary History – Comparatively". American Council of Learned Societies (ACLS) Occasional Paper No. 27. n.d. 1–13. https://tspace.library.utoronto.ca /bitstream/1807/4355/4/rethinking%20literary%20history%20 -%20comparatively.pdf.

Waugh, Patricia. "Discipline or Perish: English at the Tipping Point and Styles of Thinking in the Twenty-first Century". *Futures for English Studies: Teaching Language, Literature and Creative Writing in Higher Education.* Eds. Ann Hewings, Lynda Prescott and Philip Seargeant. New York and Basingstoke, Hampshire: Palgrave Macmillan, 2016. 19–38.

Wilkerson, Isabel. *Caste: The Lives That Divide Us.* New Delhi: Allen Lane, 2020.

CHAPTER 1

Sustaining Culture
The Oral Tradition

Oral culture has played a sustaining role in the life of the African American people. From holding a community together through shared remembrances of traditions left behind in Africa, and acting as an outlet for emotions that were otherwise suppressed by slavery, the oral tradition – made up of different kinds of expressive forms – has been present from the earliest times and has often run alongside the written tradition, influencing and enriching it, and providing succour and emotional support to a people facing the multiple traumas of slavery and racism. So while there are forms that are closely linked to the work situations on plantations, there are others that have evolved out of the interaction of lives and cultures. Work songs, corn ditties, folk tales and ballads, sorrow songs (evoked by Du Bois in *The Souls of Black Folk*) and spirituals that reference the Christian God and carry images evoking rest and final joy in heaven, are all part of early African American culture. Subsequently, the gospels carried church singing to many levels of sophistication, while the emergence of blues and jazz show an increasingly complex musical repertoire that seems to grow organically out of varied experiences of sorrow and joy. Aspects of this tradition cannot, therefore, be fixed in any period. Though many may have emerged in very specific places and contexts and times, variations have reappeared in later times and other places. These forms are important to acknowledge because they contributed powerfully to sustaining the community's spirit and unity while providing a continuing resource to subsequent cultural work in the literary and performance genres.

This brief chapter takes a look at some of the forms that begin to be seen and heard from the earliest experiences of Africans in America and then continue to grow and evolve alongside the written tradition. Much of it is difficult to date and sometimes has been given the date of the first collection. Work songs, corn ditties, ballads, spirituals and tales seem to have appeared early on during life and work on the plantations. The spiritual became available in a collection for the first time in 1801. Gospel music came much later, in the early years of the twentieth century. All of these, however, share the unique characteristic of having embedded details from the lives of slaves, their relations with their owners, the daily sufferings on the plantations, and the cruelty that found expression not just in beating and torture but in the poor quality of food and clothing. The blues and jazz forms, sophisticated expressions of mood and style, evolved out of deep tragedy and drew on these earlier traditions. All of these were significant influences on the written tradition and often came to be incorporated by authors. Frederick Douglass recounts the story of slaves singing on their way to another plantation; trickster figures inflect the representation of protagonists as literary forms developed; and blues and jazz lent their emotion and character to all literary forms. Langston Hughes, Richard Wright, Ralph Ellison, James Baldwin, Toni Morrison, August Wilson among many others, were influenced by elements of this tradition – especially its musicality – and found ways to use and transform them. If the slave narrative is the quintessentially African American literary form, the vernacular tradition fed the latent genius of the people as they found in it sources of unique expressive language and blistering content. It is also necessary to note that elements of many of these forms as well as their characteristic sounds or speech also found their way into the work of white writers – Mark Twain's awareness of racial difference in *The Adventures of Huckleberry Finn* is expressed not only through the presence of a character like Jim, but in the superstitions, fears and rituals to counter them that find believers in the slave and the white child, and in racial terms like 'nigger' and 'slave' often used in the text. William Faulkner's fiction is immersed in southern plantation life with its typical black characters and rendering of black speech (besides his infamous statements in support of slavery that invited sharp and angry criticism from the likes of Du Bois and James Baldwin).

1

The *Norton Anthology of African American Literature* suggests the constitution of a vernacular tradition (also sometimes described as "black talk", folklore, low and popular culture) out of these oral creations that is ongoing – beginning in a time before writing but becoming a strong parallel tradition. The denial of education, writing and other cultural possibilities and outlets sent the slaves back to memories of life in Africa, of songs and stories carried in the mind through the Middle Passage and into the plantations, and kept alive as a source of joy, community feeling and hope. The *Oxford Bibliographies* entry on this tradition characterises it as made up of "linguistic elements from African Languages, black English, creole, pidgin English, patois, and various dialects, as well as forms such as oral epics, folktales, the dozens, signifying, call and response, improvisational practices, sermons, line dances, ring shouts, cyphers, and music genres such as spirituals, gospel, blues, jazz, rap, hip-hop". It is seen to be both old and modern/postmodern. It "shifts and morphs across geographical spaces and bodies." And "[T]he aesthetics can be classified as southern, northern, western, transnational, local, secular, sacred, digital, analog, visual, or musical" (Horton-Stallings n.p.). This story of connections is what the retrieval of the early oral literatures of the Africans in America indicates and it is such an awareness that shows the value of the oral forms we discuss in this chapter.

Retrospective effort – the gaze back from the present that imaginatively reconstructs the earliest years of African life and pushes back the story of African American creative activity to the period of earliest arrivals – has been significant for the writing of literary histories of Africans in America. A huge scholarly programme that became systematic for the first time during the Harlem Renaissance, uncovered, compiled, anthologised and gave visibility to the oral forms that sustained the enslaved from the early years of separation from homes, families and land, while tracking and recording emerging new forms. The important role played by the oral in emotional and cultural sustenance is evident in the use of folklore and many of the early forms in the written literature from the eighteenth century onwards. As Shirley Moody-Turner writes of the crucial place of "black folklore in African American literary texts", it was an exercise "not solely driven by aesthetic motives, but [is] almost always part of a larger social, cultural, and political conversation centered on issues of survival, representation, self-determination, and freedom" (201).

The oral mode has been recognised as an important form of communication in and among the countries of Africa and one that has not been displaced by the written. The oral is dominant in "all aspects of linguistic behavior in African life and cultural expression", is "a major component of the cultural capital of African societies" and serves as "a primary foundation for the black imagination in the New World" (Irele 21). The oral has its own unique features which are realised in performance. For example, "the narrative strategies of even the simple folk tale always involve the incorporation of songs by the storyteller, accompanied by refrains from the audience, both forming an antiphonal pattern – the 'call and response' pattern that has endured in African American performance styles" (Irele 25).

F. Abiola Irele, distinguished scholar of African folk traditions, points out how "devices such as apostrophe and hyperbole, parallelism, enumeration, repetition and anaphora or iteration generally, and collocations, are reinforced in the oral mode by sound values such as ideophones, onomatopoeia, tonal balance, and effects which are sustained in oral delivery by modulations of the voice" (25). The "institutionalization of literature in oral cultures" involves "a reverence for language" giving "social status and cultural significance" leading to the "'professionalization' of the literary phenomenon" and the place of the "oral bard[s]" or *griots* who not only continue to perform the forms prevalent in a society but also innovate, add and create even as they perform (26). Even more important is their role of preservation – "the griot or dyali of West Africa and the imbongi of South Africa emerge as the guardians of the textual values consecrated by the culture which they preserve primarily through the assiduous use of memory" (26). This reading of the oral retrieves it from the lesser status that it has traditionally been assigned in histories of literature which have concentrated on the written work.

The discovery of the African oral traditions has had significant influence in the way African American literary history has come to be perceived, as it expanded the cultural experience beyond the confines of the American landmass by discovering and establishing links with the African cultures from which slaves were captured and brought. This alternative source succeeded in overturning many of the prejudices and assumptions about the oral while establishing its significance as a continuing cultural resource and inspiration.

The recovery of the oral forms and especially the rejection of dichotomies between prose and poetry in them, has been responsible for the revaluation of the folk literature that preceded and also continued simultaneously with the written. The circumstances of retrieval and the scholarship that has researched, identified, and compiled oral resources has been crucial to the development of literary culture, often as a political gesture of cultural assertion and pride. Compilations of different oral forms served to develop interest in distinctive styles, the assertion of difference from the white settler, and the articulation of oppressive circumstances that compelled the emergence of these forms, even as content and style were established to be an amalgam of African elements carried in the memory of slaves and the English language-based Christian culture to which they had been brought.

Ideas about the value of the word, *Nommo* or the spoken, the style of performance, connotation, the presence and participation of the audience, the call-and-response mode that structures the performances and binds performer and audience – all of these were recognised as essential elements of the oral forms.

Irele discusses the "interaction between form and function in African oral literature": a) "the literary quality of an utterance, whether oral or written, derives in the first instance from the recourse to metaphor, which serves to embroider language as it were, in order to emphasize its evocative and emotive potential" (24); b) "the calculated patterning of language in order to obtain an artistic effect, evident in the prosodic features – such as meter and rime" (25) (songs, call-and-response pattern etc.); c) "the institutionalization of literature in oral cultures . . . In other words, the expressive and aesthetic values embodied in the verbal arts constitute a significant component of the cultural references of oral societies" (26). The figure of the oral bard, the professional storyteller and performer, who preserves texts through a very special work of memory that involves reiteration and transformation is an important element in the performances. Stephen Henderson's "beautiful talk" (in Rickford and Rickford 15), "signifying" (defined by Gates Jr. as "repetition with revision or repetition with a signal difference" xxiv), tonal semantics (characteristic of a tradition of poetry from the beginnings to contemporary slam poetry) and defined by Smitherman as "the use of voice rhythm and vocal inflection to convey meaning in black communication" (134), and "the specific use of stress and pitch in pronouncing words in the black style" (145) are all distinctive elements of the oral performance. These stylistic features suggest the closed community within which performances took place – a fact of life conditions during slavery that determined style for a whole literature. As scholars of such intonational aspects of the oral have established, since these elements are difficult to render in print, they are only discernible by the same speech community (Smitherman, Stoudamire), and knowing the rules for interpreting the vocal inflections is essential for the effect they create but also for understanding their import (many of these forms can be heard online). Subsequently when the oral influences entered written literature, reproduction of the inflections, and pitch and sound effects, especially of black speech, lent a distinctive tone and flavour to the writing.

Given the 250 years of honing a style to record suffering, joy and effervescence, no other literature of a people comes close to the African American in being able to express experience in language and style that is so unique and that is so closely embedded and embodied in their lives. And because it has been an expression not just of actual conditions but of aspirations, desires and appreciation of beauty and harmony, despite the suffering and oppressions, it is not just tragic or angry; it is also full of fun and 'trickery'; full of laughter and exaggeration; it is reflective and philosophical and always a source of knowledge and understanding for its readers/ hearers of the world we live in, black experience that is also universal experience.

Slaves who came to North America during the seventeenth, eighteenth and nineteenth centuries carried with them elements of oral traditions from their African and Caribbean cultures. Many of these evolved into the forms in which they are known today. The African hare and jackal became Brer Rabbit and Brer Fox, but retained many of their original characteristics. The narrative traditions, especially in their performative aspects, forged community feeling and affinities while helping to keep alive the spirit of life and fun amidst sorrows. They often served a more immediate purpose in being used as vehicles for passing on information or messages while making plans for escape. The trickster tales, where the weak Brer Rabbit habitually outwits a stronger adversary like Brer Fox, were expressive of the desire on the part of the slave to outwit the slaveholder. Following the abolition of slavery in 1865 another set of tales with a character named John emerged. John, also a trickster figure, worked on a plantation and was the confidant and servant of the old master – and these stories demonstrate most powerfully the illusion of freedom offered to the slave by the new turn of events. Though John and Old Massa have a benign relationship, the power equation is not significantly different from that under slavery.

These varieties of the oral or vernacular tradition are bound up with the community – living and working together and expressing similar work and life conditions, and therefore recognised and shared by all. The community feeling is also evident in the call-and-response style where the effectiveness of the form depended on the ability of a performer, chorus or raconteur to draw the audience into the performance. One of these practices was that of the "lining-out" where the lyrics would first be called out and then the group would sing the song. Participating in this way and singing a song together would bind the group together and cause an emotional high that found expression in the swaying of many bodies to the rhythm. Form *and* content therefore, held the community together as they performed amongst themselves, secretly, away from the eyes of the masters. Eventually performances in this mode also took place in the black churches. One of the initial reasons for the prevalence and popularity of this practice was the inability to read, though in later times, when participants *could* read, the paucity of printed hymn or song books for each member of a congregation also compelled this practice.

Another aspect of such music is what is called the "ring shout", a form that is indigenous to Central and West Africa but that became mixed with elements of Christianity. "Participants moved in a circle, providing rhythm by clapping their hands and patting their feet. One individual would set the tempo by singing, and his lines would be answered in call-and-response fashion" (www.jazzhistorytree.com). The ring shout has been seen as a unifying element by Sterling Stuckey who also argues that other forms like the field hollers, work songs and spirituals, and eventually blues and jazz, all evolved from it. The "basic elements of the ring shout – dance, calls, cries, and hollers; blue notes; call-and-response; and strong rhythmic aspects" as well as improvisation are all aspects in contemporary music to this date. Dancing and shouting continue in black churches every Sunday and the ring shout continues to evolve ("Harlem Late Night Jazz Presents: Ring Shout", www.jazzhistorytree.com. Examples may also be viewed in the videos available on this site).

2

In the story of how the **oral tales** came to be part of cultural history, the name of Joel Chandler Harris figures prominently. Harris was a white man, a journalist, amateur folklorist and children's author who retold tales using a version of black speech. Though his tales come from a variety of sources – African American, Native American and European – his most famous invention was the storyteller-character of Uncle Remus, an old slave on a plantation who tells the stories to the master's young son. Harris's Uncle Remus originated from "several black storytellers he had met while working from 1862 to 1866 as a printing compositor on Joseph Addison Turner's Turnwold Plantation, outside Eatonton, in Putnam County" but more particularly from an elderly black gardener he met in Forsyth, Georgia, when he was working as an editor from 1867 to 1870, for the *Monroe Advertiser*:

> From 1876 to 1879, during the first phase of Harris's quarter-century career as associate editor of the *Atlanta Constitution*, he wrote for the newspaper several dialect sketches that

portrayed Uncle Remus as a reluctant city dweller who was fond of dropping by the paper's editorial office and sharing comic, philosophical, and sometimes cynical perspectives about city life in what he sometimes called 'Atlanta-Ma-Tantrum'. (web n.p.)

Harris's folktale collection was the largest that was put together in the nineteenth century. His work appeared in several collections. In *Nights with Uncle Remus* (1883), there are three other narrators: "Aunt Tempy, the uppity and privileged cook in the Big House; 'Tildy, the often impertinent house maid; and Daddy Jack, a sagacious old Gullah from the Sea Islands who performs stories complexly counterpointed with musical themes" (Web n.p.). But Uncle Remus remains the best developed and most popular of Harris's storytellers. Harris's original 185 tales were collected in one volume as *The Complete Tales of Uncle Remus* (1955) by Richard Chase.

Other important collections include Zora Neale Hurston's *Mules and Men* (1935), containing stories Hurston collected from Florida, including her hometown, Eatonville, and New Orleans, and *Tell My Horse: Voodoo and Life in Haiti and Jamaica* (1938); Langston Hughes and Arna Bontemps's *Book of Negro Folklore* (1958); and Julius Lester's retelling of the Uncle Remus tales, *Uncle Remus: The Complete Tales* (1999), in which the dialect used by Harris is dropped and more contemporary references are introduced.

While Harris retold one set of tales, inventing and drawing on the traditions he came to know during various stints of journalistic work and visits to the South and its plantations, there were many others that may be categorised as tales of origin, trickery and triumph especially of the weak over the strong, tales featuring supernatural beliefs where evil appears, as do ghosts and spirits, tales that carried lessons about life, and of course, tales about slaves and their masters. The folktales are a composite, made up from memories of similar tales in their home regions of Africa and tales from Native American and European sources that they happened to encounter – all of these woven closely with the actual circumstances of their lives. Besides the famous Brer Rabbit tales, are others like "All God's Chillen Had Wings" or "Big Talk" that are typically humorous, poignant, exaggerated, providing glimpses of the cruelty of masters and overseers on plantations, and the unending hard work that becomes the reason for escape or trickery even amongst themselves. In the first of these tales, the cruel master is a representative type. He overworks his slaves and when they fall from exhaustion, he brings in new Negroes. "One day, when all the worn-out Negroes were dead of overwork, he bought . . . a company of native Africans just brought into the country" and set them to work. A young woman who had a newborn child, and who repeatedly collapsed from the hard work and weakness, turns to the oldest man in the group and he identifies for her the exact moment when she can drop everything and fly away. The old man speaks to his fellows even as the master and overseer identify him as the source of the escapes, and "they all remembered what they had forgotten and recalled the power which had once been theirs". Then they all leap into the air and fly away, clapping and singing (Norton 103–05). "Big Talk" follows the tradition of the tall tale where one "ole nigger" boasts to another that he had told off his master who had annoyed him. His friend, believing him, attempts to do the same and is "whipped nearly tuh death". The first man then reveals: "When Ah cussed Ole Massa he wuz settin' on de front porch an' Ah wuz down at de big gate". The second man retaliates with a similar ruse, tempting the first by bragging that he had looked under ole Miss's drawers and she had done nothing. The first tries it, is beaten and on complaining to his friend, is told that when the peeping episode happened, the drawers were hanging out on the clothes line (Norton 105–06). Others tell of origins. For instance, the hard work that features prominently in many tales, is often given an origin in some aspect of character or luck. In "Why the Sister in Black Works Hardest," the great box, left by God on the road after he finished making the world, that lay there for thousands of years, is finally opened by the "nigger 'oman" who obeys an order from her husband who has been told by the Ole Massa to fetch it. She finds it full of hard work and that is the reason why "de sister in black works harder than anybody else" (Norton 111). In "De Reason Niggers is Working So Hard", God leaves a big bundle and a small one on the road and a black man and a white man run to them. The black reaches first and grabs the big bundle, leaving the small one for the white man. Once the bundles are opened, the black man discovers that his contains a pick and shovel, hoe, plough, and chop axe while the white man finds pen and ink (Norton 114).

Among other oral or 'vernacular' forms are parodies of prayers, sermons and satires. Many of the parodies juxtapose sharp criticism with humour. The well-known prayer, "Our Father Who Art in Heaven..." is transformed in this version: "Our Fadder, Which Art in Heaben! / White man owe me leben and pay be seben" (Project Gutenberg n.p.); or there are unkept promises of freedom made by "ole Mistiss" and "ole Mosser" in "Promises of Freedom" (Norton 39). These songs contain themes of freedom and sometimes betrayal by one of their own (seen in "Jack and Dinah want Freedom" where Uncle Billy, "a mighty good Nigger" informs the master of their plan to escape [Norton 39]), hard labour, one-sided loyalty and most poignantly, the refusal or inability of the master to see the tears behind the laughter (for instance, in "Me and My Captain" [Norton 38], the refrain of "He don't know, he don't know my mind, / When he see me laughing / Just laughing to keep from crying").

Satire, with a combination of derision and flattery was also cleverly directed at the white masters. It had its beginnings in Africa, often composed against the white men with whom Africans came into contact in the process of business, especially during their dealings in the slave trade. It was a form that is said to have been refined by the *griots* who also sang the praise songs, and is believed to have evolved from the culture of lampooning and ridiculing personal action as well as neighbourly disputes, often resulting in corrective moves by individuals and communities (Piersen 166). Satire used parody, imitation and ridicule – but with self-criticism and deflation as its base, it shielded the singer/performer from the possible anger of the master. Piersen suggests that "A satire of a master did not seem so dangerous when it followed on the heels of a self-parody of the slave condition or a series of praise-songs flattering the master's vanity" (166). He gives the following example of a Louisiana slave song where the white man is introduced into the text after the Negro and the mulatto:

Negro cannot walk without corn in his pocket,
It is to steal chickens.
Mulatto cannot walk without rope in his pocket,
It is to steal horses.
White man cannot walk without money in his pocket,
It is to steal girls. (174)

Ballads were sung to celebrate the exploits of larger-than-life figures like Railroad Bill, a black Robin Hood who had many brushes with the law but who always managed to escape, and John Henry, the worker who died in a contest with a steam drill, trying to outdo the machine that was fast replacing human labour. A well-known rendering of the John Henry song is that of Harry Belafonte. Other famous ballads include "Poor Lazarus" that tells the story of the young man shot down by the sheriff and his deputy; "The Signifying Monkey" where the monkey and the lion are engaged in a contest of wits and where the monkey "just kept on signifying," making fun of the lion, playing tricks on him and insulting him; and "Shine and the *Titanic*" where Shine, the black man, refuses to take the Captain's word that the pumps would get rid of the water from the ship and swims away to safety, out-swimming whale and shark and being happily drunk on Broadway when the news of the disaster reaches the country (all in Norton 41–52).

Other verbal forms were children's rhymes, stray lines of advice or sayings, and songs sung to help maintain the rhythm of work and keep tired bodies going through long, hard days.

Negro Spirituals (early versions were called the "corn ditties") were first gathered in book form in 1801 by the black Church leader Richard Allen. They were not only sung in churches or other religious settings but also at bush meetings where slaves gathered to meet one another or to listen to an itinerant preacher. They were seen as a source of solace and escape and sung throughout the day – during work, play and rest. Their themes of escape to a better world, of rest and joy at the throne of a benign and just God and of hopes of being reunited with family and friends clearly emerge from the harsh conditions of slave life – long days of hard labour, the cruelty and injustice of the white slaveholder and the inhuman practice of separating families. A song like "Walk Together Children" (Norton 9), with its refrain at every second line of "Don't you get weary" is as much reality as metaphor – growing out of the weariness and exhaustion of long work days. Similar pictures of slave life appear in other refrains: "Lay dis body down" in "I Know Moon-Rise"; "Didn't my Lord deliver Daniel? / An' why not everyman?" – a sharp query that includes the desire for freedom and equality – in "Didn't My Lord Deliver Daniel?" and "Soon I Will Be Done with the Troubles of the World" (with a refrain of "Goin' home to live with God"). "My home" and "Sweet Canaan" refer to the Promised Land but also express the hope of actual escape across the Ohio river (Norton 10–12). There are references in the spirituals to the Underground Railroad and to water – for example, "Wade in the water, children", repeated twice at every alternate stanza in the five stanzas of "God's A-Gonna Trouble the Water" – that obviously point to the runaway slaves stepping into water to throw off the dogs and masters pursuing them. This song and others like the "The Gospel Train" and "Swing Low, Sweet Chariot" also refer to the Underground Railroad – the network of secret routes, taken by runaway slaves on their way to the free states and Canada, that included various modes of transport, walking, and hiding in safe houses with the help of other slaves and sympathisers. One of the most powerful of the spirituals, "We Shall Overcome" began as a work song, a version of which, "I'll Overcome Someday", was published in 1901 by Charles A. Tindley. It became a Civil Rights song and was adopted by Peter Seeger, the folk singer and activist. It was sung during a strike for higher wages by workers of the American Tobacco Company and was picked up by Zilphia Horton, music director of the Highlander Folk Center in Monteagle, Tennessee, from two of the striking tobacco workers who attended the Highlander workshop where both black and white workers had been meeting for years (for details see Adams, Noah, "The Inspiring Force of 'We Shall Overcome'", www.npr.org). Other evocative spirituals include "I Been Rebuked and I Been Scorned", "No More Auction Block for Me" (that runs through four stanzas expressing the hope that the auction block, the poor food and the slave driver's whip would no longer need to be borne) and "Steal

Away to Jesus", with the refrain, "I ain't got long to stay here", (Norton 10–13).

Gospel music is of more recent origin. Drawing from the spirituals but also influenced by blues and jazz musical styles and use of instruments, it emerged in the Holiness churches, and Churches of God in Christ, especially in Chicago. Gospel quartets and singing preachers are prominent in its history. Gospel singing is rousing, energetic and joyful, full of "bounce and swing" as Sterling Brown puts it, and uses instruments like tambourines, cymbals, trumpets, trombones and bass fiddles (Brown cited in Gates Jr. and McKay 16)

Gospel music has been described as both "a repertoire and a style of singing" (Reagon 5) that is either newly composed or developed out of an existing hymn. It is described as a "song delivered as a high-powered spiritual force, with increased emphasis on vocal rhythms and calculated use of vocal textures to create greater intensity. Basic gospel song musical structures rest on the sacred music traditions within the Black community: congregational style singing with its call-and-response forms, and slow-metered, lined-out Protestant hymns" (Reagon 5).

The first collection of gospel songs was that of Philip Bliss from 1874. Though they emerged in urban churches after blacks fled to the cities of the North, the form really came into its own in the early years of the twentieth century under the influence of blues and jazz styles of vocal and instrumental music. Famous gospel singing groups include Mitchell's Christian Singers, the Golden Gate Jubilee Quartet, and the Dixie Hummingbirds. Among individual singers and composers two were exceptionally gifted: Charles A. Tindley brought together the melodies of white religious revivals and blues and other forms of black music in songs like "Stand By Me", and "Take Your Burdens to the Lord" and Thomas A. Dorsey, who drew on the work of Tindley, on the popular musical forms around him, as well as on his own rich experience as a blues player, composed songs like "Take My Hand, Precious Lord", and "I'm Going to Live the Life I Sing About in My Song". Ralph Ellison, who was also a musician and a student of jazz, has written eloquently in "The World's Greatest Gospel Singer," about the form as an art that employs

> [t]he full expressive resources of the human voice – from the rough growl employed by blues singers, the intermediate sounds, half-cry, half-recitative, which are common to Eastern music; the shouts and hollers of American Negro folk cries; the rough-edged tones and broad vibratos, the high, shrill and grating tones which rasp one's ears like the agonized flourishes of flamenco, to the gut tones, which remind us of where the jazz trombone found its human source. (Ellison cited in Gates Jr. and McKay 17)

It is a dynamic art that continues to grow.

Forms like **blues** and **jazz** (discussed at different places in the book), and **rap** emerged mostly in the twentieth century. They are standalone musical forms that have also lent their characteristics to writing. The blues mood of melancholy, for instance, is a source for the overall melancholic turn in African American studies today (Crawford).

The **blues** began to be heard in New Orleans and the southern United States at the start of the twentieth century. Similar in many ways to the spirituals, they were, however, usually sung by one person to the accompaniment of a guitar and sometimes other instruments. They had the form of a complaint or of a love song that expressed longing for closeness and companionship. And dances that accompanied blues songs were drawn from secular rituals that formed part of after work entertainment. Associated with the name of W. C. Handy, also called the father of the blues, the early lyrics of Handy were "most often twelve-bar forms: three lines of four beats each, the first line repeated twice and followed by a third end-rhymed line" (Gates Jr. and McKay 22). Among Handy's blues songs are "Yellow Dog Blues", "St Louis Blues" and "Beale Street Blues" (a line from which became the title of James Baldwin's 1974 novel, *If Beale Street Could Talk*). Ralph Ellison, who identified the blues mood in Richard Wright's *Black Boy,* gave the following definition in a 1992 essay on that novel that has not been surpassed:

> The blues is an impulse to keep the painful detail and episodes of a brutal existence alive in one's aching consciousness, to finger

its jazzed grain, and to transcend it, not by the consolation of philosophy but by squeezing from it a near-tragic, near comic lyricism. As a form, the blues is an autobiographical chronicle of personal catastrophe expressed lyrically. (cited in Gates Jr. and McKay 23)

Bessie Smith ("Down-Hearted Blues", "Backwater Blues"), Ma Rainey ("See, See Rider", "Prove it On Me Blues"), and Jimmy Rushing ("Good Morning, Blues", "Goin' to Chicago Blues") are famous blues singers who also find frequent mention in literature.

Jazz, a form where the voice was used like a musical instrument, drew on European classical music, opera, and ragtime, besides the various African American musical forms. It emerged in New Orleans in the late nineteenth and early twentieth centuries, a period of tremendous political and cultural upheaval. New Orleans in this period was a multicultural city where people of African, French, Caribbean, Italian, Mexican, Native American and German descent interacted with one another and different musical traditions came together. Jazz lent its name to a period in the early twentieth century, the Jazz Age. It is a style that is improvisatory, with players or singers making up pieces of music on the spot. It is mostly rhythmic, with a forward momentum called "swing" and it uses "bent" or "blue" notes. The call-and-response pattern of oral performances can be heard in jazz where singers, instruments and even one part of the band answers another. Many of the great jazz musicians can be heard doing this (see Ella Fitzgerald and Roy Eldridge do this at "What is Jazz?" in the "National Museum of American History" americanhistory.si.edu which is also a good source for getting a brief history of its development, its character and its major performers). Jazz captures pain and loss as much as celebration and freedom in its tone and character. It is always fresh and every new performance of a jazz song is different from those done earlier. In this it might be compared with Indian classical music traditions where finding their own voice or style is the focus of the best musicians who improvise every time they play or sing a raga and where the structure of a raga and the teaching of a guru work to liberate the musician rather than tie them down. If the slave narrative has been considered to be the quintessential American literary form, jazz is its national musical form and for students of American, and of course African American literature, *hearing* jazz is crucial to understanding and appreciating the literature. The first recordings of jazz were made in 1917 and thereafter this music spread all over the world. Some of the great musicians whose names are associated with the development of jazz are Louis Armstrong, Duke Ellington, Charlie Parker and Miles Davis, John Coltrane, and Ella Fitzgerald (a survey is available here: "The Best Jazz Musicians of All Time: 40 Legendary Jazz Artists" by Matt Fripp, www.jazzfuel.com).

Jazz entered literature in many ways. Critics have identified jazz as "the alternative to the angst" found in European and white American modernists (Leonard 291). Langston Hughes wrote about it in his essay "The Negro Artist and the Racial Mountain" as the expression of Negro life and soul. Hughes also incorporated jazz situations and rhythm in poems like "Jazzonia" where an overt sexuality is expressive of an assertion of freedom in the bold eyes of the dancing girl as she dances to the music played by "six long-headed jazzers". In many literary texts, the cabarets of Harlem where jazz was performed are featured (Claude McKay's *Home to Harlem* for instance depicts the ambience of these iconic jazz spaces). In Sterling Brown's jazz poem "Cabaret" there is a line that captures the frenzy in the music: "The Jazz band unleashes its fury". Body language is described – flashing eyes, teeth, hands, or the jerk of shoulders, the undulating hips – to celebrate freedom, intensity, joy and pain. A difference with the blues has been suggested by poets like Sonia Sanchez, according to whose poems and reviews "the existential ethos of the blues belonged to conservative, fearful, anti-revolutionary 'negroes', while jazz more actively articulated the ideals of revolutionary 'Blacks'" (Leonard 296). Sanchez (and other poets like Russell Atkins, Ted Joans, Leroi Jones and Bob Kaufman) visually represented the sounds and rhythm of jazz in what Leonard calls "visual jazz". Leonard describes how "on the printed page, the orthographic or visual reproduction of a jazz sound was meant to assert a distinctively black scream of rage, pain and 'I am', as in Sanchez's "a / coltrane / poem":

    A
    Love
    supreme, a love supreme a love supreme.

A LOVE SUPREME
scrEEEccCHHHHH screeeeEEECHHHHHHH.
(Leonard 296)

Jazz appears in the episodic structure of Ralph Ellison's novel *The Invisible Man,* in James Baldwin's short story "Sonny's Blues" and in the narrative form of Gayl Jones' novel *Corregidora.* There is a sense of liberation in the way meaning/s is/are created in novels like Morrison's *Jazz* where the liberation is that of the reader, and in the gift of meaning-making given by the novelist, but also of the way meaning is set in the reconstructions of both memory and history. "The conceptual and aesthetic breadth of jazz in literature has expanded to include anything from refrains to stream-of-consciousness narration, from elegies and odes to jazz musicians to postmodern epistemological speculation" (Leonard 299). And as the poet Yusef Komunyakaa has said of jazz poems, they "need not have an overt jazz theme as such" but only need to "embrace the whole improvisational spirit of jazz" (in Leonard 299). This would apply to much of the literature in its appropriation of such a spirit while pulling together diverse material from past and present, and all the moods and emotions that mark African American memory.

Another typical performance style is that of **rap** or hip-hop which involves DJ-ing, rapping (which is the vocal track), breakdancing, and graffiti. It originated in New York city in the 1970s as a form of cultural exchange among Black, Latino and Caribbean youth and influenced a wide range of activities including politics and fashion. Evolving from earlier and ongoing musical forms like rhythm, blues and jazz, it gave birth to many variations and subgenres like trap, grime, gangsta rap, crunk, chillhop, bounce and Latin hip-hop. The 1980s and 1990s came to be known as the golden age of the genre with major artists like Tupac Shakur, MC Hammer and Big Daddy Kane coming to the fore. The period also saw the rise of the subgenre of gangsta rap with artists like Schoolly D and Ice-T. Hip-hop continues to grow in style and popularity and is now a globally practiced genre. Its characteristic features, drawing from earlier blues and jazz styles, are a *strong rhythmic beat* that can be fast paced or slow and easy and serve as a backdrop for vocal performers; *vocals* that are a rhymed chant keeping time with the beat; and *breaks*, that as the word suggests, are breaks during a song when a percussion instrument plays and there is dancing, also called breakdancing. Among the contemporary global stars of hip hop are Afrika Bambaataa, a DJ whose song 'Planet Rock' has been influential for later artists, the Grammy award-winning singer and rapper Queen Latifah, and the group The Roots who made the album *Things Fall Apart*. (For all the musical forms a useful site to consult is www.masterclass.com, which provides lucid introductions that can help to understand the music, much of which can also be heard as individual or group performances).

These performance traditions – old, new, and evolving – are a necessary part of the process through which African American literature came to finally be written. While they served as a source of comfort and togetherness in the early days of slavery, they also evolved and grew alongside the written traditions. They retained their distinctive character as musical forms or folklore, and were also hugely influential as resources for literature. They lent style and mood and content to narratives that represented the lives of blacks as they evolved strategies, engaged in disguise and trickery and escaped from everyday brutality on the plantations by using their own wits and resolve while also relying on the help of the community. The best example of an aspect of the oral forms that is deeply enmeshed with the literature is that of call-and-response. And one specific example is that of Morrison's *Beloved* where the pattern of calling and responding is represented between and among characters, between Beloved and Sethe, between the women in the family and those in the community:

> Call-and-response patterns both structure and are the theme of Sethe and Beloved's relationship. Sethe's guilt, which she acknowledges only to her murdered child, keeps that child alive and eventually calls her back into the physical world. Beloved calls Sethe to account once Sethe realizes who she is, and Sethe responds endlessly but uselessly, since the healing response is not reciprocal. . . . When considered in a larger frame, call-and-response patterns are related to audience (reader) participation in that the text suggests, or calls, implicitly asking for a response. (Sale 43)

Aspects of different oral genres are to be found in much of the literature, closely embedded in the culture.

The literature that is featured in subsequent chapters is closely linked with these oral forms and it is useful to keep them in mind while exploring the works of authors who are discussed in this book.

Works Cited

Benezet, Anthony. *Some Historical Account of Guinea, Its Situation, Produce, and the General Disposition of Its Inhabitants*. The Project Gutenberg EBook. Release date: 7 March 2004.

Bruce Jr., Dickson D. *The Origins of African American Literature, 1680–1865*.Charlottesville and London: UP of Virginia, 2001.

Crawford, Margo Natalie. "The Twenty-First-Century Black Studies Turn to Melancholy". *American Literary History*, Vol. 29, No. 4 (Winter 2017). 799–807 (Review) doi:10.1093/alh/ajx032. Advance Access publication 16 October 2017.

Ellison, Ralph. "Richard Wright's Blues". *The Antioch Review*, Vol. 50, No. 1/2, 50th Anniversary Issue (Winter–Spring, 1992). 61–74. https://www.jstor.org/stable/4612492.

Gates Jr., Henry Louis and Nellie Y. McKay. Eds. *The Norton Anthology of African American Literature*. New York and London: W.W. Norton & Company, 1997.

"Harlem Late Night Jazz Presents: Ring Shout". jazzhistorytree.com.

Horton-Stallings, LaMonda. "African American Vernacular Tradition". oxfordbibliographies.com DOI: 10.1093/OBO/9780199827251-0154. Last reviewed: 16 December 2021.

Irele, F. Abiola. "Sounds of a Tradition: The Souls of Black Folk". *The Cambridge History of African American Literature*. Eds. Maryemma Graham and Jerry Ward. New York and Cambridge: Cambridge UP. 2011. 21–38. Kindle EBook (Paginated).

Leonard, Keith D. "Jazz and African American Literature". *A Companion to African American Literature*. Ed. Gene Andrew Jarrett. Malden MA, Oxford, Chichester: Wiley-Blackwell, 2013. 286–301.

Moody-Turner, Shirley. "Folklore and African American Literature in the Post-Reconstruction Era". *A Companion to African American*

Literature. Ed. Gene Andrew Jarrett. Malden MA, Oxford, Chichester: Wiley–Blackwell, 2013. 200–11.

National Museum of American History. "What is Jazz". https://americanhistory.si.edu/smithsonian-jazz/education/what-jazz.

Negro Folk Rhymes: Wise and Otherwise. New York: The Macmillan Company, 1922. Project Gutenberg EBook.

Piersen, William D. "Puttin' down Ole Massa: African Satire in the New World". *Research in African Literatures,* Vol. 7, No. 2 (Autumn 1976). 166–80. http://www.jstor.com/stable/3818714. Accessed 12 June 2022.

Reagon, Bernice Johnson. Ed. *We'll Understand It Better By and By: Pioneering African American Gospel Composers*. Washington, D.C., and London: Smithsonian Institution Press, 1992.

Rickford, John, and Russell Rickford. *Spoken Soul: The Story of Black English*. NY: John Wiley, 2000.

Rosenbaum, Art. *Shout Because You're Free: The African American Ring Shout Tradition in Coastal Georgia*. U of Georgia P, 2013.

Sale, Maggie. "Call and Response as Critical Method: African-American Oral Traditions and *Beloved*". *African American Review*, Vol. 26, No. 1, Women Writers Issue (Spring 1992). 41–50 https://www.jstor.org/stable/3042075. Accessed 30 May 2020.

Sassi, Jonathan D. "Africans in the Quaker Image: Anthony Benezet, African Travel Narratives, and Revolutionary-Era Antislavery". *Bringing the World to Early Modern Europe*. 95–130 DOI: https://doi.org/10.1163/9789047418702_006.

Smitherman, Geneva. *Talkin and Testifyin*. Boston: Houghton Mifflin Company, 1977.

Stoudamire, Shawnkeisha. "From the African American Oral Tradition to Slam Poetry: Rhetoric and Stylistics". *McNair Scholars Journal* (2012), Vol. 16, No.1, Article 10. N.p. http://scholarworks.gvsu.edu/mcnair/vol16/iss1/10. Accessed 20 Feb. 2021.

Stuckey, Sterling. *Slave Culture: Nationalist Theory and the Foundations of Black America*. Oxford UP, 1987.

Uncle Remus Tales. Original entry by R. Bruce Bickley, Florida State University, Tallahassee, 10/03/2002. Last edited by *NGE* (*New Georgia Encyclopedia*) staff on 07/23/2018. https://www.georgiaencyclopedia.org/articles/arts- culture/uncle- remus-tales.

Chapter 2

Struggling for Literacy and Literate Identities
Slavery and Freedom: 1619–1865

Timeline

1619: Twenty Africans brought on a Dutch ship to Virginia and sold as indentured servants.

1624: The first African American child born free in the English colonies, William Tucker, is baptised in Virginia.

1625: The first enslaved Africans reach the Dutch Colony of New Amsterdam (now New York City) with the Dutch West India Company and are used as the city's first municipal labour force.

1636: Dutch minister Everadus Bogardus brings a teacher from Holland to Manhattan Island to provide religious training to Dutch and African children. This is the earliest educational effort in Colonial North America for blacks.

1641: Massachusetts becomes first colony to legalise slavery.

1642: Virginia passes a Fugitive Slave law. As part of the penalties, those helping escapees to be fined, and an enslaved person making a second attempt to escape is to be branded.

1645: Merchant ships arrive in Boston from Barbados. They trade their cargo of captured Africans for sugar and tobacco. This exchange encourages the slave trade in New England. First American slave ships sail from Boston. Dutch colonists transfer some of their landholdings in New Amsterdam to their former enslaved Africans as compensation for their support in battles with Native Americans.

1646: First slave couple freed in New England.

1651: Anthony Johnson, a free African American, imports several Africans and is given a grant of land on Virginia's Puwgoteague River. Other free African Americans follow suit.

1652: First law against slavery passed in Rhode Island.

1653: Enslaved African and Native American workers build a wall across Manhattan Island to protect the Dutch colony from British invasion. The site of the wall is now Wall Street.

1662: Virginia declares that a mother's status will decide whether a child is free or enslaved.

1663: Black and white indentured servants plan a rebellion in Gloucester County, Virginia, but are discovered and the leaders are executed. Maryland slave law rules that all Africans arriving in the colony are presumed to be slaves. Free European American women who marry enslaved men lose their freedom. Children of European American women and enslaved men are enslaved.

1664: In Virginia, the enslaved African's status is differentiated from that of the indentured servants, with laws decreeing that enslavement is for life and is transferred to the children through the mother.

1667: Virginia declares that baptism does not free a slave from bondage, thereby abandoning the Christian tradition of not enslaving other Christians.

1672: King Charles II of England charters the Royal African Company, which dominates the slave trade to North America for the next half century.

1682: A new Slave-code in Virginia prohibits weapons for slaves, requires passes beyond the limits of the plantation and forbids self-defence by any African American against any European American. New York enacts its first slave codes. They restrict the freedom of movement and the ability to trade of all enslaved people in the colony.

1688: Quakers in Pennsylvania make the first written official protest against slavery.

1690: At this point all English colonies in America have enslaved Africans.

1695: Rev. Samuel Thomas, a white cleric in Charleston, South Carolina, establishes the first school for African Americans in the British North American colonies.

1700: The publication of Samuel Sewall's *The Selling of Joseph*, is considered the first major condemnation of slavery in print in British North America.

1708: Africans in South Carolina outnumber Europeans, making it the first English colony with a black majority.

1711: A public slave market opens in New York City at the east end of Wall Street.

1712: The New York City slave revolt begins on April 6. Nine whites are killed and an unknown number of blacks die in the uprising. Colonial authorities execute 21 slaves and six commit suicide. Pennsylvania outlaws slave trade.

1724: The French colonial government in Louisiana enacts the Code Noir, the first body of laws that govern both slaves and free blacks in North America.

1727: Enslaved Africans and Native Americans revolt in Middlesex and Gloucester Counties in Virginia.

1734: Religious revival known as the Great Awakening begins. Blacks attracted to Christianity through Methodist and Baptist churches.

1738: The first permanent black settlement is established by fugitive slaves at Gracia Real de Santa Teresa de Mose (Fort Mose), Florida.

1739: Stono Rebellion by slaves in South Carolina. 30 whites and twice as many blacks are killed.

1740: South Carolina bans teaching of reading and writing to slaves.

1741: During the New York Slave Conspiracy Trials, New York City officials execute 34 people for planning to burn down the town. Thirteen African American men are burned at the stake and another 17 black men, two white men and two white women are hanged.

1746: Lucy Terry's only poem 'Bars Fight' published.

1752: Twenty-one-year old Benjamin Banneker of Maryland constructs one of the first clocks in Colonial America, the first of a long line of inventions and innovations until his death in 1806.

1756–1763: African Americans fight in the French and Indian War.

1758: First Black Baptist Church set up in Virginia.

1773: Slaves in Massachusetts petition for freedom for the first time.

1773: Phillis Wheatley's poems published in London.

1774: Continental Congress prohibits importation of slaves after 1 December, 1774.

1775–83: American Revolutionary War. African Americans fight at the battles of Bunker Hill, Lexington and Concord.

1775: First anti-slavery society organised by Philadelphia Quakers. Royal governor of Virginia offers freedom to any slave joining the British army: 800 respond to form Ethiopian regiment. Second Continental Congress resolves against import of slaves.

1776: Declaration of Independence adopted without the anti-slavery statement proposed by Jefferson.

1777: Vermont becomes the first state to abolish slavery in the state constitution. New York first state to extend vote to black males but limits voting in 1815 and 1821 with permit, property and residency requirements.

1780: Pennsylvania becomes the first state to permit interracial marriage. Free blacks protest taxation without representation.

1783: Massachusetts Supreme Court grants suffrage to black taxpayers.

1786: Free blacks join in Shay's Rebellion, protesting the lack of concern over harsh conditions of farmers by Massachusetts Govt.

1787: Constitution ratified, classifying one slave as three-fifths of one person for congressional apportionment, postponing prohibition of import of slaves till 1808, and demanding return of fugitive slaves to masters. Congress passes Northwest Ordinance, banning slavery in Northwest Territories and all land north of the Ohio River. Philadelphia Free African Society is established and free blacks of Rhode Island set up African Union Society to promote repatriation to Africa, though this is opposed by the former.

1789: Equiano's *Narrative* published in England. Appears in the US in 1791.

1793: US Congress passes first Fugitive Slave Law. Invention of cotton gin increases demand for slaves in the South.

1794: US Congress prohibits slave trade with foreign countries. French National Convention abolishes slavery in French territories (ban would be repealed by Napoleon in 1802). Richard Allen founds the first African Methodist Episcopal Church in Philadelphia.

1798: Georgia is the last state to abolish slavery.

1800: Pennsylvania free blacks petition US Congress to outlaw slavery. Gabriel Prosser and Jack Bowler organise 1000 fellow slaves to seize Richmond but plan is quelled by militia, and leaders and others executed.

1802: Haitians force French government to end slavery in Haiti. Francois-Dominique Touissant-Louverture is made governor.

1803: Louisiana Purchase doubles size of US territory.

1804: York, a slave, serves as guide to the Lewis and Clark expedition to the Pacific. Ohio passes the first 'Black Laws' restricting rights and movements of free blacks in the North.

1807: Britain abolishes slave trade.

1811: Slave revolt in Louisiana led by Charles Deslondes ends with over 100 slaves killed or executed by US troops.

1812: Slaves and free blacks fight in war of 1812.

1815: The Underground Railroad is established by the Quaker Levi Coffin to help slaves escape to Canada. Between 1800 and 1865, the railroad helped approximately 70,000 slaves to escape.

1816–18: First Seminole War involving runaway slaves and Native Americans fighting US federal government in Florida.

1816: American Colonization Society formed in Washington D.C. to promote repatriation of freed slaves to Africa to ease race problems. It is supported by leading white Congressmen.

1817: Over 3000 free blacks in Philadelphia meet to oppose American Colonization Society.

1820: The Missouri Compromise allowed Maine into the Union as a free state and Missouri was allowed as a slave state in 1821, and slavery was outlawed in all new Northern Plains States. American Colonization Society sends expedition to establish Liberia, a black republic in West Africa. First repatriation ship, *Mayflower of Liberia* leaves from New York City with 86 blacks.

1821: African Theatre also known as African Grove, Minor Theatre and African Company set up by William Alexander Brown, and with it the first all-black US acting troupe, begins performances in New York City.

1822: Denmark Vesey organises slave revolt to take over Charleston, South Carolina but is betrayed. Liberia formally founded by African American colonisers.

1823: The first African American, Alexander L. Twilight, graduates from Middlebury College, Vermont. William Alexander Brown's play, *The Drama of King Shotaway,* believed to be the first by an African American, produced in New York City.

1826: First US colony for free blacks, Nashoba, established near Memphis, Tennessee.

1827: *Freedom's Journal,* the first African American run newspaper published

1829: Publication of David Walker's *Appeal and* Horton's *The Hope of Liberty.* Three-day race riots in Cincinnati; over 1000 blacks flee to Canada after whites attack them and burn their homes.

1830: First National Negro Convention in Philadelphia. The Jim Crow character is performed by white blackface performer Thomas Dartmouth Rice. Rice is believed to have started this brand of performance and toured with it throughout the United States and Europe, presenting various stereotypical black characters, dressed in ragged attire, and singing and dancing on stage.

1831: Maria W. Stewart publishes *Religion and the Pure Principles of Morality.* Nat Turner leads a slave uprising in Southampton County,

Virginia; at least 57 whites are killed; Soldiers and militiamen react and kill blacks indiscriminately. Nat Turner is captured and hanged.

1832: Maria Stewart begins lecture tour in Boston, the first African American woman to engage in public political debates.

1833: Oberlin College is founded as the first co-educational US college, and is integrated from the start. Ira Aldridge, a black actor, performs Shakespeare in London.

1834: Henry Blair, inventor of the corn planter is the first recorded African American to receive a patent. Anti-abolitionist riots in Philadelphia and New York.

1835–42: Second Seminole War.

1836: The first "gag rule" is passed in the House of Representatives, preventing anti-slavery bills and petitions from being introduced, read or discussed.

1837: Victor Sejour's *The Mulatto* published.

1838: Frederick Douglass escapes from slavery.

1839: Successful slave revolt on the Spanish ship *Amistad*. Passport application by Philadelphia black man rejected by the State Department on the basis that African Americans are not citizens.

1841: Douglass makes first anti-slavery speech in Massachusetts.

1843: Henry Highland Garnet delivers *An Address to the Slaves of the United States* at National Negro Convention, Buffalo, New York.

1845: Douglass's *Narrative* appears.

1847: William Wells Brown's *Narrative* published.

1848: Douglass speaks at Women's Rights Convention, Seneca Falls, New York. Ohio reverses 'Black Laws'.

1849: Harriet Tubman escapes from slavery and begins work with the Underground Railroad.

1850: Clay Compromise strengthens the Fugitive Slave Act of 1793. Lucy Session becomes first African American woman college graduate from Oberlin College.

1851: Sojourner Truth delivers her *Aren't I a Woman?* Speech at Women's Rights Conference in Akron, Ohio.

1852: Harriet Beecher Stowe publishes *Uncle Tom's Cabin*.

1853: Wells Brown's *Clotel*, J.M. Whitfield's *America and Other Poems* appear.

1854: Frances F.W. Harper, *Poems on Miscellaneous Subjects* appears. Republican Party founded to oppose extension of slavery.

1855: Douglass's *My Bondage and My Freedom* published.

1857: Supreme Court Dred Scott decision declares that African Americans are not citizens.

1859: Harriet Adams Wilson's *Our Nig* is published. John Brown's raid on Harper's Ferry, West Virginia. Last US slave ship docks in Alabama.

1860: South Carolina secedes from Union.

1861–65: Civil War

1861: Harriet Jacobs, *Incidents in the Life of a Slave Girl* and Francis Harper's short story, *Two Offers* published.

1862: Emancipation Proclamation issued by President Lincoln.

1863: Slavery abolished in all Dutch colonies.

1864: Fugitive Slave Laws repealed.

1865: Slavery outlawed by Thirteenth Amendment; Freedmen's Bureau established; Black Codes issued in former Confederate states, limiting the rights of freed slaves; President Lincoln assassinated; Ku Klux Klan founded in Tennessee.

1865: Approximately 3.9 million slaves freed.

While the first Africans came to the Americas as explorers, the twenty Africans who arrived on a Dutch slave ship that reached Jamestown in Virginia in 1619 were brought as labourers. They were indentured servants who could work their way to freedom by satisfying a master for a fixed number of years. This relatively innocuous episode (innocuous because enslavement of defeated peoples had been part of the wars amongst kingdoms from ancient times) has gained in significance because it developed so quickly into institutionalised slavery as the black person became the property of white planters whose commercial success with cotton, tobacco and rice plantations depended heavily on slave labour.

The period of early experience is worth noting. The African American and white settler relationships were complex, and varied according to region. In many places there were black property holders, owners of small businesses and maritime industry workers as well as social and economic contacts. A more systematic segregation began only in the late seventeenth and early eighteenth centuries with the institutionalisation of slavery through legislations on issues like regulation of movement, prohibition on slave gatherings, and penalties for runaway slaves and for those helping them.

An idea of universalism at work in the characterisation of races made it possible to conclude that the Africans were lower order members of society, denying their distinctiveness through this discursive incorporation. These were views already prevailing in England through the writings of returning travelers and their accounts of interactions with Africans:

> John Hawkins, the first important English slave trader, spoke in the 1560s particularly of the basic dishonesty of 'the Negro (in which nation is seldome or never found truth),' and he and others told stories of African treachery giving substance to such a charge. Such concrete views were supplemented by a scientific belief that questioned African humanity in significant ways, not to mention a biblical thinking that, drawing on the story of Noah, described black Africans as the descendants of Noah's son Ham, cursed as a result of his own indiscretions to a state of permanent and eternal servitude. (Bruce 2)

Bruce goes on to note that there were different "modes of exclusion" in different British colonial societies with "haphazard" "segregation and discrimination". In New England, blacks and whites appear to have been treated equally before the law, and in all the colonies, courts were open to, and used by, everyone including African slaves. In all the colonies as well, social contacts between blacks and whites, especially outside elite circles, were frequent and extensive, as were economic relations, particularly those involving free people of colour and non-gentry whites (Bruce 3). Such relations appear to have been conducted on relatively equal terms. Even interracial marriage, if uncommon, was not unknown (4).

It was the growing plantation economy (based on tobacco, cotton and rice) in the southern region of North America that by 1700, gave birth to the institution of chattel slavery where the slave became the property of the planters. This is a significant point in history because it is from here onwards that systematic enslavement, based on physical and psychological control, began. Certain basic steps taken at this stage laid the foundations. The most powerful of these was the separation of the slave from all sources of personhood and happiness – alienation from family (slave families were separated, with husbands, wives and children sold away to other plantations or to the slave traders), from cultural practices (conversion to Christianity and insertion into alien religious practices of worship but also into the Genesis story that helped establish racial difference and inferiority), and from community (while the slave lived with and amidst other slaves on plantations, each slave was alone in a structure of punishment and reward, and any signs of cooperation or collaboration were quickly nipped in the bud by exemplary tortures and death). As the history of the institution and the literature would show, while pride and aspiration, self-reliance and freedom were the basic principles of the young nation, these were denied to the slaves. The blatant division of races that this represented – the ability on the part of the white race to live with and indeed thrive in the midst of the horrors they created, and to continuously improve on the details and effectiveness of oppressive practices – also provided the socioeconomic and psychological groundwork for the entrenchment of racism which continued long after slavery itself was abolished. "The intention of slavery was to create in the slave a sense of complete alienation from all human ties except those that bound him or her in absolute dependence to the master's will" (Gates Jr. and McKay 130).

Hawkins's early assessment was given a strong rationale through a basic interpretation of racial difference where physical features like colour of skin, kind of hair, facial features and body structure became signs of racial superiority and inferiority – preliminary steps in the consolidation that assumed blacks to be intellectually and morally inferior to whites. The success of the institution and its continuation was the result of a major discursive exercise on the part of powerful men like Thomas Jefferson, a slave owner himself, who in his *Notes on the State of Virginia* (1787) both condemned slavery and provided intellectual ballast for it when he wrote of the "eternal monotony" of their countenances and the "immoveable veil of black which covers all the emotions of the other race" (Jefferson 669). He adds that they require "less sleep" despite being engaged in hard labour from dawn to dusk, "their griefs are transient" and their "numberless afflictions . . . are less felt" (670). The differences he establishes in this piece are then seen as "a powerful obstacle to the emancipation of these people", adding that if and when they are freed, they should "be removed beyond the reach of mixture" (673). This text appears to summarise "lessons" learnt by whites about blacks and offers explanations for black inferiority from the social and natural sciences despite Jefferson's acknowledgment in the *Notes* that slavery is an unfortunate if unavoidable institution.

The idea of a usable past is a possible way to consider how the horrors of slavery were to be processed. In the history of this literature, if the past was where all the horrors lay, it was also where the glimmerings of creativity are to be found. In what might appear as a version of Van Wyck Brooks' "usable past" or a "practical past" that can serve as a resource for literature, we have, in the case of slave and race history, a past that is always present, that has never quite settled and that is a never-depleted resource for the collective imagination, precisely because of how unspeakably terrible and comprehensive it was; a past that, no matter how often it is mined and how deeply it is investigated, still reveals more. The reality competes with the imagination in trying to find the forms that will re-present it anew in ever different character.

Scholarship into the discrete experiences in the different slaveholding states of the South and the cities of the North shows the complexity of intermingling, cultural resistance and practices during festivities that were responsible for the preservation and evolution of a distinct culture with moorings in African culture but influenced by European forms and styles even as these were parodied and their stereotypical images of Africans mocked and played with. Occasions were available for the evolution of such practices. Bruce Jr. mentions "Negro Election Days" and "Negro Training Days". In the first of these "local blacks chose 'kings,' 'governors,' and other officials," who dealt with "social and even legal offenses committed by members of the community". In the second, "through motley dress and an intentional incompetence, [they] ridiculed white pretensions and even played with white stereotypes of black 'limitations'" (6–7).

Such carnivalesque practices are an early indication of the modes of critique that African American literature would use as it developed in sophistication and found ways to represent and satirise the evils of slavery and racism.

Religion was another site where we can see the Africans making a space for themselves. From the first recorded African slave who spoke to an all-white congregation using the story of Ham, to Elizabeth Key, a Virginia slave, and other later slave voices, the Christian religion offered opportunities for the participation of slaves and slaveholders alike. Missionary effort among the slaves particularly, was egalitarian in its ends. All of this brought about a confusing and complicated situation that contributed to the emergence of literary work. With historical research opening up, accounts of slaves expressing themselves on different matters, the fact of African influence on their forms is hardly surprising. This might be seen to constitute a kind of agency or as Bruce Jr. terms it, "authority" (11) that would offer a sense of worth in otherwise unbearable situations.

The import of slaves continued into the eighteenth century and many of them recounted stories of how they were captured and forcibly brought back. Their lives and tales were a continuous reassertion of a discrete African life and culture that fed and kept alive a sense of selfhood. One story, often recounted by the Quaker abolitionist Anthony Benezet in his anti-slavery tracts in the 1760s, is of a man captured and brought away when he was on his way to fetch water for his sick children (Benezet n.p.). Such stories circulated among slaves and often assumed the status of folklore, and many identified with the predicament. The taking on of another's story and retelling it as if it were one's own – accessing another's memory – is what Toni Morrison means by the term 'rememory' that she uses in *Beloved*. Such a process is not appropriation but an inhabitation, entering into the space of another's memory. It became possible because of the empathy at work, of the sameness of experience as well as the evolution of a more representative, better narrated experience.

1

In 1740, South Carolina passed one of the first anti-literacy acts, known as the Negro Act which declared:

> Whereas the having of slaves taught to write, or suffering them to be employed in writing may be attended with great inconveniences, *Be it enacted*, That all and every person or persons whatsoever who shall hereafter teach or cause any slave or slaves to be taught to write, or shall use or employ any slave as a scribe in any manner of writing . . . every such person or persons shall for every such offence forfeit the sum of one hundred pounds of current money. (web n.p.)

Similar laws were enacted in 1800 and 1834. Other slaveholding states followed: Virginia in 1819 and 1849, Mississippi in 1823, Georgia in 1829 and 1833, Louisiana and North Carolina in 1830, Alabama in 1833 and 1856 and Missouri in 1847. These laws were part of the effort to uphold white supremacy and were among the major hurdles that blacks had to overcome in order to write. Their existence places in perspective the importance given to reading and writing, to written communication and its central role in raising political consciousness seen in the ex-slave narratives, in the newspapers and periodicals established by men like Frederick Douglass, and in the orations and lectures that were also circulated in printed form. One striking instance of its effect is seen in Douglass's *Narrative,* which carries the phrase "Written by Himself" in the title.

The legal framework for denial of education was only one of the strategies through which the slaveholding states sought to preserve their power. The other legal recourse taken by white slaveholders was the Fugitive Slave law that evoked fear in all those who would help slaves to escape. In fact this systematic legalisation of all aspects of slavery (and correspondingly the protection provided by the absence of any punitive action against slaveholders who habitually murdered their slaves for petty, often merely perceived, aberrations) shows up more brightly the immense resolve, care and cunning that underlines the narrative of slavery and escape.

Jefferson's complex but finally unambiguously racist *Notes* represents assumptions that must be seen in their contemporary influence but also in the actions such assumptions set in motion – the huge exercise to lift themselves from a state of degradation to self-respect and identity. Writing, giving birth to a literature, formed a crucial foundation for this ambition even as it provided the necessary articulation of past experience, present condition and future aspiration. As Jarrett (2011) has shown, the response of David Walker to Jefferson through his *Four Articles,* placed on the table all that the slave had suffered and everything that would be required to turn the darkness to light.

Early forms of writing include poetry and the first autobiographical accounts like captivity and slave narratives, and spiritual autobiographies, letters, pamphlets, articles, sermons, speeches/orations, and the first play written by an African American. Lucy Terry Prince, Briton Hammon, Gronniosaw, Olaudah Equiano, Jupiter Hammon, Phillis Wheatley, George Moses Horton, John Marrant and David Walker represent themes of identity and spiritual enlightenment alongside pictures of racial difference, transatlantic journeys, the Middle Passage and escape from slavery. Overall, there is a tendency to balance the desire to be part of a reading and writing community with awareness of the obstacles. The struggle for literacy is pre-eminent, seen as the only possible way for slaves and free blacks to lift themselves up from their condition of inferiority, and achieve a respectable place in society under the equality promises of the Constitution. A running theme in much of the first generation writing is that of spiritual enlightenment, which "served rhetorically to assert the humanity of Africans and, of equal importance, their qualification for admission to the early national polity" (Jarrett Vol 1, 5). The Great Awakening and the influence of George Whitefield are factors that showed people of African descent a way to reconcile to their abject condition with the promise of salvation.

In this chapter we look at the forms of writing that became popular, the reasons for their emergence and the ways in which this literature was the product of the political and cultural aspirations of a community.

In the early writings there is a picture of human relations that is yet to crystallise into the rigid master-slave dynamic that would be described in the slave narratives. Masters are reasonably generous and kind, and slaves seemed to have had opportunities and leisure –

opportunities to travel alone or with their masters and leisure to read and write (as was the case with Wheatley). The theme of community is presented as enabling interracial relationships and slaves were relatively mobile. Identities are still fluid and there is little sense of belonging to a nation whether Africa or America, nationalist conceptions that enter into political and cultural discourse much later with the Revolution and its definition of Americanness. The Revolution and the Constitution, while giving birth to a strong discourse of freedom, and equality within a free nation, in actuality failed to ensure equality of belonging and citizenship, and in fact compelled the search for other identities, giving rise to the idea of people of African origin in America constituting a nation but also having access to a diasporic identity as 'sons of Africa'. However, this was yet to come. In these early years, since those transported from Africa on slave ships belonged to different ethnic groups with their own cultures and politics; there is no sense of a homogenous Africanness. This is an idea that geographical and temporal distance created in later years.

Identity is a theme that appears early. The passage from the darkness of African life to enlightenment seen in works by Wheatley and many others reveals the pursuit of a fervent Christian identity. Participation in a common religious identity with the whites became a way of alleviating current distress and achieving a sense of belonging in an alien space. Such identity aspirations are closely aligned to achieving literacy that would mean speaking about themselves but also speaking to a white readership. Jefferson's contemptuous comments about Wheatley pose a challenge that authors tacitly accept as they begin to present themselves in various literate personas. There is also the running theme of racial difference in many of these texts – Douglass's *Narrative* is explicit about it but all narratives that speak of the cruel white master and the downtrodden slave participate in an oppositional discourse that clearly demarcates two racial groups set at two opposing ends of a scale – in big house and slave hut, in plenty and want, in white and black, in cruel exercise of absolute power and powerless victimhood. These binaries run through the slave narratives and feature in other works, especially the orations delivered by many on the lecture circuit. The primary literary forms are poetry, the slave narrative, articles and lectures.

2

The single poem by **Lucy Terry Prince** (1730–1821), "Bars Fight" is the earliest known written work and was published after her death in Josiah Gilbert Holland's *History of Western Massachusetts* in 1855. It is a 28-line poem with seven four-line stanzas, on the Abenaki Indian attack of 1746 and is mainly an account that remembers the men who were killed, one woman who was left for dead, and a child who was captured and carried off by the attackers. Born in Africa, purchased in Rhode island and eventually marrying a free black man, Abijah Prince, a war veteran who purchased her freedom and who went on to become a prosperous landowner and helped found the town of Sutherland in Vermont, Terry's circumstances enabled her to become a prominent orator and eventually to become a protector of her family's interests against her predominantly white neighbours (she was the first woman to argue against a white man trying to seize her land, in the Supreme Court), but no other written work by her is extant. Her poem can be seen as an assertion of equality through the written word and like the later Wheatley, proof of her ease with the newly learnt language.

Phillis Wheatley (1753?–84) was the first black poet who published her work in her lifetime and had some role in the way it reached its readership, having taken pains to promote it, by meeting the right people and generally making herself known to her potential readers. Her only volume of poetry, *Poems on Various Subjects, Religious and Moral*, appeared in 1773. It was published with the help of the religious leader and literary patron, the Countess of Huntingdon, and released in London. In its preface appear signatures of several important people, possibly collected by Wheatley herself, attesting to her authenticity as a poet. The volume was published in 1774 in the colonies, making her the second poet, after Anne Bradstreet, to have a public reception of her work.

Young Phillis was kidnapped from her native Gambia in West Africa and brought to Boston in 1761 when she must have been eight or nine years old. She was bought by John Wheatley, a rich merchant who named her Phillis after the slave ship, *The Phillis*, in which she was transported. Scholars have speculated that she must have belonged to the Fulani tribe (from her features), and to an elite Muslim family. This was the story of many Africans who fell victim to the slave trade in which African slave traders collaborated with British (and other colonial) slave merchants who were part of this lucrative human trafficking. But Wheatley, unlike many slaves who were lost in the terrible new world they were brought to, was lucky. While the family that she came to was kind to her and attentive to the intelligence and brightness of the little girl, she herself was quick to take advantage of the opportunities available. The Wheatleys assigned her duties to other slaves in the household, encouraging her to learn her letters and study the Bible, and Latin and Greek literature. At the same time, she was also able to read in the extensive library of Boston's Old South Church (which she attended with the family). She was mentored by some of the well-known intellectuals of Boston, among them Joseph Sewell, pastor of the Old South Church. One of Phillis Wheatley's dedicatory poems was "On the Death of the Rev. Dr. Sewell, 1769" where she refers to him as her "monitor". She later wrote a second elegy on his death. Other influences included Samuel Cooper, minister at Boston's Brattle Street Meeting House, and Mather Byles, Cotton Mather's nephew and a neighbour of the Wheatleys. This environment was crucial to Phillis Wheatley's development as a writer and thinker. The reading she did in these libraries is evident in her frequent references to the Greek and Latin classics, to Homer, to the poets Horace and Virgil and the comic playwright Terence, to legendary heroes and gods and goddesses and frequently to the Muses. Many of these appear in the poem "To Maecenas", the patron of Horace and Virgil, a poem that clearly suggests her own awareness of the role played by white patrons like the Countess of Huntingdon and all those others who facilitated her emergence as a poet.

Wheatley's life is as interesting as her work. Her exceptional abilities, her strong urge to overcome the disadvantages of her state, and her alertness to everything around her distinguish her and is an early example of the importance of individual ability. She was quick to adapt to the new life, even as she was keenly conscious of the injustice and cruelty represented by the slave trade. However, despite her prominence in literary history as the first African American poet, controversy has dogged her reputation especially because of her ostensible acceptance of the white view of slavery and slaves. J. Saunders Redding has accused Phillis of going along with the belief held by the Wheatleys "that Christianized Negroes, even though slaves, were better off in America than free Negroes in 'benighted, heathen, Africa'" (640). This problematic notion remains an undercurrent in the early literature, as several of the writers from that time demonstrate an unquestioning absorption in the Christian religion that they found all around them and into which they were initiated on the plantations as well as by preachers and missionaries who sought to draw them in as members of the 'saved'.

Many of Wheatley's poems represent aspects of her early slave experience. "On Being Brought from Africa to America" has her playing on the duality of the slave's life, conceding to the Christian rhetoric of saving 'pagan lives' – "'Twas mercy brought me from my *Pagan* land" while demonstrating awareness of the racist mindset behind the benevolence:

> Some view our sable race with scornful eye,
> 'Their colour is a diabolic die.'
> Remember *Christians, Negroes*, black as *Cain*,
> May be refin'd, and join th' angelic train" (Norton 171).

While a poem like this appears to look on the slaves' capture and transport to America in terms of an escape from darkness and paganism, the fact of writing about this passage tacitly suggests all that she does not mention. As historians have uncovered the details of the Middle Passage and the circumstances in which Africans were captured, 'stored' like cargo in barracks before being packed in the holds of slave ships, transported to America and put up for auction, the deliberate forgetting or the deliberate suppressing of this stage in her life becomes a point worthy of attention as we read Wheatley's poetry. Her absorption in the intellectual and emotional life of America – religion, the Great Awakening of George Whitefield, the opening up of a cultural world that was made up of the Muses and other figures from classical mythology – all of which is referenced in her poetry, appears as a comprehensive exercise in forgetting the dehumanising journey, the fact of being bought and owned, the poverty following marriage and the lifelong subservience of one race to another. The poet and scholar drea brown's rumination on that phrase "being brought" opens up the hidden corners of this poem that is ostensibly a prayer of gratitude for being saved from the pagan land: the discomfort, the darkness in the hold, filth. It also suggests the darkness behind the spirit that finds expression in other poems, inviting speculation about the disguises and the quality of 'masking' that has come to be seen as an element in many slave narratives (brown n.p.). (Margareta Matilda Odell's 1834 *Memoir and Poems of Phillis Wheatley* is the only early documentation of her life).

"Phillis Wheatley's mastery of popular belletristic conventions, her deployment of Christian evangelical rhetoric, and her manipulation of the colonist-as-slave analogy have all been cited as tactics that enabled her to adopt an intelligible and therefore consumable subjectivity" (Hodgson 663). But Hodgson's point is not only these generally accepted notions about Wheatley's work but rather her use of childhood as a trope: "The child figure of the early 1770s was simultaneously affiliated with varied and contradictory – yet primarily positive– characteristics, including malleability, obedience, and faith in authority. This constellation of attributes enabled Wheatley's literary child persona to speak to her social superiors about family, religion, and politics while mitigating the threat associated with her wronged and enslaved African body" (663).

Hodgson's essay makes a distinction between the child characters in her poetry and the child authorial persona that helps explain her use of a subliminal critique even in poems where she seems steeped in a culture of thought and expression that included her Christian metaphors and her references to Greek and Latin mythology, imbibed from her surroundings and her reading. Her use of this persona allowed her to speak of the supposed emancipated and saved condition while subversively gesturing at what this immersion would have meant in terms of cultural erasure and displacement of an African child. The place of patronage and white mediation in the formation of her creative self is a theme that will recur through this period as Africans, removed from their countries, tried to find in the guise of gratitude and humility to their white amanuenses, a distinct and identifiable voice.

Wheatley's poetry has been read as epic hymns that are "a powerful representation of: woman in nature... in art... in society ... and in politics" (Shields 237 in Anderson 4). But they also speak of the larger condition of slavery and what it must have meant to those snatched away from their homes and lands. In "To the Right Honourable William, Earl of Dartmouth", she mentions the source of her "love of *Freedom*":

I, young in life, by seeming cruel fate
Was snatch'd from *Afric's* fancy'd happy seat:
What pangs excruciating must molest,
What sorrows labour in my parent's breast?
Steel'd was that soul and by no misery mov'd
That from a father seiz'd his babe belov'd:
Such, such my case. And can I then but pray
Others may never feel tyrannic sway? (Norton 173)

Wheatley's poetry, innocuous and polite on the surface, offers an unmistakable critique of the domination of one race by another. Marlon B. Ross sees her work as a precursor in an alternative mode to the narrative of racial uplift of a later time. Using this "oblique, seemingly deferential strategy" and apparently "pleading the case on behalf of her masters" against the tyranny of the colonial British power, "she inserts at the very heart of the poem her own 'grievance' as an 'unredress'd' complaint" (Ross 155) – a strategy of masking that is also evident in Jacobs' narrative.

A theme of cultural recovery and agency runs through figures like that of the "Young African Painter" and in poems like "On Recollection" and "On Imagination". Invoking first the Muse of Memory and then the nine Muses, in the first of these two poems she asks for inspiration for the "vent'rous *Afric*" (Norton 175) so that she remembers the past – which is both the eighteen years mentioned in the poem and implicitly the life left behind.

"On Imagination" is about the opening up of vision facilitated by this faculty. In writing this as accessible to all she is clearly participating in a community of creativity that transcends race and other inequalities:
> We on thy pinions can surpass the wind,
> And leave the rolling universe behind:
> From star to star the mental optics rove,
> Measure the skies, and range the realms above.
> There in one view we grasp the mighty whole,
> Or with new worlds amaze th' unbounded soul. (Norton 174).

Wheatley's work also sets in perspective the contempt with which she was dismissed by Thomas Jefferson. Jefferson, who owned slaves, had sexual relations with female slaves and expressed strong reservation about racial mixture, represents the obstacles many of these early writers faced. What Jefferson stood for also renders complex the apparently unquestioning entry into and acceptance of Christian redemption for themselves and the races back home in Africa that is seen in many of the early writers. In the case of Wheatley, her strong feelings about the treatment of blacks is evident in her letter to Samson Occom with whom she had a lifelong friendship: "in every human Breast, God has implanted a Principle, which we call Love of Freedom; it is impatient of Oppression, and pants for Deliverance; and by the Leave of our modern Egyptians I will assert, that the same Principle lives in us. God grant Deliverance in his own Way and Time . . ." (Norton 176). This statement opens up her poetry to interesting possibilities of interpretation.

Jupiter Hammon (1711–1806?), with his poem "An Evening Thought: Salvation by Christ with Penitential Cries" (1760), became the first published poet of African origin. He is, however, better known for the poem, "An Address to Phillis Wheatly (sic), Ethiopian Poetess, in Boston, Who Came from Africa at Eight Years of Age, and Soon Became Acquainted with the Gospel of Jesus Christ". Both these poems are based on the Christian belief with which these early writers rationalised the condition of slavery, repeatedly assuring themselves of the fact of having been saved from pagan Africa by the "wisdom", "mercy" and "grace" of Christ. The poem is in twenty-one four-line stanzas, each referring to a Biblical text or Psalm and built around a tacit denial of "dark" and "danger[ous]" Africa from which Phillis (and by implication all other Africans in America) has been rescued and saved by the Christian God – a theme of fortuitous escape through God's grace that is similar to the sentiment running through Phillis Wheatley's own poetry. Hammon's four poems are said to carry the influence of Negro spirituals and religious folk poetry (Ransom 12). Ransom mentions the important role of Oscar Wegelin in bringing Hammon into literary history through first, his article, "Was Phillis Wheatley America's First Negro Poet?" in the *Literary Collector* for August, 1904, and then the more substantial *Jupiter Hammon; American Negro Poet* (Ransom 15).

Ransom uses the word "intoxication" about the religious fervour in Hammon's poetry and this would describe much of the writing by African Americans at this period. Jupiter Hammon, who had access to the library of his master Henry Lloyd in Long Island and made the most of this opportunity, not only wrote poetry but also published several sermons, besides being a leader in New York's African Society. (Four poems and three prose pieces have been discovered and are all collected in Ransom's volume.) He was witness to the American Revolution and its promise of freedom as well as the many inequalities embedded in the Constitution that followed.

The other important poet of these early years is **George Moses Horton** (1797?–1883?). His two collections are *The Hope of Liberty* (1829) and *The Poetical Works of George M. Horton, The Colored Bard of North Carolina, to Which is Prefixed the Life of the Author, Written by Himself* (1845). Unlike Wheatley whose poetry often sidestepped the real conditions of the slave's life, Horton's poetry expressed the frustrations of trying to be a poet while enslaved to three generations of the Horton family. The circumstances of his initiation into a life of letters were unique. Having taught himself to read, he began composing hymns in his head as a young teenager. By the time he was twenty he had started writing love poems on demand for the students of the nearby state university of Chapel Hill for a fee of twenty-five to seventy-five cents per lyric. Some students paid for his efforts with collections of poetry and this is how he came to read Homer, Virgil, Shakespeare, Milton and Byron – poets who became his models when he started to write, taught by the wife of a Chapel Hill professor, Caroline Lee Hentz. Horton wrote most often of religion, romantic love and death; but in poems like "On Hearing of the Intention of a Gentleman to Purchase the Poet's Freedom" (from the 1829 volume) and "Division of an Estate", and "George Moses Horton, Myself" (from the 1845 volume) there is direct reference to his life.

From the careers of these writers and from examples of other African Americans who prospered and had whites helping rather than obstructing them, we have evidence of some of the opportunities available for those who could avail of them (the career of Benjamin Banneker [1731–1806], scientist, naturalist, inventor, astronomer and surveyor, and maker of almanacs is a good example). It is only in later years when slavery was institutionalised and racism became ingrained that the ugly picture of social division, oppression and inequality becomes visible. Nevertheless, while educational opportunities were not entirely denied and in fact often facilitated, these writers experienced the ignominy of being owned by a white master. The moral dilemma of dealing with kindness and benevolence on the one hand and the soul-destroying reality of an enslaved condition was carefully disguised in many of these early writings as their authors attempted to reconcile themselves to circumstances. While they remained slaves or lived free in extreme poverty, they also found readers and publishers and a share in the intellectual life of the time. The running theme of mobility and transnationalism is already beginning to be seen as these writers wrote of the journeys that brought them to America, took them to England or that they experienced as they followed white masters to different places within the country. The narrative accounts use the journey as a trope for spiritual progress, detailing the stages through which they moved from ignorance and sin to enlightenment – a feature of the slave narratives that also became a literary trope in later, more sophisticated examples of the genre.

3

The slave narrative is a genre of writing which is deeply embedded in the circumstances of slave education, freedom and selfhood, giving a realistic picture of society and introducing readers to conditions of the slave's life. The slave narrative is usually the first-person account of the life of a former slave, often told to someone who acts as an amanuensis, or sometimes written by himself/herself. It graphically depicts whippings and other tortures, unbelievable punishments for petty crimes and mistakes, the inhuman behaviour of the cruel master, mistress and overseer, sexual exploitation, relationships amongst slaves, the acquiring of literacy and the dangerous and harrowing circumstances of escape. The trajectory from slavery to freedom traced in these narratives usually culminates in the author taking a new name and starting a new life.

The slave narrative became an important instrument in the abolitionist movement, and contributed to the national debate about slavery. The direct, autobiographical style, the variation of tone and voice, the ruminations on slavery, freedom and the future, the use of dialogue and the overall structure were also features that would eventually contribute to the increasingly sophisticated use of it by later fiction writers. It is possible to see the style of the sentimental novel already being used in many of these narratives with their quite undisguised appeals to the reader's sympathy, even as the political potential of the form is realized in the narratives of Frederick Douglass and Booker T. Washington. By the end of the Civil War about one hundred slave narratives had appeared. Following the abolition of slavery, many former slaves wrote or dictated accounts of their lives. And in the period from 1936 to 1940, the Federal Writers' Project of the US Work Projects Administration gathered oral testimonies from 2500 former slaves that eventually ran to 40 volumes (these manuscripts are available at https://www.loc.gov).

The slave narrative has been called "an autobiography and a sociology of slavery and freedom" (Gordon 517). It made the immorality of slavery tangible, finding ways to describe the indescribable. As Gordon writes, "It accomplished its task of laying bare slavery by producing a morality of verisimilitude, by forging a congruence between realism and sympathy. It told the bare, real truth of slavery, from the point of view of one who was or had been in it", but in this design it "was greatly constrained by the demands placed on it by the abolition movement, its primary sponsor and its largest consumer" (517). Gordon's essay, which is essentially a reading of Toni Morrison's *Beloved* as a novel drawing on the slave narrative but with the added edge lent by the freedom and space of fiction, shows how the novel "remembers some of what the slave narrative forgot, creating a palimpsest, a document that has been inscribed several times, where the remnants of earlier, imperfectly erased scripting is still detectable" (518–19).

Alongside this is the caustic description given by Henry Louis Gates: "The slave's texts could not be taken as specimens of a black 'literary culture'. Rather these texts could only be read as testimony of defilement: the slave's *representation* of the master's attempts to transform a human being into a commodity, and the slave's simultaneous verbal witness of the possession of a 'humanity' shared in common with Europeans" (*James Gronniosaw*, 52).

Du Bois has identified **Olaudah Equiano** (1745–97) as the founder of the genre of the African American slave narrative with good reason. In his expansive and rich account, Equiano, who calls himself a "citizen of the world", explores the many dimensions that a slave narrative could have. Making travel a central experience, he demonstrates how the escaped slave could aspire to several identities and become a world traveler, leaving behind the demeaning and soul-destroying slave experience, and embracing life as a realm of hope and possibilities. Olaudah Equiano was apparently born in a village in what is present day Nigeria, kidnapped along with his younger sister when he was eleven and enslaved in a neighbouring village before falling into the hands of European slave traders. He was separated from his sister, taken first to Barbados and eventually landed up in Virginia. He writes about village life before his capture and gives an account of the Middle Passage that evokes its utmost horrors. The doubt that scholars have raised about the veracity of the account of his early years, especially on the basis of records that suggest he was born in South Carolina, does not take away from the imaginative power with which Equiano presents what must have been a typical series of events for most Africans as they were torn from their homes and carried like cargo on the slave ships to the New World. Equiano went on to become part of the British abolitionist movement along with Ottobah Cuguano, a former slave who had organised a protest group called the Sons of Africa. He lectured on behalf of the movement on tours around the country, and became part of a group of radicals that included the English Romantic poet, William Blake. *The Interesting Narrative of the Life of Olaudah Equiano, or Gustavus Vassa, the African, Written by Himself* ran into many editions, was translated into several European languages and reached the US in 1791. The *Narrative* is an account of his life and travels and his sharply evocative style is evident in the description of the Middle Passage. After a picture of his village that shows a people living well and harmoniously, cultivating the land, possessing clean personal habits, and believing in one Creator, he presents the dramatic interruption of this idyllic state with the initial capture by a rival tribe and then the transport to the sea coast and the slave ship "waiting for its cargo". He recounts his shock, surprise and dismay as the ship gets underway and the captives are sent below decks into the holds where human bodies were packed close together, and forced to live there in filth:

> The closeness of the place, and the heat of the climate, added to the number in the ship, which was so crowded that each had scarcely room to turn himself, almost suffocated us. This produced copious perspirations, so that the air soon became unfit for respiration, from a variety of loathsome smells, and brought on a sickness among the slaves, of which many died.
> (Wiley 1, 68)

Equiano also gives more pleasant pictures, of being on deck, seeing flying fish and being allowed to watch the use of the quadrant. Once they arrive in Barbados, there is a description of the slave market where families are separated forever. He himself reaches Virginia and is set to work on a plantation where he sees a "black woman slave" who was cooking dinner and who was wearing an iron muzzle that prevented her from speaking or eating and drinking (68–70). While there are other shocking incidents that he recounts, the narrative is fast paced and moves from incident to incident, through a variety of people whom he met, journeys and adventures he undertook in different parts of the world – England, the Mediterranean, Turkey – and interspersed with reflections on the relations of humans with one another, his conversion to Christianity and his work as a missionary.

Briton Hammon (no dates available) wrote what is considered to be the first autobiographical work by an African American. Very little is known about him except from what he himself tells us in the *Narrative of the Uncommon Sufferings and Surprizing Deliverance of Briton Hammon, a Negro Man* (1760). This work is in equal measure a captivity narrative, an autobiography and a travel narrative, flagging motifs that will appear in subsequent slave narratives. He writes of his thirteen-year-long wanderings and experiences after leaving the house of his master, General Winslow, in 1747; the cruelty and barbarism of the Native Americans who attacked the ship he was in and his captivity among them; his years in a dungeon and the fortuitous meeting with his old master in London and his return with him to Boston. Following a brief synopsis of the narrative, there is a note to the Reader where he announces that because of his poor "Capacities and Condition" he would present facts but refrain from commenting or analysing them.

John Marrant (1755–91), born free in New York, moved to the South after his father's death and happened to hear George Whitefield speak. He became a fervent Christian and set out into the wilderness on a spiritual quest. He was captured by Cherokees, was sentenced to death but after the miraculous conversion of his executioner, he lived among the Native American tribes for about two years before returning as a missionary to work among slaves in Charleston. He worked as a carpenter before conscription by the Royal Navy during the Revolutionary War. He served in the Navy for six years. He subsequently went on to become a Methodist minister with an evangelical sect that had separated from the Church of England, and was ordained in Bath in 1785. In the same year *A Narrative of the Lord's Wonderful Dealings with John Marrant, a Black* was published in London, telling of his conversion, miraculous experiences and his captivity. The narrative expresses deep religious fervour and is a litany of self-castigations for minor aberrations that precede the writer's discovery of God. His sudden awakening to religion is central in the narrative and it is this that carries him through the troubles he is faced with in captivity. Marrant went on to a full-fledged missionary career, ministering to a group of Revolutionary War refugees in Nova Scotia and then returning as chaplain of the Prince Hall Grand Lodge in Boston. He married on a visit to Nova Scotia and then travelled to England where his second work, *A Journal of the Rev. John Marrant, From August the 18th, 1785 to the 16th of March, 1790*, on his missionary work, was published. He died in England in 1791.

The first female slave narrative is *The History of Mary Prince* (1831), dictated by Mary to Susanna Strickland and published in London. But it was **Harriet Jacobs** (1813–97) who wrote the first female slave narrative, *Incidents in the Life of a Slave Girl* (published in 1861 with the support of Lydia Maria Child who edited and condensed the text and wrote an introductory note). This narrative is both representative and unique. It is predominantly a tale of sexual abuse of the female slave, and Child, in her introduction, refers to it as experiences that could be considered both "delicate" and "indelicate", but that "the public ought to be made acquainted with its monstrous features" (Wiley 1, 368).

Harriet Jacobs only discovered that she was a slave at the age of six when her mother died. Her early years were spent with her biological family (her father was a carpenter much in demand for his skills, who died when she was thirteen) – unlike most other slave children who were usually sold away from their families. She was also luckier than most in having a kind mistress who taught her reading and spelling. But her fortunes changed at the death of her mistress when she discovered that she had been willed away to a five-year-old niece, the daughter of Dr Flint who had married her mistress's sister. This episode constitutes a betrayal that she feels very strongly and that aligns her story to that of all those others who were passed on from master to master. From this point the narrative recounts the many kinds and degrees of cruelty that the institution of slavery seems to have engendered in slave owners. In the chapter on "The New Master and Mistress", she tells the story of the plantation slave brought to Dr Flint's town house for disciplining because he had dared to suggest that the fair child his wife had given birth to was the owner's. The "piteous groans" as he is whipped and "the cowhide still wet with blood, and the boards all covered with gore" (Wiley 1, 374), discovered by the narrator next morning is a graphic example of many such accounts that record the inhuman practices that went with the institution of slavery. The narrative is as much an indictment of slavery as it is a testimony to the indomitable spirit that made Jacobs escape from the Flint family, spend seven years in the dark, airless garret of her grandmother's house and eventually escape to the North. From Edenton, North Carolina, to Philadelphia and then to New York is a journey that traces her transformation from slave to writer and active worker against slavery, and also reveals many of the powerful themes and tropes that mark the slave narrative as a literary genre. She not only bears witness to the institution of slavery as she experienced it but also records some of the notable episodes of slave revolt (she mentions Nat Turner's revolt).

One critic, Novian Whitsitt, has pointed to Jacobs's use of the black cultural tradition of "masking" with regard to her manipulation of Flint and Sands, as

> [a] technique of double meaning that allows the storyteller to make accessible a hidden message only to those readers attuned to the secretive signs embedded within the story. 'Masking' thus allows Jacobs to compose an acceptable explanation of events that will satisfy the majority of her immediate readers, white middle-class women in the North, while revealing the complete and actual experience to a select group of readers who can detect the cipher and appreciate Jacobs's impressive cunning given her desperate circumstances. (73)

The specific instance Whitsitt points to is the manipulation by the pregnant Jacobs (or Brent as she was known) of two men, the actual father of the unborn child, Flint, and Mr Sands with whom she has an affair. Each of the men is led to believe that he is the father. Flint, as was the practice with slave owners who impregnated their slaves, willingly sells the child and Sands, believing that the child is his, is relieved to be able to buy him. "This intentional complicating of paternity served Brent's purposes perfectly, leaving Flint to willingly sell the child, thinking that the child was his, and Sands anxious to buy the child, thinking that the boy was his. Jacobs's oblique and duplicitous narrative style offers information that points to this truth" (Whitsitt 74).

Frederick Douglass (1818–95) is a central figure in the early struggle against slavery. Writer of one of the best known slave narratives, *Narrative of the Life of Frederick Douglass, an American Slave, Written by Himself* (1845), he wrote two subsequent autobiographies, *My Bondage and My Freedom* in 1855 (written after his split from William Lloyd Garrison and representing his reassessment of his philosophy of reform), and the final, most comprehensive version, *The Life and Times of Frederick Douglass* in 1881, expanded in 1892 (serving as an epilogue to his life in its quieter, more ruminative tone and the image of the community elder that it projects).This was a long exercise in self-making that saw him move from a life of slavery to becoming one of the most eminent men of his time – the first African American to be given a vice-presidential ticket (in 1872) besides being appointed president of the Freedman's Bureau Bank, and federal marshall and recorder of deeds for the district of Columbia, serving as consul to Haiti and as charge d'affaires for the Dominican Republic.

From his first anti-slavery speech delivered before the Massachusetts Anti-Slavery Society in 1841, after he escaped, married and settled down in New Bedford, Massachusetts, he went on to become part of the American Anti-Slavery Society's Hundred Conventions Project and undertook a six-month tour of lectures in the East and the Midwest. His growing fame also endangered his freedom and in a strategic step he was advised by his white abolitionist friends to undertake a two-year lecture tour of Great Britain (1845–47). Here he met the Irish nationalist, Daniel O'Connell, and the British abolitionist, Thomas Clarkson. The trip was also significant because during this period British supporters raised money to buy his freedom. On his return Douglass launched his first newspaper, *The North Star* (it ran from 1847–63). Besides writing regularly in it, he also published his novella, *The Heroic Slave* in 1853, first in the volume of anti-slavery writings, *Autographs for Freedom,* and then reprinted as a four-part serial in his newspaper.

This was based on the real story of Madison Washington who led eighteen slaves in a revolt against the white crew on the slave ship *Creole* in 1841, killing an officer and then piloting the ship to Nassau in the British Bahamas. The British freed the slaves and also released Washington. Douglass first mentioned Madison Washington in a speech in Ireland and continued to refer to the episode as an example of other possible insurrections.

Douglass's growing command over language and his sense of literary style is seen in his most well-known work, the *Narrative*. Beginning with the place and circumstances of his birth (like most slave narratives), he runs through experiences that are representative and that he dwells on and analyses. Mentioning the possibility of his father being a white man and of never having seen his mother in daylight, because he was separated from her while still an infant and she could only visit him at night after walking the twelve miles from the home of her master, he says that this was the condition of most slave families. He speculates that this was done "to hinder the development of a child's affection toward his mother, and to blunt and destroy the natural affection of the mother for the child" (Wiley 1, 157). The fact of father and master being the same man is a matter he comments on even as he speaks of the lives of female slaves who were at the mercy of their master's sexual appetites. He also mentions how the children of such unions were a "constant offence to their mistress . . . she is never better pleased than when she sees them under the lash" and "The master is frequently compelled to sell this class of his slaves, out of deference to the feelings of his white wife" (157). Adopting a judicious tone he argues that a master often has to sell his own children out of humanity because otherwise "he must not only whip them himself, but must stand by and see one white son tie up his brother, of but few shades darker complexion than himself, and ply the gory lash to his naked back". Predictably "[E]very year brings with it multitudes of this class of slaves" (158). The *Narrative* is filled with anecdotes and reflections that gradually build up a picture of the slave institution as dehumanising not only for the slaves but also for their masters and for all those engaged in sustaining it. Scenes of violence (which are found in all slave narratives) are used to show the gulf between the slaves and their owners, but each scene is also part of an archive of cruelty and unimaginable tortures that left slaves maimed for life. Escape in these circumstances testifies to the immense resolve and mental strength of all those who succeeded in leaving and made lives for themselves. Douglass was exceptional but the many others who escaped to the North, remained anonymous while becoming part of an ever-swelling resistance.

Early in the *Narrative* there is an account of slaves "selected to go to the Great House Farm, for the monthly allowance for themselves and their fellow slaves" and singing their way through the dense woods "revealing at once the highest joy and the deepest sadness". This is a moment when the slaves get a tantalising glimpse of what freedom might be but that they can only taste briefly:

> The mere hearing of those songs would do more to impress some minds with the horrible character of slavery than the reading of whole volumes of philosophy on the subject could do... They told a tale of woe... they breathed the prayer and complaint of souls boiling over with the bitterest anguish...
> Slaves sing most when they are most unhappy. (Wiley 1, 162)

Here we find an early characterisation of slave music in terms that will eventually be used to describe the blues – a deep-seated sadness of spirit that accompanies the moment of joy that would go on to become one of the most important features of the literature. The germ of what has been called the "melancholy turn" in African American studies in recent years is recognised and articulated here. Scholars of African American theatre and performance have identified these "wild songs" as instances of performativity that go back to the coerced singing and dancing on the decks of ships during the Middle Passage. While the captors were primarily interested in keeping their captives healthy by giving them some exercise and fresh air, these occasions also provided them with an opportunity to form collectivities. Alexander Falconbridge, the surgeon mentioned earlier in the book, called the songs, performed to the accompaniment of makeshift drums, "melancholy lamentations" (cited in Jones, Jr. 16) and declared that slaves were forced to cut across ethnic differences "forg[ed]ing bonds of *African* solidarity... in order to endure, and eventually resist, the wretchedness of their captivity"

(Jones, Jr. 16). Critics have noted the power of "black noise" (Best and Hartman 9), and the way slaves "communed through rhythm, tone, and gesture" (Jones, Jr. 17) and not necessarily through words. Jones, Jr. also however points out that these performances were used by white masters to compel slaves to appear content with their lot and praise the benevolence of their masters as well as appear happy when displayed in the slave market (18–19). He suggests that "slave performances such as plantation wild songs or the on-deck 'lamentations' helped facilitate the transformation of black grief to black grievance, what in Hartman's terms might be called the move from 'sorrow' to an 'oppositional culture'" (Jones, Jr. 22).

The "battle with Mr Covey", a leader of the Methodist Church, to whom Douglass was sent by his master "to be broken" is, in his own words a "turning-point". Recounted in detail, this passage has him rise from the ground and grab Mr Covey and eventually bring him down, and is a rare and exceptional event in the sad history found in most slave narratives. Though Douglass remained for some more time as a slave and was hired out again to a Mr Freeland, his spirit remained unbroken. His observations and assessments get sharper and he is particularly caustic about "the religion of the south" (many of the slave holders he met or heard of were churchmen), which is "a mere covering for the most horrid crimes – a justifier of the most appalling barbarity – a sanctifier of the most hateful frauds – and a dark shelter under which the darkest, foulest, grossest, and most infernal deeds of slave holders find the strongest protection" (Wiley 1, 188).

Douglass writes about the society of his fellow slaves during his stay with Mr Freeland, suggesting a sense of community and brotherhood that is rare because isolating slaves from one another was one of the most powerful methods through which the slaveholders kept their power. Douglass writes: "We were linked and interlinked with each other. I loved them with a love stronger than anything I have experienced since . . . We never undertook to do anything of importance, without a mutual consultation" (Wiley 1, 190). This was the community with whom Douglass discussed the inhumanity of slavery and the first, failed attempt at escape was made in their company. The final escape came on

3 September 1838 when, he writes, that he reached New York without any "interruptions". This is merely stated, Douglass believing that giving details about the Underground Railroad would only endanger other aspirants and escapees. After this point the narrative goes on to his marriage, employment, the meeting with abolitionists and the launching of his career as an abolitionist speaker. One of his most important speeches is "What to the Slave is the Fourth of July?: An Address Delivered in Rochester, New York, on 5 July 1852" where he elaborates on this most uncomfortable of questions for a free nation:
> What have I, or those I represent, to do with your national independence? Are the great principles of political freedom and of natural justice, embodied in that Declaration of Independence, extended to us? . . . Fellow citizens; above your national, tumultuous joy, I hear the mournful wail of millions! whose chains, heavy and grievous yesterday, are, to-day rendered more intolerable by the jubilee shouts that reach them. (Wiley 1, 215)

Douglass' overall awareness about continuing prejudice is noted by one critic who writes, "As with so many aspects of life in America for blacks, their participation in the crusade against slavery was largely controlled by white leaders. Even among the Abolitionists there were strong racial prejudices. Douglass said in the mid-1850s: 'Opposing slavery and hating its victims has come to be a very common form of abolitionism'" (from *Frederick Douglass's Paper*, 5 April 1856 cited in Matlack 15).

In 1855, Douglass published his second autobiography, *My Bondage and My Freedom,* taking stock of the fifteen years he had spent as a free man. By now his relations with William Lloyd Garrison had soured and he was beginning to wonder about the effectiveness of the anti-slavery actions that had been undertaken so far. It is an account that provides explanations for many of his actions, and also gives glimpses of his time in England, Ireland, Scotland and Wales. The tone of melancholy in this work is, however, set aside at the end when he rededicates himself to the anti-slavery cause, asserting that though he could have remained in England, he knew that it was his duty to "labor and suffer with the oppressed in my native land" (Norton 379). The third and final autobiography, *Life and Times of Frederick Douglass*, came in 1881. It sums up his experiences and thoughts on his life, his achievements in the anti-slavery movement and looks forward to more objective assessments of the history of slavery in the future. It is written in a slightly elegiac tone as Douglass reflects on how he has been perceived, what remains still to be done and the divisions within the movement, especially with regard to the exodus from south to north encouraged by many leaders of the movement. But there is also satisfaction at "hav[e]ing had some small share in the great events" that occurred during his lifetime, and as "more than most men, I have been the thin edge of the wedge to open for my people a way in many directions and places never before occupied by them" (Norton 199). The retrospective narrative is especially significant in the case of Douglass as his experience of life in the North, his travels and his involvement in the lecture circuit as a speaker for the abolitionist movement enabled him to constantly review his own experience of slavery, note the cultural, political and psychological significance of many such episodes and understand their contribution to the making of the American nation.

With the rise of black studies in the 1960s as Gates Jr. and McKay have noted, Douglass's second autobiography began to be recognised, alongside the first-person writings of Thoreau and Whitman as one of the "crucial 'I-narratives' of the American 1850s" (301). In the record of his early struggles and the lifelong effort to articulate the meaning of the suffering undergone by his people, he is a representative figure in the mode proposed by Emerson, one who best expressed what an entire community had felt and thought and experienced. Recognising his historical role and responsibility, Douglass transformed his life and writings into a political instrument, more comprehensively than any other before him.

William Wells Brown (1814–84) like Douglass, embodies the new kind of drive that shifts the story of black emancipation into a different gear. From enslavement to escape, and then to becoming a conductor on the Underground Railroad and a much-in-demand abolitionist orator, Brown was also one of the most prolific writers of this period, using several genres to project different aspects of slavery. He wrote eight books including his best-selling slave narrative, *Narrative of William Wells Brown, A Fugitive Slave* (1847). An interesting facet of his literary personality is his practice of reading from his plays during his anti-slavery lectures. There is no extant text of the first play he wrote, titled *Experience; or, How to Give a Northern Man a Backbone* (1856) but Cato, who appears as a buffoon, fawning over his master and spying on fellow slaves, in Brown's *Escape; or, A Leap to Freedom,* the first extant play by an African American, was a useful figure to capture audience attention, especially when in his moments alone he dreams of escape and how he would show them once he reached Canada. This play was never performed during its author's lifetime (it was finally staged in 1971 at Emerson College) though Brown frequently read from it at anti-slavery meetings. But its arrival is an important intervention in the American theatre which, at this time, primarily consisted of minstrel shows and some adaptations of novels like Harriet Beecher Stowe's *Uncle Tom's Cabin,* and Anna Cora Mowatt's *Fashion* (1845) that depended heavily on stereotypical images of the black servant as primitive, childishly simple, and by turns helpless, loyal and dignified (like Uncle Tom), or willing to renounce his ethnic identity and ape his master (as with Zeke in *Fashion*). Brown exploits these stereotypes through Cato's childish behaviour and predilection for lying as well as his efforts to imitate his master – leading to comic situations. The play presents a picture of the slave's life – the frequent displacements, the absence of a stable identity, and the diverse exploitations of the slave's body especially in miscegenation (when a slave in the house is mistaken for Dr. Gaines' son). Brown is keenly aware of the impact of a dramatic presentation. As he wrote of his practice of reading excerpts from his plays, "[p]eople will pay to hear the Drama that would not give a cent in an anti-slavery meeting" (quoted in Farrison 294).

The context of reform, emancipation and abolitionism serves to frame the multi-generic work of Brown – sociological accounts like *The American Fugitive in Europe* (1854), a history of the race in *The Black Man, His Achievements, His Genius and His Antecedents* (1863), a military history in *The Negro in the American Rebellion:*

His Heroism and His Fidelity (1867), a travel book, *Three Years in Europe*, *The Anti-Slavery Harp: A Collection of Songs* (1848) for use at meetings, and the first novel by an African American, *Clotel; or The President's Daughter* (1867), about the daughter that Thomas Jefferson had with his slave mistress Sally Hemings. These diverse texts and genres repeatedly highlight the most urgent concerns of this time, balancing the long historical view with sharp attention to specifics. They also make Brown one of the most important figures in African American literary history, a trendsetter who demonstrates the power of the various genres of writing he practiced in the long battle for emancipation.

The three powerful narrators here, Douglass, Brown and Jacobs serve to show the gendered nature of the slave narrative and the different levels and kinds of torture and bodily violation that men and women suffered. They reveal the male slave narrative to be much more self-focused, highlighting obstacles in order to show the resolve and determination of the individual who overcame them. In contrast the female slave narrative of Jacobs is interested in revealing the support of people who helped her at various stages of her journey to freedom and publication of her narrative. One critic who has written on this aspect of the slave narratives suggests that: "While male fugitives stressed their individuality, their ability to stand alone and assume adult male responsibility for themselves, women fugitives generally saw themselves as part of their communities" (Morgan 83). Morgan also suggests that slave narratives countered the prevailing racial stereotypes: "Black men combated the stereotype that they were 'boys' while black women contested the idea that they were either helpless victims or whores" (76).

Though Brown had written the first novel by an African American, it was published in England. The first novel by an African American to be published in the US was written by **Harriet E. Adams Wilson** (1825–1900). *Our Nig; or, Sketches from the Life of a Poor Black* (1859) told the story of racism in the antebellum North. Harriet Wilson had a colourful if hard life. She was born in Milford, New Hampshire, to an African American father and an Irish mother. Her father's death left the family in abject poverty.

Her mother abandoned young Harriet to the life of an indentured servant in the home of a well-to-do Milford farmer. Here Harriet suffered abuse that she later used in her novel. At the end of her period of indenture, Harriet left and married Thomas Wilson with whom she had a child. The marriage was a source of unhappiness, with her husband leaving her when she was pregnant. He returned some years later and rescued mother and child from the Poor Farm where they were forced to live, but left again on a sea voyage to earn money. He died at sea leaving Harriet to fend for herself and her son. This was when she wrote *Our Nig*, but meanwhile her son died at the Poor Farm where she had left him to earn a living in Boston. Wilson continued to live in the Poor Farm at Milford for a few years after the tragedy of her son's death, before moving to Cambridge, Massachusetts in 1867, and joining the Spiritualist Movement as a "colored medium". She married a second time, but this marriage, too, did not last long. She reinvented herself as a popular lecturer at camp meetings and even at private homes, now going by the name of "Dr. Hattie E. Wilson, the trance medium". The autobiographical novel, *Our Nig*, tells the story of young Frado or Nig, a mulatto like Harriet Wilson, whose white mother abandons her to work as an indentured servant in a rich, white family, the Bellmonts. Here the young black child is subjected to unimaginable little cruelties by Mrs. Bellmont and her daughter Mary, making it difficult for the more sympathetic members of the family to openly support or be kind to the child. At a climactic moment in the book, after having endured Mrs. Bellmont's beatings, Frado suddenly shouts out to her to stop or she would not work for her again. After this the novel loses its momentum, quickly winding up with the final chapter, "The Winding Up of the Matter" telling of Frado's departure, only to continue in a life of poverty. She has a failed marriage, and is finally left physically and psychologically damaged. The novel ends with an appeal to the sympathy of the reader.

4

As we traverse this period, besides the autobiographical accounts, we begin to see several other forms being used: David Walker's

Appeal, Sojourner Truth's speech "A'int I a Woman?", and Martha Stewart's political lectures and essays are breakthrough events in that they made available forms of discourse that could directly address questions of slavery, women's selfhood and rights, and methods to counter the concerted efforts to keep African Americans, free or enslaved, in ignorance.

David Walker (1785–1830) was born in North Carolina to a slave father and free mother. His *Appeal in Four Articles, Together with a Preamble, to the Coloured Citizens of the World* (1829) is a culmination of his years of travelling in the slaveholding states of the South and studying and lecturing on slavery. It is a radical indictment and a call to violent resistance against racial injustice. During his lifetime two significant events took place that suggest a rising groundswell of resistance to slavery and parallel Walker's own convictions. These were the violent, organised revolt of Denmark Vesey in Charleston, South Carolina in 1822 and the founding in 1826 of the abolitionist Massachussetts General Colored Association by free blacks. While Vesey's revolt failed and he and others were tried and hanged, organised abolitionism went on to become an important movement for freedom and emancipation, and Walker's *Appeal* can be read alongside as a record of growing awareness and determination to find means of resistance. The *Appeal* has been read as an early nationalist document (Finseth 2001, Levine 2010) and as a riposte to Jefferson's *Notes on the State of Virginia* (Jarrett 2011). In the Preamble and the first Article of the *Appeal*, Walker offers a historical account and analysis of slavery from ancient times, calling it an "inhuman system" and a "curse to nations"(Norton 180), arriving at an assessment that he states in unambiguous terms: "The whites have always been an unjust, jealous, unmerciful, avaricious and blood-thirsty set of beings, always seeking after power and authority" (Norton 189). In the next three Articles he chalks out a programme for educational upliftment, renewal of the spirit and political awareness and action. Distinguishing the American version of slavery for its unequalled cruelty, he writes in Article 1,

> we (the coloured people of these United States of America) are the most wretched, degraded and abject set of beings that ever lived since the world began, and [that] the white Americans

having reduced us to the wretched state of slavery, treat us in that condition more cruel (they being an enlightened and Christian people) than any heathen nation did any people whom it had reduced to our condition. (Norton 183)

He justifies taking the offensive throughout the Appeal, urging fellow blacks to recognise the strength of the enemy while preparing to fight: "Fear not the number and education of our *enemies*, against whom we shall have to contend for our lawful right; guaranteed to us by our Maker; for why should we be afraid, when God is, and will continue (if we continue humble) to be on our side" (Norton 186, emphasis in original).

As African American print culture began to strengthen and spread, a number of other forms of writing emerged and *The Christian Recorder,* a magazine founded in 1852 and continuing into the present, gave a platform to a unique set of writers and readers – black ministers, soldiers and single women. It carried serialised novels, elegies, letters and sketches and was also a site for black editorial work that defined and shaped what it published (Eric Gardner's 2015 study notes the importance of black print culture). Works on print culture in the nineteenth century record the varieties of black writing that included broadsides, pamphlets, tracts and various other kinds of documents and this serves to show the diversity of writing without which what we put into a canon of African American literature would not have been possible. Ideas of literariness, of the black author and the reader were formed in the vibrant black print culture of this period. The careers of a number of men and women who came into prominence in these years and the growing participation in the abolitionist movement attest to the important role played by the press and print in disseminating the critique of slavery and racism.

Martin Robison Delany (1812–85), most famously associated with the Niger River Valley experiment for emigration of African Americans to Africa, and a proponent of African American nationhood (as a "nation within a nation", was born free in West Virginia. He began learning his letters from a Yankee peddler and eventually when the family fled to Pennsylvania because of threats to his mother for trying to educate her children, attended night school at the local African Methodist Episcopal Church. He also studied medicine with a doctor while working as an officer in the Pittsburg Anti-Slavery Society. He began his programme of emancipation of the race by starting a weekly newspaper, *The Mystery,* in 1843, writing fearlessly on issues of race. This was followed by two years of working as co-editor on Frederick Douglass's *The North Star.* In 1852 he published *The Condition, Elevation, Emigration, and Destiny of the Colored People of the United States.* He begins this text with the statement that in nations with "the greatest claim to civilization and enlightenment [there have been] classes of people who have been deprived of equal privileges, political, religious and social" who have "been looked upon as inferior to their oppressors, and have ever been mainly the domestics and menials of society" (Wiley 1, 300). This is the setting against which he sees the condition of the "colored people" who as "freemen even in the non-slaveholding States, occupy the very same position politically, religiously, civilly and socially (with but few exceptions) as the bondman occupies in the slave States" (301). He is caustic and sad that through long and habitual "maltreatment and abuse," they have become like the spaniel that still crouches at the feet of the master who kicks him, or the canary and the eagle that become tame: "[I]t has been so with us in our position among our oppressors; we have been so prone to such positions that we have learned to love them" (Wiley 1, 321). Here Delany argues for black resistance in a mode and tone that was characteristic but it is in his novel *Blake; or The Huts of America* (1860), the story of Henry Blake's escape and his travels in America, Canada, Africa and Cuba, that he explores more freely the theme of transnational resistance, echoing the actual revolutions that had taken place or were to come. Blake is imagined as a combination of the qualities of Nat Turner (a slave who led a rebellion in Virginia and was hanged) and Touissant (leader of the successful slave revolution in the French colony, Haiti). He starts a revolt after his wife is sold to a planter in Cuba, then follows her there, buys her freedom and forms the "Army of Emancipation" to free slaves in Cuba and spread the idea of revolt to America. Eric J. Sundquist writes that "throughout the Cuba section of the novel Cuba appears as a representative object of the increase of

Slave Power; in Cuba itself the American residents term themselves 'patriots' and 'rebels' who engineer false alarms of black rebellion against planters in order to increase their political power with the Spanish and to set the stage for American annexation" (21–22).

In depicting these expansionist designs, Delany is referencing the mood of the 1840s and '50s when it was argued that the US should annex Cuba, Haiti, Mexico and Latin America "because freedom for blacks in those regions posed a genuine threat to white life and institutions in the South" (Sundquist 21). Delany is an important early figure in the history of African American nationalism and emigration, who used his writing to articulate a critique of slavery but also analysed the effects of slavery on the victims. As he writes at the end of *The Condition*, "A child born under oppression has all the elements of servility in its constitution" and cites William Whipper, an African American businessman and abolitionist to drive home his point: "'they cannot be raised in this country, without being stoop shouldered'"(Wiley 1, 322).

Maria W. Stewart (1803–79), essayist, orator, abolitionist and women's rights activist is known for four powerful speeches she delivered in Boston at a time when women were not yet visible on public platforms as speakers. Maria Stewart was born Maria Miller in Hartford, Connecticut. She lost both her parents when she was five and entered the house of a white clergyman as a servant, living there for the next ten years. Here she was given religious instruction but educated herself as best she could by reading books from the family's library. She left at fifteen to fend for herself as a domestic while continuing her efforts at education in the Sabbath schools. She moved to Boston and married James Stewart, a war veteran who made a fair living by fitting out whaling vessels. Her husband died after three years of marriage and Maria returned to domestic service to support herself. In 1830 following a religious experience and conversion she became convinced that she had to dedicate herself to the freedom of her people. Gates Jr. and McKay suggest that the publication of David Walker's *Appeal* in 1829 influenced her in her resolve to become an activist and speaker for black rights (201). Her first publication was a pamphlet, *Religion and the Pure Principles of Morality* (1831) that urged African Americans to resist slavery in the South and racism in the North while calling for the education and economic upliftment of African Americans as well as rights for women. Around the same time, she also published several essays on these subjects in William Lloyd Garrison's abolitionist newspaper, the *Liberator*. Her collection of speeches and essays, *Productions of Mrs. Maria J. Stewart*, was published in 1835. Stewart's career as a speaker began with a speech, *An Address*, delivered before the African American Female Intelligence Society of Boston, on 28 April 1832, followed by a speech delivered before the New England Anti-Slavery Society at Franklin Hall in Boston on 21 September of the same year. The second speech begins with the shocking exhortation, "Why sit ye here and die?" and goes on to fearlessly speak of prejudices and economic deprivation that keep a whole race down:

> [w]e feel a common desire to rise above the condition of servants and drudges. I have learnt, by bitter experience, that continual hard labor deadens the energies of the soul, and benumbs the faculties of the mind: the ideas become confined, the mind barren, and, like the scorching sands of Arabia, produces nothing; or like the uncultivated soil, brings forth thorns and thistles. (Norton 205)

Stewart speaks also of the condition of "the wretched and miserable daughters of the descendants of fallen Africa" from her own experience of repeated episodes of domestic service and of the lack of prospects for young men who are otherwise "smart, active, and energetic" (206). Stewart's third speech, "African Rights and Liberty" was delivered at the African Masonic Hall on February 27, 1833 and the fourth and last one, "Mrs. Stewart's Farewell Address to Her Friends in the City of Boston" on 21 September 1833 (all the speeches are accessible at the Iowa State University Archives of Women's Political Communication, awpc.cattcenter.iastate.edu).

The transcripts of all her speeches were published by Garrison in the *Liberator*, ironically in its "Ladies Department" section. Garrison also published a second pamphlet, *Meditations from the Pen of Mrs. Maria J. Stewart*, in 1832.

In most of the writers discussed above we notice a common resolve to empower themselves through education and pursue upliftment for the whole community. This was achieved across genres. Against immense odds these writers demonstrated a sharp awareness of what was necessary to fight the long fight, but they were also confident that they, as individual members of the community, had the intellectual and moral resources and resourcefulness to engage in the many stages and forms of protest and awakening that were increasing in intensity as the North and South, abolitionists and slaveholders, moved towards Civil War. As the nation stood poised on the cusp of change, already we begin to discern the formation of strong and literate identities that would be necessary to speak for and about the community and push it out of the darkness of years of enslavement.

WORKS CITED

Anderson, Maureen. "Phillis Wheatley's Dido: An Analysis of 'An Hymn to Humanity, To S.P.G. Esq'." *New Essays on Phillis Wheatley*. Eds. John C. Shields and Eric D. Lamore. Knoxville: U of Tennessee P, 2011. 3–17.

Baym, Nina and Robert S. Levine. General Editors. *The Norton Anthology of American Literature.* Vol. A: Beginnings to 1820. New York and London: W.W. Norton & Company, 2012.

Best, Stephen and Saidiya Hartman. "Fugitive Justice." *Representations,* Vol. 92, No. 1 (2005). 1–15.

Brooks, Van Wyck. "On Creating a Usable Past." *The Dial* (11 April 1918). 337–41.

brown, drea. "The Multiple Truths in the Works of the Enslaved Poet Phillis Wheatley." Women Who Shaped History: A *Smithsonian Magazine* Special Report (24 June, 2020). smithsonianmag.com. n.p.

Bruce Jr., Dickson D. *The Origins of African American Literature, 1680–1865.* Charlottesville and London: UP of Virginia, 2001.

Davis, Charles T. and Henry Louis Gates Jr. Eds. *The Slave's Narrative.* New York: Oxford UP, 1985.

Documenting the American South (DocSouth), a digital publishing initiative sponsored by the University Library at the University of North Carolina at Chapel Hill, provides access to digitized primary materials that offer Southern perspectives on American history and culture

Farrison, William Edward. *William Wells Brown: Author and Reformer.* Chicago: U of Chicago P, 1969.

Gardner, Eric. *Black Print Unbound: The "Christian Recorder," African American Literature, and Periodical Culture.* New York: Oxford UP, 2015.

Gates Jr., Henry Louis. "James Gronniosaw and the Trope of the Talking Book." *Studies in Autobiography.* Ed James Olney. New York: Oxford UP, 1988. 51–72.

Gates Jr., Henry Louis and Nellie Y. McKay. Eds. *The Norton Anthology of African American Literature.* New York and London: W.W. Norton & Company, 1997.

Gordon, Avery. "Not Only the Footprints but the Water Too and What is Down There." *American Studies: An Anthology.* Eds. Janice A. Radway, Kevin K. Gaines, Barry Shank and Penny Von Eschen. Malden, Oxford, Chichester: Wiley-Blackwell, 2009.

Hartman, Saidiya. *Scenes of Subjection: Terror, Slavery, and Self-Making in Nineteenth-Century America.* New York: Oxford UP, 1997.

Hodgson, Lucia. "Infant Muse: Phillis Wheatley and the Revolutionary Rhetoric of Childhood." *Early American Literature*, Vol. 49, No. 3 (2014). 663–82.

Isani, Mukhtar Ali. "'Gambia on My Soul': Africa and the African in the Writings of Phillis Wheatley." *MELUS.* Vol. 6, No. 1, Oppression and Ethnic Literature (Spring 1979). 64–72. http://www.jstor.com/stable/467520.

Jarrett, Gene Andrew. *Representing the Race: A New Political History of African American Literature.* New York and London: New York UP, 2011.

Jarrett, Gene Andrew. Ed. *The Wiley-Blackwell Anthology of African American Literature.* 2 Vols. Malden, Oxford, Chichester: Wiley–Blackwell, 2014.

Jefferson, Thomas. "Query XIV: Laws [Slavery]." *Norton Anthology of American Literature: Vol A, Beginnings to 1820.* Eds. Nina Baym and Robert S. Levine. New York and London: W.W. Norton & Company, 2012. 669–73.

Jones Jr., Douglas. "Slavery, Performance, and the Design of African American Theatre." *The Cambridge Companion to the African American Theatre.* Ed. Harvey Young. Cambridge and New York: Cambridge UP, 2013. 15–33.

Matlack, James. "The Autobiographies of Frederick Douglass". *Phylon* (1960–), Vol. 40, No. 1 (1st Qtr., 1979). 15–28. https://www.jstor.org/stable/274419. Accessed 2 Aug. 2021.

Moody-Turner, Shirley. "Folklore and African American Literature in the Post-Reconstruction Era." *A Companion to African American Literature*. Ed. Gene Andrew Jarrett. Malden, Oxford, Chichester: Wiley–Blackwell, 2013. 200–11.

Morgan, Winifred. "Gender-Related Difference in the Slave Narratives of Harriet Jacobs and Frederick Douglass." *American Studies*, Vol. 35, No. 2 (Fall, 1994). 73–94. https://www.jstor.org/stable/40642688. Accessed 2 February, 2021.

Ransom Jr, Stanley Austin. Ed and Introd. *America's First Negro Poet: The Complete Works of Jupiter Hammon of Long Island*. Lloyd Manor, Long Island, NY. 1970. (Electronic Texts in American Studies/Libraries at University of Nebraska-Lincoln). https://digitalcommons.unl.edu.etas.

Redding, J. Saunders. "Phillis Wheatley." *The Dictionary of American Negro Biography*. Ed. Rayford W. Logan and Michael R. Winston. New York: Norton, 1982. 640.

Slavery and the Making of America: Original Documents https://www.thirteen.org/wnet/ slavery/ experience/education/docs1.html.

Sundquist, Eric J. "Slavery, revolution and the American Renaissance." *The American Renaissance Reconsidered*. Eds. Walter Benn Michaels and Donald E. Pease. Baltimore and London: The Johns Hopkins UP, 1985. 1–33.

Theatre Journal. Vol. 57, No. 4 (2005) Special issue on black performance.

Whitsitt, Novian. "Reading between the Lines: The Black Cultural Tradition of Masking in Harriet Jacobs's *Incidents in the Life of a Slave Girl*." *Frontiers: A Journal of Women Studies*, Vol. 31, No. 1 (2010). 73–88. https://www.jstor.org/stable/10.5250/fronjwomestud.31.1.73. Accessed on 11 May 2021.

Williams, Heather Andrea. *Self-Taught: African American Education in Slavery and Freedom*. Chapel Hill: U of North Carolina P, 2005.

CHAPTER 3

Up from Slavery
Reconstruction to the New Negro Renaissance: 1865–1919

TIMELINE

1867: First Reconstruction Act passed granting some rights to blacks and suffrage to black males.

1868: Fourteenth Amendment passed granting equal citizenship and civil rights.

1869: National Women's Suffrage Association formed; Wyoming Territory grants first suffrage to women

1870: Fifteenth Amendment passed granting suffrage to all male US citizens; Congress passed Enforcement Acts to check the Ku Klux Klan and to federally guarantee civil and political rights; A number of blacks are elected to the US House of Representatives; The first black Harvard graduate is Richard T. Greener.

1871: Second Act to enforce the Fourteenth Amendment

1875: A second Civil Rights Act passed giving equal treatment in public places and access to jury duty

1877: Federal troops withdraw from the South officially ending Reconstruction.

1881: Booker T. Washington establishes the Tuskegee Institute

1883: Supreme Court overturns Civil Rights Act of 1875

1890: The "understanding test" introduced in Mississippi to limit black suffrage and is followed by other southern states

1894: *The Woman's Era*, which later became the official organ of the National Association of Colored Women, begins publication.

1895: Washington's *Atlanta Exposition Speech*

1896: Supreme Court approves segregation with 'separate but equal' ruling in the *Plessy v. Ferguson* case. National League of Colored Women and National Federation of Afro-American Women merge to form National Association of Colored Women.

1898: Spanish-American War

1900: *Up from Slavery*

1902: Williams and Walker put up *In Dahomey*, a full length musical, the first by African Americans, on Broadway.

1903: Du Bois' *The Souls of Black Folk* is published.

1904: Braithwaite, *Lyrics of Life and Love*. *AME Church Review* calls for a "New Negro Renaissance".

1905: Niagara Movement dedicated to "aggressive action" for equal rights founded by Du Bois and others.

1907: Alain Locke becomes the first African American Rhodes Scholar.

1909: National Association for the Advancement of Colored People (NAACP) founded by Du Bois

1910–30: Great Migration of a million southern blacks to northern cities.

1912: The Lafayette Theatre becomes the first New York City Theatre to desegregate.

1914–18: World War I. US enters the war in 1917.

1916: Grimke's *Rachel,* performed in Washington, D.C., becomes the first full-length play written, performed and produced by African Americans in the twentieth century. Marcus Garvey comes to the US from Jamaica and begins "Back to Africa" movement with the establishment of the Universal Negro Improvement Association (UNIA).

1918: Marcus Garvey establishes the newspaper *Negro World*.

1919: Du Bois organises first Pan-African Congress in Paris. Eighty-three recorded lynchings during what came to be known as the "Red Summer of Hate". American Communist Party organised.

1920: Nineteenth Amendment grants suffrage to women.

After slavery was outlawed by the Thirteenth Amendment, the US Congress passed the first Civil Rights Act in 1866, declaring freed male African Americans to be US citizens and nullifying black codes. This marks the starting point of a decade of hope and related actions known as the Reconstruction that resulted in several important constitutional amendments, and provided free and newly freed blacks with a glimpse of hope and change. Even though the period quickly came to an end and was followed by new forms of racism and discrimination, the thought of what was possible remained in the collective consciousness, to be addressed and developed towards a fresh awakening in society and letters.

While our concern with one body of literature dominates the emphasis of this book, it is impossible to ignore that what happens here is actually set against a period of tremendous upheaval as the American nation shapes itself, and debates questions about the slave-based, agricultural economy of the South and the immigrant-dominated industrial economy of the North. These debates take place against the arrival of several immigrants and former slaves in the cities of the East and North, raising quite as many problems over integration as the post-slavery South did. The emergence of women in a big way in the public sphere, as a result of the anti-slavery movement and the women's movement which virtually ran alongside each other, was a significant development. As is likely when so many contradictions exist, development and change were uneven and often the prospects looked bleak. The African American literary corpus is a remarkable mirror of this national churning as it is affected by most of these questions over national integration, freedom and equality, the making of a multiracial society and political and economic upliftment. But more than mere reflection of the times, much of this literary outpouring articulated resistance, intervening and creating a discourse that was expected to be politically effective and bring about change for African Americans.

As we examine texts in this period it will also be evident that the debates within the African American society were equally debates that would impact the nation, especially over issues of educational opportunities, human rights (particularly in the context of what has come to be called the 'red summer of hate'), economic and employment avenues and most importantly, universal suffrage that would be *actually* available to all. The most significant period in which these developments first began to be seen is the decade of the Reconstruction, followed by its swift disintegration. The promise, the realisation and the failure of what was essentially a dream of change, are seen in the writings but also in the social and economic processes of this period. The conception of a New Negro identity (distinguishing it from the idea of the Old Negro) articulated in the works of many writers is a site of complexity that shows how diverse were the aspirations held by the community with regard to methods of racial uplift. For many freed slaves the material changes were minimal. Where they had earlier worked as slaves they were now employed, often by the same masters, for the same kinds of work, with their employers continuing to exercise nearly the same kinds of authority as they had earlier done.

Racial uplift in many forms is the emphasis of this chapter. It can be seen in direct and indirect forms in the literature, in subversions of existing conceptions of the Negro, in the use of realism, in fictional relationships between blacks and whites representing actual ones in various subversive ways, imagining utopias, using dialect and thereby acknowledging the value of the folk experience, recording various aspects and phases of social change including interracial relationships, mixed blood individuals and the phenomenon of passing (that is addressed by many writers who are themselves of mixed race), and newer forms of racial violence that grow out of the old.

Amendments to the US constitution made slavery illegal and African American men were given the right to vote. Newly freed individuals experienced the euphoria of freedom and dreams of equality (that quickly proved to be illusory). They were now suddenly able to move freely, take part in "constitutional conventions and the electoral process that enabled a number of African Americans to hold public offices" (Carson 154). But the area of most visible work and change was education. The Freedmen's Bureau, established in 1865, to protect the rights of black people of the South, sent thousands of educators of both sexes, and both black and white, to the South to variously work for upliftment of the Negroes – setting up schools and establishing cooperatives. Some four thousand schools were established by the Bureau. Independent colleges and universities like Fisk, Morehouse, Howard, Atlanta, Talladega and Hampton came into being between 1866 and 1868. Schools and colleges were also set up by different denominations of the Church, like the African Methodist Episcopal (AME), AME Zion, and Baptist churches. "Preparation for teaching, training for the Christian ministry and the skilled trades were principal curricula. Indeed, the nature and direction of black education formed one of the crucial divisions in black thought and educational policy well into the twentieth century" (Carson 155). Among the many cultural achievements were those in music. The Fisk Jubilee Singers and other college choirs contributed to establishing the spiritual as "an original American music form" while "Scott Joplin brought ragtime to a national audience" and writers started including early blues forms in their works. Literary examples of influences, as well as straightforward inclusion are "The Sorrow Songs" from *The Souls of Black Folk* by Du Bois, James Weldon Johnson's poem, "O Black and Unknown Bards" (1908) and Paul Laurence Dunbar's musical comedy *Clorindy, or the Origin of the Cakewalk* (1898) (Carson 155). Carson cites the opinion of Long and Collier that "the major form of literature [in this period] was the essay" often finding publication space in the many newspapers and magazines that began to emerge, with 154 papers in circulation by 1890 (156). These papers offered platforms for some of the debates – on the nature of education that African Americans should have (the two significant opposing views represented most vocally by Booker T. Washington and W. E. B. Du Bois), and "whether blacks should migrate to the North or remain in the South, or whether they should recolonize Africa or organize their own black state within the United States" (Carson 156). Most African American writers were published by presses run by their black compatriots (though some like Dunbar and Chesnutt found mainstream publishers for a few of their works). An interesting case is that of Pauline Hopkins who established her own book publishing company and edited the *Colored American Magazine,* using both to provide space to black writers.

The brief period of optimism and indeed euphoria ended with the election of Rutherford B. Hayes to the presidency, the removal of federal troops and backlash against African American progress, "suppression of the Negro vote" as Du Bois put it (Du Bois recounts this phase and the many examples of 'betrayal' and reversal in *The Souls of Black Folk*) through methods like "poll taxes, grandfather clauses and literacy tests, and underscored by the intimidation tactics of the Ku Klux Klan and other white vigilante groups" (Carson 157). The Jim Crow laws legalised segregation while lynching virtually became a norm for punishing black offenders.

But even as these regressive processes gained momentum, the already existing positives from education and movement out of the South ensured that a certain degree of improvement and empowerment continued and many black families and individuals succeeded in moving into the middle class, received education at the institutions set up during the Reconstruction, and found jobs (in spite of the competition from the constant stream of immigrants from Europe who were taking up the jobs of carpenters, blacksmiths, and shipbuilders earlier held by blacks, and who served in factories and formed all-white unions). As Gates Jr. and McKay colourfully put it,

> Nannies replaced mammies, and black butlers became corner bootblacks. Waiters were demoted to dishwashers, and cooks were replaced by European chefs. Barbers could not use their scissors on the hair of blacks if they wished to keep a white clientele, and even bootblacks could not use the same rag on shoes worn by Africans Americans and on those that shod the feet of Anglo-Americans. (465)

While old stereotypes shifted into newer ones, and racial discrimination took new forms, larger conceptions of identity were also forming. In the course of the educational and social programmes for racial uplift, a number of ideas of the "New Negro" emerged. These are listed by Marlon B. Ross as the Bookerite New Negro (to be realised through economic and industrial enterprise), the Garveyite nationalist New Negro (fostered by the nationalist 'Back to Africa' movement of Marcus Garvey and his Universal Negro Improvement Association), the New Negro of the NAACP and Du Bois (that would be legally integrated into US society at every level) and the red New Negro advocated by the black communists through communist consciousness raising and revolution. The New Negro identity was also the result of "class and regionalist dimensions" as well as "assumptions of gender roles and sexual conduct" (Ross 152). Tacitly masculine, this identity was, however, complicated by the emergence of women in the New Negro enterprise, "shaping not only its quotidian practice but also its intellectual, iconographic, and discursive frameworks" (Ross 153).

The failure of Reconstruction was primarily the result of the reassertion of racial superiority by whites who "mounted a public campaign to reaffirm white power as naturally ordered, divinely ordained, and scientifically justified" or "romanticiz[ing]ed the antebellum plantation culture of happy, docile, primitive slaves and beneficent, knowing, civilized slaveholders in fiction" seen in the novels of Thomas Nelson Page and Joel Chandler Harris (Ross 153). Within the period between 1865 and 1919, the Reconstruction decade was followed by the "Decades of Disappointment" also labelled as "the Nadir of Black Experience" by the historian Rayford Logan (cited in Gates Jr. and McKay 464).

1

The literature that developed in this climate was one of intense protest and equally intense aspiration. These were the reasons why the most popular form of literary engagement was the essay, with its flexibility and scope as well as its capacity to state the ideological resistance much more overtly than other forms. But it is also a literature that assessed black-white relations anew in the context of the reality of the Reconstruction.

It is necessary to place on record the growing importance of the press, printing and publishers in the programmes of this period. Many of the writers began their careers in magazines and newspapers as editors or occasional writers; some published novels serially in them; and many of the short stories that went into collections initially appeared in magazines. The press also played a significant role in consciousness raising, a key element in the programmes for racial uplift. Gene Andrew Jarrett notes an interesting shift that was apparent in the subject and emphases of popular magazines and periodicals from the earlier *Anglo-African Magazine, Freedom's Journal, National Reformer, Mirror of Liberty* and *Douglass' Monthly* to the contemporary *Colored American Magazine, Voice of the Negro* and *Horizon* in their "focus on the intellectual responsibility of African American literature to racial uplift and on the kind of forms and themes that could best facilitate the expression and impact of this doctrine" (Jarrett, *Representing the Race* 81). Themes of "African American social marginalization, economic disfranchisement and political disempowerment" as well as "literature that ... implied the collective racial progress of African

American writers in the realm of belles lettres" found place in the newer magazines. Hopkins' novels were serialised in the *Colored American Magazine* which she edited, while her essays and short stories regularly featured in it. In much of the racial uplift literature emerging in this latter part of the period there is recognition of the need for a distinct literary style that would attract readers and establish literary ability. Equally important was the conviction that "themes of African American *civilization*" (Jarrett, *Representing the Race* 83, emphasis added) should be asserted to educate but also to create a sense of worth amongst their readers. Statements by Hopkins and William Braithwaite in issues of the *Colored American Magazine* attest to the consciousness about a programmatic literary approach to uplift. Hopkins wrote in one of the editorials of her magazine on how the short stories were "becoming more and more literary in style" while Braithwaite declared the "commencement of a 'Negroid' renaissance"– the Harlem Renaissance of the 1920s (in Jarrett, *Representing the Race* 83).

The other instrument of upliftment and empowerment, education, was primarily of the two types represented by Washington and Du Bois – one for training at technical institutes that would equip black people for various skilled trades, and the other that would feed the 'soul' or give emotional content to their education. The polarisation of these two men and their views is indicative of larger implications, with each representing a view of the race, opinions about racism and methods to counter it, as well as showing awareness of the state of black-white relations and responses to dealing with it.

Booker T. Washington (1856–1915), born in Franklin County, Virginia, was the son of a white father and slave mother, who was a cook on a plantation until the Civil War and emancipation, after which the family of four children and their mother moved to Malden, West Virginia, where Washington worked at a salt furnace and later in the coal mines. At Malden he started attending night classes until 1872, before undertaking a 500-mile journey to Hampton, Virginia, to enroll in the Hampton Institute that imparted training in industry to blacks and Native Americans. Washington graduated from Hampton in 1875 and then joined as a faculty member, before leaving in 1881 to establish a school for black teachers in Alabama.

This was the famous Tuskegee Normal and Industrial Institute that was at the heart of the educational programme and philosophy upheld by Washington all his life – and that was based on industrial education and training felt by Washington to be crucial in bringing African Americans out of their poverty and historical subjugation, equipping them with skills for employment. This kind of training, while ensuring the upliftment of blacks would also accommodate the feelings of southern whites – essentially meaning that each would retain their place in the social hierarchy. Washington became a towering figure during this time, able to equally communicate with white businessmen and politicians and with the black community, working at transforming their condition. He travelled around the country, lecturing on his views and creating the accomodationist discourse with which he is associated. He is believed to have had ghost writers who wrote articles in his name for magazines, but he is known as the author of a biography of Frederick Douglass and a history of black America in two volumes. However, it is the autobiographical account *Up from Slavery,* a new version of *The Story of My Life and Work* (1900) that most fully represents the personality and views of Washington. A taste for the slave narrative had already been created by several significant earlier publications (discussed in the previous chapter) that contained themes of suffering and struggle, escape and finally the finding of voice, with authors learning how to identify and woo a readership. Washington clearly follows this pattern in catering to readers, white and black, who would each find something to match their expectations. He recounts details of his life as a slave child on the plantation – the poor meals, wooden shoes, rough flax shirts that needed to be broken in for the younger children, no time or occasion for play, no schooling and yet he claims every slave would have been willing to lay down his life for his master and his family, a tie that he says was mutual (Norton 492–95). Possibly the most startling aspect of his narrative is the declaration that slavery had actually turned out to be a good thing, with the black man and the white both benefiting from it: "notwithstanding the cruelty and moral wrong of slavery, the ten million Negroes inhabiting this country, who themselves or whose ancestors went through the school of American slavery, are in a stronger and more hopeful condition, materially, intellectually, morally, and religiously, than is true of an equal number of black people in any other portion of the globe" (496).

Recounting life in the period before and after the Civil War, Washington shares the excitements and fears on the day of freedom, the initial euphoria followed by worries about "a home, a living, the rearing of children, education, citizenship, and the establishment and support of churches." No wonder that the "wild rejoicing" was so soon replaced by "a feeling of deep gloom" in the slave quarters (Norton 498). Washington also narrates his intense aspiration to learn to read and write and generally educate himself – a desire that is eventually transformed into a collective aspiration for his people: "a whole race beginning to go to school for the first time" (Norton 500–01). His account of education at Hampton and subsequent work in educating his fellows provides glimpses of Washington's own understanding of the urgencies of the time – the commitment and the application in the cause of racial uplift and acknowledging the role of the "Yankees" who worked tirelessly in the cause, not only educating their wards and serving as role models, but also providing support in the setting up of other such institutions.

Up from Slavery contains the famous "Atlanta Exposition Address" which expressed most pithily Washington's view of the kind of education and training in skills that blacks should get at this early stage of their emancipation. This was a speech delivered at the Cotton States and International Exposition, a trade fair held in September 1895, to which Washington was invited as a representative of his race. His views set the terms of the ensuing debate, on the nature of education required by the mass of African Americans in the new era, with Du Bois, who took him on most vocally in his almost diametrically opposite text, *The Souls of Black Folk*. In Washington's address there is a sense of his mixed audience as he expands on what he has said at the start of his book: "[w]hen it comes to business, it is in the South that the Negro is given a man's chance in the commercial world". He speaks of the need to "glorify common labour", to begin at the bottom and not at the top and not "permit our grievances to overshadow our opportunities" (Norton 514).

He follows this up by urging the whites to throw in their lot with the "eight millions of Negroes, whose habits you know" instead of waiting for foreign labour of "strange tongue and habits" (Norton 515). Washington's expressed views ensured his position as the favoured spokesperson of the African Americans to the whites and also enabled him to be heard by powerful white business and political leaders. But in the process the narrative mode and structure of the uplift-autobiography form had to undergo "a shift that entail[s]ed curtailment of manly self-assertion and thus a demasculinization of the form, even while its virile structure of heroic ascent remain[s]ed intact" (Ross 159). Marlon B. Ross, who identifies this formal shift, compares Frederick Douglass's "violent resistance as a liberating rite of manhood" to Washington's habit of "repeatedly imag[es]ing the tenderness and fidelity of the enslaved." Ross refers to the "most vivid iconography" of *Up from Slavery* as that which "captures Washington in matronly poses and acts, meticulously sweeping the floor to gain entry to Hampton Institute, preaching 'the gospel of the toothbrush,' instructing the Tuskegee students on how to make their beds properly, and extolling the virtues of domestic servitude as a nursery for the tutelage of thrift, discipline, and entrepreneurship" (159). The sharpest criticism of this stand came from Du Bois who wrote in *The Souls of Black Folk*: "He insists on thrift and self-respect, but at the same time counsels a silent submission to civic inferiority such as is bound to sap the manhood of any race in the long run" (Norton 639).

William Edward Burghardt Du Bois (1869–1963) was the voice that gave the intellectual understructure to the struggles of the race. He is regarded as the founder of black studies with his training in the disciplines of history and sociology, and his years of teaching at several prestigious universities. His writings on many subjects provided the language and the ideas for resistance to the Washingtonian positions of compromise and accommodation.

In two papers "The History of the Negro Home" and "Negro Labor in Lowndes County", Du Bois

> [s]ought to refute the dominant belief in blacks' mental and physical inferiority – sometimes called the "retrogression

hypothesis" – by presenting historical evidence of the flourishing of domestic life and virtue among black Americans. . . . The study of the predominantly black Lowndes County aimed to amass extensive empirical evidence of black American vitality and health through house-to-house canvassing of more than twenty-five thousand homes . . . collecting data on . . . Negro schools, homes, landownership, and mortality. (Farland 1017)

These studies represent the scholarly rigour with which Du Bois approached the problems of the community and the lifelong attention he gave to the multiple questions that needed addressing in the programme of racial uplift through his writings on the history and sociology of the African American community.

Du Bois was born in Great Barrington, Massachusetts, and attended the local white school from where he graduated with honours in 1884, apparently without facing any discrimination from his white fellows. In 1885, he went to Fisk University to do his bachelor's degree and for the first time found himself exposed to the racism of the South and observed the condition of the African Americans there. In 1888, passing out of Fisk he entered Harvard University and received both a bachelor's and a master's degree. In 1895, he received his PhD degree from Harvard with his dissertation on "The Suppression of the African Slave-Trade to the United States" which was published in the Harvard Historical Studies series in 1896. He began his teaching career at Wilberforce University, a black institution, and then joined the University of Pennsylvania and produced the first sociological study of the race, *The Philadelphia Negro*, which was published in 1899. Meanwhile in 1897 he had moved on to Atlanta University where he remained for the next thirteen years, organising conferences and producing annual reports on subjects like black landowners, the black church, the black family, black urbanisation, and black mortality that laid the foundation for twentieth century African American sociology (Gates Jr. and McKay 607). This was a discipline that was critical in laying the foundation for the huge intellectual effort of understanding and resistance that would be manifested in literature and culture but that also helped educate both blacks and whites in the history of the race and the real conditions of black life.

Du Bois is most familiar to us through *The Souls of Black Folk*, a text that acquaints us with the idea of "soul", with "double consciousness" and with the metaphor of the "Veil". In the "Forethought" to *The Souls*, Du Bois mentions "the problem of the color-line", the key fact running through the book and implicit in the synopsis that he provides at its opening:

> I have sought here to sketch . . . the spiritual world in which ten thousand Americans live and strive. . . . Emancipation . . . and . . . its aftermath . . . . I have sketched . . . the two worlds within and without the Veil, and thus have come to the central problem of training men for life. (Norton 613)

He follows this up with an emphasis on "soul" – tacitly opposing the utilitarian, economic and industrial training programme of Washington – "I have stepped within the Veil, raising it that you may view faintly its deeper recesses, – the meaning of its religion, the passion of its human sorrow, and the struggle of its greater souls" (Norton 613).

The first chapter, "Of Our Spiritual Strivings" expresses this discursive shift in the pedagogic programmes as well as the "strivings" to emerge from the historical duality of being an American and a Negro and become "a co-worker in the kingdom of culture, to escape both death and isolation, to husband and use his best powers and his latent genius" (Norton 615). Subsequent chapters like "Of the Dawn of Freedom", "Of Mr. Booker T. Washington and Others", "Of the Meaning of Progress", "Of the Training of Black Men", "Of the Black Belt", "Of the Sons of Master and Man", and "Of the Sorrow Songs" trace the history, conditions, mental and spiritual aspirations and the possible ways of achieving them, as well as the distinct cultural character that is represented not only in the chapter on sorrow songs ("of undoubted Negro origin and wide popular currency") but also in the sorrow songs that serve as epigraphs to each chapter. The "Afterthought" with which he ends his book is an address to the reader who is urged to ensure that the book "fall not still-born into the world-wilderness" but be used to generate "vigor of thought and thoughtful deed" while "the ears of a guilty people tingle with truth" (Norton 740).

On the training of black men, his criticism is particularly sharp as he points to "boundless, planless enthusiasm and sacrifice . . . preparation of teachers for a vast public-school system . . . launching and expansion of that school system amid increasing difficulties . . . and finally the training of workmen for the new and growing industries" (Norton 658–59) – a programme that is at odds with his own conception of the need to give equal emphasis to the economic and cultural uplift of the race.

Du Bois's other works include five novels, *The Quest of the Silver Fleece* (1911), a love story set against the cotton industry of the South, *Dark Princess* (1928), which has Indian characters (derived from Du Bois's interest in the Indian freedom movement and especially in Mahatma Gandhi), and a trilogy written several decades later – *The Black Flame* (1957), *Mansart Builds a School* (1959), and *Worlds of Color* (1961). Besides there is the poem "A Litany of Atlanta" (poets.org) written in response to a three-day race riot in Atlanta, Georgia, in 1906, that is a prayer to God to take notice of black suffering and contains stark images of violence and blood lust – "A city lay in travail, God our Lord, and from her loins sprang twin Murder and Black Hate", or "Behold this maimed and broken thing; dear God it was an humble black man who toiled and sweat to save a bit from the pittance paid him" – in equal parts angry and helpless.

In 1911 he launched the magazine *Crisis,* the official organ of the NAACP which had grown out of the Niagara Movement and in both of which he was a prominent leader and member. The incipient nationalism of his early positions and writings received a strong boost from his Marxist sympathies and this crystallised into, on the one hand, the interest in cooperatives as a basis for social and economic uplift, and on the other, in his conviction about pan Africanism as a solution to the African American problem. In 1935 he published a major history, *Black Reconstruction: An Essay Toward a History of the Part which Black Folk Played in the Attempt to Reconstruct Democracy in America, 1860–1880,* followed by a book that might be said to represent his lifelong conviction about the unique blend of the individual and the collective, *Dusk of Dawn: An Essay Toward an Autobiography of a Race Concept* (1940) in which he used his own life and career as a representative case to study the problem of race and racial conflict.

In his writings in the many genres he practised there is a sense of the intermingling of sociological and historical inquiry stemming from his academic training and profession, with the imaginative and creative processes that he writes of so evocatively in *The Souls*. His philosophy of art is best represented in the essay "Criteria for Negro Art" (1925) where he takes issue with the views of Alain Locke on the relationship between art and propaganda, holding that: "all art is propaganda and ever must be, despite the wailing of the purists. I stand in utter shamelessness and say that whatever art I have for writing has been used always for propaganda for gaining the right of black folk to love and enjoy" (Norton 757). In another essay, "Two Novels", he compares Nella Larsen's *Quicksand* and Claude McKay's *Home to Harlem,* calling the first, "fine, thoughtful and courageous . . . the best piece of fiction that Negro America has produced since the heyday of Chesnutt" while the other "for the most part nauseates", catering to the "prurient demand on the part of white folk for a portrayal in Negroes of that utter licentiousness which conventional civilization holds white folk back from enjoying" (Norton 759).

In all of his work there is an integration of his primary concerns: the ideological is as much a part of personal experience as is the historical understanding of slavery and racism and the clear judgment of his own time as he observes and critiques the many phases of political and social development through the course of his long life. It is probably appropriate that this significant intellectual of the first half of the twentieth century should have had his prolific career end in death while still working on the ambitiously planned multivolume *Encyclopedia Africana.*

2

A number of powerful female voices emerged alongside those of the men. These women were writers, editors and important agents of emancipation for the community. They protested against injustice, supported other writers, used their own writings to critique and analyse and stood as exemplars. Among them are women like Pauline E. Hopkins, Ida Wells-Barnett and Anna Julia Cooper.

Pauline Elizabeth Hopkins (1859–1930), whose work was rediscovered in the middle of the twentieth century, was born in Portland and brought up in Boston. She first came to literary prominence as a contributor to the *Colored American Magazine* (founded in 1900) for which she was literary editor from 1900 to 1904 and where she wrote short fiction, historical articles and biographical sketches. She wrote a musical, *Slave's Escape, or the Underground Railroad* (performed on tour by the family's singing group, the Hopkins' Colored Troubadors) and a play, *One Scene from the Drama of Early Days,* and then went on to write the four novels for which she is best known.

Also called the magazine novels, these were published serially in the *Colored American Magazine*. The first is *Contending Forces: A Romance Illustrative of Negro Life North and South* (1900), the one hundred year saga of a mixed race family in the backdrop of racist violence in the post-Civil War era. This was followed by *Hagar's Daughter: A Story of Southern Caste Prejudice* (serially published, 1901–02), on the wife of a white landowner whose dark secret is black blood; *Winona: A Tale of Negro Life in the South and Southwest* (serially published, May–October, 1902), a tale of interracial marriage, abduction into slavery and escape; and the fantasy, *Of One Blood; or, The Hidden Self* (serialised, 1902–03), about a medical student who finds himself transported to a city beneath a pyramid in Ethiopia where he is proclaimed king. Hopkins' interest in themes of racial ambiguity and passing are most well represented in this novel which seems to have refined the techniques of sensationalism used in the earlier works. This last is a more complex examination of passing, especially in its presentation of the protagonist Reuel Briggs as a physically impressive man whose breadth of nostril initially suggests Italian and Japanese origins.

One critic has written that Hopkins was drawing on the two nineteenth century interests – the new psychology associated with William James and race – in figuring racial ambiguity: "[r]acial difference becomes something that lies inside an individual. Race is here construed as an interior element, as a secret buried within the personality, as a 'submerged' side of the self" (Otten 229). *Of One's Blood* "attempts to reopen questions of character and to offer new ways in which body, mind, and race can, as indices of identity, be understood in terms of each other" (Otten 230). Hopkins took recourse to one of the most popular forms of the nineteenth century, the sensationalist novel, to depict suffering, violence, interracial tensions and concerns over identity as well as the romantic escape from these situations. Her final work is *A Primer of Facts Pertaining to the Early Greatness of the African Race and the Possibility of Restoration by its Descendants – with Epilogue*.

Seen as a whole, this corpus of writing suggests her position as someone who was working with the history of the race, and its present while looking forward to a post-racial future, using the magazine as a platform to speak to the community about black heroes and heroines and the possibilities of race revival and uplift, and offering a version of the American Dream that would be accessible to African Americans.

Consciousness-raising is an important aspect of the community theme that is discernible in all writers of this phase. All of them were concerned with articulating a programme and carrying the community with them; the difference was only in how they imagined that such uplift could be achieved. If Washington focused on technical education and training, Du Bois spoke of the spirit and the soul, and these other writers seem to have been influenced by the same goal in writing about the history of the race and its greatness while articulating critiques of their contemporary condition. One such writer is **Ida B. Wells-Barnett** (1862–1931), a name we have come to associate with searing accounts and analyses of lynching. Wells-Barnett was born to slave parents, went to a school opened by the Freedman's Aid association in Holly Springs, Mississippi, but dropped out at sixteen and started teaching to support the family after her parents died in the yellow fever epidemic of 1878. She eventually moved to Memphis where alongside teaching she also attended Fisk University during summer breaks. She edited two newspapers in succession, *The Evening Star* and *The Living Way*, and later became the editor and part owner of the *Memphis Free Speech* where she continued her crusades against injustice and inequality. After three of her friends, owners of the People's Grocery Company, were lynched, she wrote in her editorial that there was little that could be done against lynching, urging blacks to leave a town where they would get neither security nor justice. A mob attacked the offices of the *Free Speech* newspaper while she was out of town, making it difficult for her to return to Memphis. She moved to Chicago, continuing her anti-lynching crusade, and writing and taking active part in all the public efforts that were going on for racial uplift. She joined the Niagara Movement of Du Bois and was one of the founding members of the NAACP; but because of the radical nature of her views and her unhesitating criticism of men like Booker T. Washington, her role was not acknowledged. As one critic has written of her command over rhetoric, she "engaged in writing as swordsmanship, demonstrating that in the right hands the pen can indeed become a mighty sword" (Royster 169). Her career of activism, directed through a lifetime of journalism and writing to convince and educate, besides showing up the many dimensions of lynching, offers an example of the place of the essay and the speech as forms that were wielded by hundreds of blacks in the service of the community. The word became a weapon that could demolish and persuade and show up – an aesthetics of literary activism which would elevate these prose forms into a national literature.

Wells-Barnett's books, all of which dealt with the murderous violence against the African American community in the post-Civil War period, include *On Lynchings,* a collection of three of her pieces on the subject, *Mob Rule in New Orleans* (1900), and two pamphlets, *Southern Horrors: Lynch Law in all its Phases* and *The Red Record: Tabulated Statistics and Alleged Causes of Lynching in the United States* (1895). Her unfinished autobiography, *Crusade for Justice,* was published after her death. The challenges against which such writing emerged included not only the direct racial invective and the assumptions about inferiority, corruption and sexual promiscuity expressed by white supremacists to downplay the increasing visibility of blacks in the educational and economic fields, and the always-present danger of the Ku Klux Klan, but also the romanticisation of the plantation culture, of "happy, docile, primitive slaves and beneficent, knowing civilised slaveholders in fiction like that penned by Thomas Nelson Page and Joel Chandler Harris" (Ross 155). As Ross argues, what was needed against these challenges was emphatic rebuttal: "American Negroes had to do more than disconnect their identity from that of the preternatural slave as fashioned by the postbellum Redemptionists and plantation apologists; they also had to claim aggressively a racial identity allied with newness, modernity, progress, urbanity, and self-empowerment against the assault of racial invective and violence that defined their status as Negro" (157).

The work of women like Ida B. Wells-Barnett, Pauline Hopkins and **Anna Julia Cooper** (1858–1964), is particularly important in this process because of the overall masculinist assumption that underlies much of the uplift literature from Douglass to Washington. Cooper was a teacher of science and mathematics, with a PhD in history from the University of Paris-Sorbonne and edited several important magazines. In one of the essays in her only published book, *A Voice from the South by a Black Woman of the South,* titled "Womanhood a Vital Element in the Regeneration and Progress of a Race", she writes,

> Only the Black Woman can say 'when and where I enter, in the quiet, undisputed dignity of my womanhood, without violence and without suing or special patronage, then and there the whole *Negro race enters with me*'. . . . We need men who can let their interest and gallantry extend outside the circle of their aesthetic appreciation; men who can be a father, a brother, a friend to every weak, struggling, unshielded girl. We need women who are so sure of their own social footing that they need not fear leaning to lend a hand to a fallen or falling sister.
> (Norton 563)

Cooper was born a slave in North Carolina, but after the Civil War, at the age of nine, she entered St Augustine's Normal School on a scholarship and embarked on a career of teaching and lecturing. Her book is interesting for the variety of issues she discusses alongside the central argument for educating and empowering women. In the first half she writes of the role of the educational institutions run by the African Methodist Church. She argues for practical training that will make it possible for students to go out and earn a living, while suggesting that only those with special aptitude should be encouraged to study further in different subjects. Other topics that concern her in this part of the book are the vote for women and the damaging effects of segregation. In the second half she studies the representation of African Americans by authors like Harriet Beecher Stowe and William Dean Howells (the text can be read at docsouth.unc.edu).

Cooper's sentiments about women's education are echoed in the work of Wells-Barnett and Hopkins, both of whom realised the importance of uplifting women alongside men, and who engaged in unique projects towards this end. They used their journalistic skills to good purpose as they edited several newspapers, and participated in the coloured women's club movement, especially the National Association of Colored Women with its motto of "Lifting as we rise", contributing to the many different exercises in consciousness-raising being undertaken at this time.

The wide-ranging nature of these exercises can be seen in the many great-man/great-woman histories, race albums with photographic displays, and histories of a great race in books like William Wells Brown's *The Rising Son; or, The Antecedents and Advancement of the Colored Race* (1874), Carter G. Woodson's *The Negro in Our History* (1922) and *A New Negro for a New Century* (1900), the latter a collected volume of photographs and text, displaying the achievements of the race (Ross 160).

3

Paul Laurence Dunbar (1872–1906) was the son of former slaves and was born in Dayton, Ohio. His father escaped to Canada and then returned to fight in the Civil War as part of the Fifty-fifth Massachusetts Infantry and the Fifth Massachusetts Cavalry, and his mother worked as a washerwoman in her early years. From them he learned the stories and oral culture of the African American slave past and wrote his first poem when he was six. His mother worked for a while with the Wrights whose sons, Orville and Wilbur (inventors of the airplane) attended the same school as young Paul, the Dayton Central High School, and who eventually supported the printing of

Dunbar's first, short-lived newspaper, *The Tattler*, in 1890. Despite his academic abilities Dunbar could only find employment as an elevator operator after graduating from school. But he continued to write poems and his first collection, *Oak and Ivy*, was published in 1893 by the United Brethren Publishing House. At a meeting of the Western Association of Writers in Dayton in 1892, his poems came to the notice of several poets. The Illinois poet James Newton Matthews wrote a letter praising Dunbar's poetry that was printed by several newspapers across the country, making his work known to a wider readership. His second volume of poems, *Majors and Minors* (1895), a mix of poems in standard English (majors) and dialect (minors), was reviewed favorably by William Dean Howells.

Many of the best poems from the two volumes were put together and published in one volume as *Lyrics of Lowly Life* in 1896. Dunbar gained national and international renown as a result of his poems effectively reaching readers and he undertook a six-month lecture tour of England in 1897. On his return he found employment as a clerk at the Library of Congress and married the poet Alice Ruth Moore. Two collections of poems, *Lyrics of the Hearthside* and *Poems of Cabin and Field* came out in 1899. Three more poetry volumes, *Lyrics of Love and Laughter* (1903), *Lyrics of Sunshine and Shadow* (1903) and *Howdy, Howdy, Howdy* (1905), written when he was already very ill, confirmed his stature as a poet.

Dunbar was also the author of four collections of short stories – *Folks from Dixie* (1898), *The Strength of Gideon and Other Stories* (1900), *In Old Plantation Days* (1903), and *The Heart of Happy Hollow* (1904) – and four novels, three of which were about white characters while the fourth, *The Sport of the Gods* (1901), about an African American family that migrates to the North is a dark representation of urban America. These realistic pictures of life on the plantation and generally in the antebellum South, that seem to offer rationales for migration are set alongside equally convincing accounts of characters who show loyalty to the master and his family (as in the story "The Strength of Gideon") and who, even after the formal end of slavery, prefer to stay and take their chances with freedom in familiar territory. This stance (also recounted by Washington in *Up from Slavery*, of slaves who preferred plantation life to an uncertain future) in Dunbar's fiction appears to be at odds with the racial uplift theme that he expressed more directly in his essays, as did many others. But this is one phase in the changing emphases discernible during these years from Reconstruction to its aftermath as the initial euphoria gave way to cynicism and literature adapted itself to other needs.

Best remembered for his use of black dialect in his verse and fiction, Dunbar also used standard diction in poems like "The Poet and his Song" with its refrain of "And so I sing and all is well" (Wiley 1, 869–70), "Frederick Douglass" an elegy written on the death of Douglass which records that "'Twas for his race, not for himself he spoke" (Wiley 1, 871–72) or the stirring lines of the "Ode to Ethiopia" which speak of the pride and nobility of the race (Wiley 1, 876–77). His use of dialect is seen in poems like "An Ante-Bellum Sermon": "We is gathahed hyeah, my brothahs, / In dis howlin' wildaness" (Wiley 1, 873–75), or the wonderful "When Malindy Sings" which is structured around the natural musical ability of Malindy set off by the futile effort of "Miss Lucy" who "ain't got de nachel o'gans / Fu' to make de soun' come right". Malindy on the other hand "jes' spreads huh mouf and hollahs" (Wiley 1, 891–93).

Towards the end of his life he also wrote a play, *Herrick* (discovered only in 1993), in the style of a comedy of manners, besides a few fragments like *The Gambler's Wife* and *The Island of Tanawana*. The diversity of his writings attests to the range of his aesthetic capabilities especially in the light of his early struggles to make a living as a writer.

The many conditions from which writers emerged and the influence of their environment and early advantages or disadvantages on the roles they played during the period covered in this chapter is perhaps best represented by another figure, **James Weldon Johnson** (1871–1938), whose stature is often considered to rival that of Du Bois and Alain Locke.

Johnson was born in Jacksonville, Florida, to James and Helen Louise Johnson who had emigrated from the Bahamas in 1866 and had settled into comfortable middleclass life, with James Johnson employed as headwaiter in St. James Hotel and Helen Louise becoming the first African American public school teacher in Florida. James Weldon, the second of their three children imbibed her love and knowledge of literature and music, graduated at sixteen from the Stanton School, an all-black grammar school, went on to Atlanta University, where he excelled at academics, sport and music, touring New England as a member of the Atlanta University Quartet. While still a freshman at Atlanta he spent a summer teaching the children of former slaves in rural Georgia, encountering a side of black life that he had himself not experienced and about which he wrote in his autobiography, *Along This Way* (1933). After graduating from Atlanta he returned to head his own school and during this time, founded and edited *The Daily American* (1895–96), was admitted to the bar in Duval County, Florida, before leaving for New York to collaborate with his brother John Rosamond and another performer as a song writer for Broadway productions. While at New York he also studied literature at Columbia University.

His first collection of poetry, *Fifty Years and Other Poems* (1917) is generally considered to be conventional in form, though recent criticism has identified interesting contradictions in the early writings: "clichéd comedy songs about black life as well as uncompromising editorials on the race question, imitative poems as well as attacks on imitative poetry" (Müller 85). The first poem of this collection and the most famous of his songs, "Lift Every Voice and Sing" was adopted by the NAACP as the "Negro National Anthem". His second collection, *God's Trombones* (1927), is a set of seven free verse sermons. *The Autobiography of an Ex-Colored Man* (1912/1927) with its Preface and text has been called "parodic, a new and radical variation on conventional slave narratives" (Goellnicht 21), as it deals with the theme of 'passing', with its unnamed black narrator passing for a white man, marrying a white woman and agonising over what looks like betrayal of the racial cause – a story that draws on Johnson's legal partner of early years, a black man who passed as white, in a complicated depiction of identity problems. This text with its reference to the genres of both the modern novel and the slave narrative represents an important stage in the development of African American modernism.

Another role that Johnson performed was that of an editor, and in the Preface to *The Book of American Negro Poetry*, he lists four "creations" by African Americans that were "the only things artistic that have sprung from American soil". These were the Uncle Remus stories collected by Joel Chandler Harris, the spirituals, the cakewalk (a style of dancing that eventually disappeared but that paved the way for forms like "buck and wing", "stop-time", "turkey-trot", "eagle-rock", "ballin' the jack" and the "tango" from Cuba) and ragtime (Norton 862). Ragtime in fact began as songs "written in Negro dialect" about "Negroes in the cabin or in the cotton field or on the levee or at a jubilee" (863). These were what Johnson calls "jes' grew" songs and he tells of one that he and his brother and Bob Cole appropriated, rewrote the verses and published as "Oh, Didn't He Ramble" (Norton 864).

Racial uplift remained the big theme and purpose of literature with **Charles Chesnutt** (1858–1932), the most prominent and popular novelist and short story writer of the day. Born to free blacks in Cleveland, Ohio, Chesnutt grew up in Fayetteville, North Carolina, attended a Freedmen's Bureau school, headed the State Colored Normal School from 1877 to 1883, first as assistant principal and then as principal before moving, first to New York City, and then back to Cleveland where he passed the bar, became an attorney and established a successful legal stenography firm. For a brief period of six years from 1899 he shut the firm and became a full time author, writing his three novels, but reopened his firm when he realised that his novels were not commercially successful enough to supplant his profession. His literary contributions include *The Conjure Woman* (1899), a collection of seven tales about the Old South ostensibly in the plantation tradition, of benign masters and loyal and loving slaves, created by white writers like Joel Chandler Harris and Thomas Nelson Page. Set in North Carolina and featuring a white frame narrator who acts as a mediator for Uncle Julius McAdoo, the ex-slave story teller who not only uses his own recollections to tell stories of clever and imaginative responses to slavery, but also presents the African American hoodoo traditions or "conjuration" – magic and spells that help slaves to deal with their often cruel masters, and that sometimes transform humans into animals.

These tales established Chesnutt's reputation as a major writer of the post Reconstruction era. The collection contained "The Goophered Grapevine", the first short story by a black to be published in *The Atlantic Monthly* in 1887. This story begins with the white narrator, a man engaged in grape-culture, looking for a change of scene for the sake of his sick wife, and fixing on North Carolina on the advice of a cousin. Here they finally discover the McAdoo grape plantation, and Julius McAdoo himself, sitting on a log eating grapes. McAdoo, the character who would be the source of all the stories in the collection, is a tall and aged black man with bushy hair except for a bald patch on the top of his head, and apparently of mixed blood. On being questioned about the vineyard he declares: "Lawd bless you, suh, I knows all about it. Dey ain' na'er a man in dis settlement w'at won' tell you ole Julius McAdoo 'uz bawn en raise' on dis yer same plantation" (Norton 526). On discovering their interest in buying the vineyard he tells them: "dis yer ole vimya'd is goophered . . . Is goophered, – cunju'd, bewitch'", introducing this key aspect of the stories, the magical and fantastical elements of hoodoo. He elaborates on his claims with the story of Aunt Peggy who was hired to 'goopher' the vineyard to prevent the slaves from eating the grapes before they could be made into wine. Aunt Peggy

> [s]a'ntered 'roun' 'mongs' de vimes, en tuk a leaf fum dis one, en a grape-hul fum dat one, en a grape-seed fum anudder one, en den a little twig fum here, en a little pinch er dirt fum dere, – en put it all in a big black bottle, wid a snake's toof en a speckle' hen's gall en some ha'rs fum a black cat's tail, en den fill' de bottle wid scuppernon' wine. W'en she got de gopher all ready en fix', she tuk 'n went out in de woods en buried it under de root uv a red oak tree. (Norton 527)

She follows this up with a warning to "de niggers" that anyone who ate the grapes now would die within twelve months. This is followed by several tales of death following quickly after the grapes are eaten. And then comes the account of the new slave Henry who unknowingly eats the ripe grapes and has to be taken to Aunt Peggy to be ungoophered. The remedy she gives him makes him grow alternatively young and old with the grape season and his master discovers another way of making profit, selling him when he is young and hardy and buying him back when he is old and cheap. This was of course too good to last and one year when Henry was getting younger and younger, the master decided to keep him but when it was time for the grapes to come the vines started to wither, and nothing Master Dugal did could stop them dying. Henry too started to sicken and finally died. The Civil War begins, the master goes off to fight and the vineyard is abandoned. Uncle Julius story is designed to discourage new buyers who might put a stop to his free use of its produce but the narrator buys it anyway and gives a new lease of life not only to the vineyard but also to Uncle Julius who now becomes a coachman. This story with its use of dialect and the representation of African American magic is typical of the style and subjects that Chesnutt used often in his work – local colour and folklore alongside realistic depictions of plantation life, entertaining even while offering subtly embedded critiques of the institution of slavery by showing apparently benign slave owners whose primary motive of profit from their slaves is revealed in sly, sideways remarks like the one about Master Dugal in "The Goophered Grapevine" that "it ha' ter be a mighty rainy day when he could n' fine sump'n fer his niggers ter do" (Norton 529).

Another tale in this collection, "Mars Jeems's Nightmare", also subverts the plantation tradition with its white master transformed into a black slave who is whipped frequently by the overseer before he is able to revert back to his original self with the intervention of Aunt Peggy. Uncle Julius is a parody of Joel Chandler Harris's Uncle Remus and Mars Jeems is drawn from his white master.

Other works by Chesnutt are *The Wife of His Youth and Other Stories of the Color Line* (1899) and several novels. The first of his novels, *The House Behind the Cedars* (1900), is a novel on 'passing' about a brother and sister whose mother has one-quarter black ancestry, but who are determined to succeed despite racial odds. *The Marrow of Tradition* (1901) is a historical novel on the Wilmington riot of 1898 and is set in the fictional town of Wellington. It shows how white residents use the press to spread rumours and create fears against blacks, leading to the outbreak of violence on both sides, even as many blacks flee to escape it. The novel portrays the complex state of race relations at this time through the interwoven lives of two families, the Millers and the Carterets. Major Philip Carteret is the editor of *The Morning Chronicle* and along with two other military men represents the anti-Negro white sentiment that is outraged by black prosperity. Dr. William Miller on the other hand has returned after his medical education to serve his people by setting up a hospital for blacks. His wife, Janet is the half-sister of Philip Carteret's wife, Olivia, whose father had married his black servant. This explosive mix of racial themes emerging in the postbellum South – white supremacist sentiment, miscegenation, fears of black economic and social advance, and organised violence against blacks – makes this Chesnutt's most powerful novel and one that is representative of the concerns in fiction emerging at the turn of the century. His third novel, *The Colonel's Dream,* is a story of disillusionment and disappointment for Colonel Henry French, who makes a nostalgic trip to his birthplace, Clarendon, with his young son, only to discover that the place of his childhood is plagued by persisting race divisions and continuing exploitation, now of convict labour, at the hands of a wealthy contractor. The novel shows the difficulty of actual transformation of the entrenched racism and fresh resentment in the southern states. Chesnutt's critical essays and lectures represent his efforts to come to terms with these realities while inviting examination of the emerging nature of race relations. In "What is a White Man?" he begins caustically, "The fiat having gone forth from the wise men of the South that the 'all-pervading, all-conquering Anglo-Saxon race' must continue forever to exercise exclusive control and direction of the government of this so-called Republic, it becomes important to every citizen who values his birthright to know who are included in this grandiloquent term" (Wiley 1, 567).

The purpose of this query emerges when he subsequently raises the issue of the intermingling of races that must surely reorient the question raised in the title. In 1905 he lectured before the Boston Historical and Literary Association on "Race Prejudice: Its Causes and its Cure". In this piece he analyses the historical and psychological bases of prejudice and argues for education, alleviation of poverty and unemployment, and access to civil and political rights as necessary to its removal. In keeping with his interest in the mingling of races he briefly touches upon the calls for retaining racial purity as one more strategy on the part of whites to perpetuate the colour line. He ends the speech with a prophecy: "I see an epoch in our nation's history . . . when there shall be in the United States but one people, moulded by the same culture, swayed by the same patriotic ideals, holding their citizenship in such high esteem that for another to share it is of itself to entitle him to fraternal regard" (Chesnutt n.p.). In another important essay, "The Negro in Books" (1916), Chesnutt makes the interesting suggestion that realism needed to be blended with "a little idealism". As one critic commenting on this, writes,

> While black writers recognized the period's literary trend towards realism, they also valued what appeared to be 'a little idealism' in conveying their aims of racial progress. Since both realism and romance seemed ill fitted to express varied black experiences, black writers drew freely from both traditions, sometimes merging the aesthetic or ideological conventions of the two approaches to create a form more flexible for politically conscious art. (Williams 186)

This blended mode is seen in other writers, certainly in Pauline Hopkins but also in **Sutton E. Griggs** (1872–1933), a prolific author who is best known for five novels where he expressed strong political views, and who is often considered as a forerunner to the overt black nationalist literary responses of a later period. Griggs was a Baptist minister who held positions in Memphis and Nashville and wrote extensively against the backdrop of his activities in both these cities. Himself the son of a Baptist minister, Griggs attended Bishop College and Richmond Theological Seminary in his birthplace, Chatfield, Texas. In the course of his profession he came into contact with the poorer black working class and his novels address this special readership. His first novel, the utopian *Imperium in Imperio* (1899) expresses his radical views in its representation of an underground organisation of educated and militant African Americans who are determined to wipe out injustice and inequality in America. Through his two main characters, the organisation's leader, Bernard Belgrade, a mulatto, and Belton Piedmont, who is modelled on Booker T. Washington, Griggs, however, points to the dangers in any programme of action that calls for outright war, or is led by people who are solely interested in grabbing power, at the cost of the very people for whom they are presumably fighting. Piedmont who stands for a more moderate position that recognizes that many whites may be willing to participate in the fight against injustice, urges a method of compromise and dialogue and suggests a four year period of waiting, after which if things remain the same, they might take over Texas and set up a separate government there. Belgrade declares Belton a traitor and orders his execution. At the end the organisation and Belton himself are about to be destroyed by the very forces their activities released. The novel flags themes like the need to acquaint whites with black sentiment and educate them to understand black aspiration while assessing the respective merits of compromise and militant opposition. However, it refuses to offer a definitive theory of revolution. Griggs seems to issue a warning through the events narrated in the novel about the potential disillusionment of the emerging educated black youth. He uses an interesting narrative method, presenting a set of documents collected from a character named Berl Trout who appears with a dying declaration at the start of the novel – a method that allows him to keep a distance from the views expressed in the text even while offering them for the reader to evaluate. Griggs also stresses the importance of speaking and using language well in referring to the eloquence and oratorical skills of both the protagonists – a political point about suitability for citizenship and participation in democratic processes in the US that was perceived as important.

Eric Curry makes a connection between this novel and Griggs' late political work, *Guide to Racial Greatness; or, The Science of Collective Efficiency* (1923), commenting on the concept of "collective efficiency": "The principles of collective efficiency as elaborated in the *Guide* are intended to inspire or even provoke a community-based and collectively-driven black leadership that includes the farmer and the philosopher, as well as the mechanic and medical student, all of whom are necessary parts of a collective national consciousness" (Curry 24).

The goal of collective work continues as this ideal and strategy are adapted for newer challenges that arise during each period.

Among Griggs' other novels is *Overshadowed* (1901), about the struggle of the African American race against Anglo Saxon superiority, told through the growing love between childhood friends Astral and Erma that is affected by the fact of Erma's biological father being a white man. Another novel, *Unfettered* (1902), dealing with themes of forced migration in the face of violence, obstacles to racial equality, and lynching, shows the assertion of authority by Lemuel Dalton who has just inherited his father's estate that is run by an ex-slave Samuel. During the course of the novel Lemuel, and Samuel's son, Harry, have an altercation and Lemuel shoots and gravely injures Harry. Against the backdrop of rising race tensions Beulah, Harry's sister, is lynched by a group of white men. The black community is disillusioned at the failure of the government to ensure safety and many of them leave town. *The Hindered Hand; or, The Reign of the Repressionist* (1905) continues the exploration of lingering racism and the unwillingness of the white plantation owners to accept the changes. It represents three Spanish-American war veterans and includes a love story. But it is the realistic account of lynching that grabs attention. The young couple, Bud and Foresta, who kill Sidney Fletcher in self-defence, are caught and ordered to be lynched in front of the Negro church. The horror is graphically presented before an eager mob. Foresta's hair is chopped off and people scramble for bits as souvenirs; her fingers are cut off one by one and flung into the crowd; a corkscrew is bored into her bared breast and flesh pulled out. Then it is Bud's turn to have his fingers cut off, the corkscrew bored into his legs and arms, and his head battered so that an eyeball hangs out and is snatched by the nearest man as his souvenir. After three hours of torture, the brother of Fletcher is invited to set fire to the two mangled humans. One of the most horrific elements of the novel is the little boy, Melville Brant, who defies his mother and escapes from his bedroom window to watch the lynching, carrying a piece of the charred flesh home. At the end of the episode the people who had arrived to watch the lynching by special trains, leave while a newcomer, Ramon Mansford, is told by a resident: "We lynch niggers down here for anything. We lynch them for being sassy and sometimes lynch them on general principles. The truth of the matter is the real 'one crime' that paves the way for a lynching whenever we have the notion, is the crime of being black" (Gutenberg EBook, n.p.).

Pointing the Way (1908) is the story of an ex-slave Uncle Jack who appears as a social activist and also features a young lawyer, Baug Peppers who believes he can marshall the support of liberal white politicians of the South in arguing for full African American voting rights in the Supreme Court. Pepper represents the New Negro professional and is an advance on the failed project of *Imperium* where Belgrade is killed by his own followers, though the novel ends unsatisfactorily, with the reader left wondering about the citizenship case.

Hopkins, Chesnutt and Griggs all offered "a better historical alternative" through "racial equality as an essential condition for socio-economic equality" and "the utopian genre was singular in the degree to which its very conventions required the explicit articulation of social criticism, offering the opportunity to assert an oppositional stance in new ways and to new effects" (Fabi 114). Fabi argues that Griggs was actually using sophisticated ways to engage in a dialogue with peers like Chesnutt, setting the utopian *Pointing the Way* as a counter to Chesnutt's dystopian *The Colonel's Dream*. According to her, "Griggs builds on his knowledge of contemporary legal challenges to the grandfather clause in Louisiana and Alabama in order to articulate a civil rights utopia of black enfranchisement" through the figure of the elderly ex-slave and social activist, Uncle Jack (115).

Andrea N. Williams has argued that writers like Hopkins, Chesnutt, Griggs and Dunbar "intended their literature not only to reflect social conditions with a near ethnological accuracy, but also to contemplate . . . possible solutions to race and gender relations". Therefore, not making "a clear distinction between the genres of realism and romance" was obviously a convenient literary strategy, producing instead what Jarrett calls "racial realism" (Williams 189). Explicating further on racial realism, Williams calls it "a literary phenomenon or imperative that energized black

writers' experimentation in multiple forms of prose and poetry
. . . produc[e]ing . . . regionalism or local color writing, domestic
realism, and naturalism" (189). She mentions as examples, the
local color writing of Alice Dunbar and Chesnutt's conjure tales;
domestic realism mostly by women writers like Pauline Hopkins
and Frances E. W. Harper, but also Chesnutt and Griggs; and the
naturalism of Dunbar (189–96).

Many of the fictional works present powerful images of the black
man and woman that counter the stereotypes used repeatedly in the
works of white practitioners of the plantation romance tradition like
Thomas Nelson Page and Thomas Dixon. One early essay mentions
glorification of the black man: "Aroused by the literary libels of
the schools of Page and Dixon as well as by political, social, and
economic discrimination and persecution, Negro authors undertook
to offset the misrepresentations of Southern propagandists by
defending and glorifying the black man" (Gloster 336). This may
have been a strong impulse but as the fiction of Hopkins, Chesnutt
and Griggs demonstrate, these novels were nuanced and complex
in their responses to the prevailing representations.

Among a group of lesser-known writers during this period is
Fenton Johnson (1888–1958), who produced three volumes of
poetry, *A Little Dreaming* (1913), *Visions of the Dusk* (1915), and
Songs of the Soil (1916), edited two short-lived magazines, *Champion
Magazine* and *Favorite Magazine* and wrote a collection of essays, *For
the Highest Good* (1920) and one of short stories, *Tales of Darkest
America* (1920). After this brief period of productivity he slipped
into literary oblivion. His most striking contributions according to
Gates Jr. and McKay are the spirituals, "Singing Hallelujia" and
"The Lonely Mother", and poems like "Tired" with its reckless
abandonment of work and "somebody else's civilization", and "The
Scarlet Woman" that is a take on one of the common stereotypes
of black women, the seductive Jezebel, as it ironically traces the
degeneration from "the Virgin Mary" and "the Minister's wife"
through bowing to Vice (all poems in Norton 925–28).

Many of the practices from this period as well as conceptions like
the New Negro, and convictions about African American cultural

richness, and intellectual and aesthetic abilities and taste, form the base on which the literary flowering of the next period, the New Negro or Harlem Renaissance takes place.

WORKS CITED

Carson, Warren J. "Racial Ideologies in Theory and Practice: Political and Cultural Nationalism, 1865–1910." *The Cambridge History of African American Literature.* Eds. Maryemma Graham and Jerry Ward. New York and Cambridge: Cambridge UP, 2011. 154–76. Kindle EBook (paginated).

Chesnutt, Charles. "Race Prejudice; Its Causes and Its Cure." *Alexander's Magazine* (1905). 21–26. chesnuttarchive.org. Accessed 15 Jan. 2022.

Curry, Eric. "'The Power of Combinations': Sutton Griggs' *Imperium in Imperio* and the Science of Collective Efficiency." *American Literary Realism*, Vol. 43, No. 1 (Fall 2010). 23–40. https://www.jstor.org/stable/10.5406/amerlitereal.43.1.0023. Accessed 16 Jan. 2022.

Fabi, M. Giulia. "Desegregating the Future: Sutton E. Griggs' Pointing the Way and American Utopian Fiction in the Age of Jim Crow." *American Literary Realism*, Vol. 44, No. 2 (Winter 2012). 113–32. https://www.jstor.org/stable/10.5406/amerlitereal.44.2.0113. Accessed 16 Jan. 2022.

Farland, Maria. "W. E. B. Du Bois, Anthropometric Science, and the Limits of Racial Uplift." *American Quarterly*, Vol. 58, No. 4 (December 2006). 1017–45. https://www.jstor.org/stable/40068404. Accessed 16 Jan. 2022.

Gates Jr, Henry Louis and Nellie Y McKay. Eds. *The Norton Anthology of African American Literature.* New York and London: W.W. Norton & Company, 1997.

Gloster, Hugh M. "Sutton E. Griggs, Novelist of the New Negro." *Phylon* (1940–1956), Vol. 4, No. 4 (4th Qtr., 1943). 335–45. https://www.jstor.org/stable/271503. Accessed 16 Jan. 2022.

Goellnicht, Donald C. "Passing as Autobiography: James Weldon Johnson's *The Autobiography of an ExColoured Man.*" *African American Review*, Vol. 30, No. 1 (Spring 1996). 17–33. https://www.jstor.org/stable/3042092. Accessed 7 Jan. 2022.

Jarrett, Gene Andrew. *Representing the Race: A New Political History of African American Literature*. New York and London: New York UP, 2011.

Jarrett, Gene Andrew. Ed. *The Wiley-Blackwell Anthology of African American Literature*. 2 Vols. Malden, Oxford, Chichester: Wiley–Blackwell, 2014.

Lehman, Cynthia L. "The Social and Political Views of Charles Chestnutt: Reflections on His Major Writings." *Journal of Black Studies*, Vol. 26, No. 3 (Jan., 1996). 274–86. https://www.jstor.org/stable/2784823. Accessed 15 Jan. 2022.

Massiah, Louis. Produced and directed. *Du Bois, W. E. B.: A Biography in Four Voices*. Distributed by California Newsreel, San Francisco, Calif., 1995, 116 mins. (Documentary).

Müller, Timo. "James Weldon Johnson and the Genteel Tradition." *Arizona Quarterly: A Journal of American Literature, Culture, and Theory*, Volume 69, Number 2, (Summer 2013). 85–102. https://doi.org/10.1353/arq.2013.0012. Accessed 7 Jan. 2022.

Otten, Thomas J. "Pauline Hopkins and the Hidden Self of Race." *ELH*, Vol. 59, No. 1 (Spring 1992). 227–56. https://www.jstor.org/stable/2873425. Accessed 16 Jan. 2022.

Ross, Marlon B. "Racial Uplift and the Literature of the New Negro." *A Companion to African American Literature*. Ed. Gene Andrew Jarrett. Oxford and Malden: Wiley-Blackwell, 2013. 151–67.

Royster, Jacqueline, Jones. "To Call a Thing by its True Name: The Rhetoric of Ida B. Wells." In *Reclaiming Rhetorica: Women in the Rhetorical Tradition*. Ed. Andrea A. Lunsford. Pittsburg and London: U of Pittsburg P, 1995. 167–84.

Williams, Andreá N. "African American Literary Realism, 1865–1914." *A Companion to African American Literature*. Ed. Gene Andrew Jarrett. Oxford and Malden: Wiley-Blackwell, 2013. 185–89.

Chapter 4

Cultural Awakening
The New Negro or Harlem Renaissance: 1919–40

Timeline

1920: Nineteenth Amendment to US Constitution granting suffrage to women.

1922: Johnson, *The Book of American Negro Poetry;* Claude McKay, *Harlem Shadows*. Anti-lynching Bill passed in House of Representatives but fails to be passed in Senate.

1923–25: Marcus Garvey, *The Philosophy and Opinions of Marcus Garvey*.

1923: Jean Toomer, *Cane*. Oklahoma declares martial law to curb the KKK.

1925–27: Annual literary contests sponsored by *Crisis* and *Opportunity* magazines.

1925: Alain Locke, *The New Negro;* Countee Cullen, *Color*. 40,000 KKK members parade in Washington D.C.

1926: Eric Walrond, *Tropic Death;* Langston Hughes, *The Weary Blues*.

1927: Charles S. Johnson's anthology, *Ebony and Topaz;* Cullen's anthology of black poetry, *Caroling the Dusk*. The first talkie, *Jazz Singer* made with a white actor, Al Jolson as black-faced minstrel singer.

1928: McKay, *Home to Harlem;* Marita Bonner, *The Purple Flower;* Nella Larsen, *Quicksand* and *Passing*.

1929: Jessie Fauset, *Plum Bun;* Wallace Thurman, *The Blacker the Berry*. Stock Market crashes, beginning the Great Depression.

1930: Nation of Islam founded by W. D. Fard.

1931: Arna Bontemps, *God Sends Sunday*. Scottsboro boys unjustly convicted of raping two white women in Alabama, prompting nationwide protests.

1932: Sterling Brown, *Southern Road;* Thurman, *Infants of the Spring*.

1933: President Roosevelt pushes "New Deal" through Congress.

1934: Nancy Cunard, *Negro, An Anthology*.

1935: Hurston, *Mules and Men*. National Council of Negro Women founded.

1936: Bontemps, *Black Thunder*. Jesse Owens wins four golds at Berlin Olympics.

1937: Hurston, *Their Eyes were Watching God*. Joe Louis becomes world boxing heavyweight champion.

1938: Richard Wright, *Uncle Tom's Children*. Crystal Bird Fauset elected to Pennsylvania House of Representatives to become the first African American woman state legislator.

1939–45: World War II

1939: Contralto Marian Anderson sings at Lincoln Memorial for an unprecedented audience of 75,000 after her concert at Constitution Hall was prevented by Daughters of American Revolution.

1940: Wright, *Native Son;* Hughes, *The Big Sea;* Robert Hayden, *Heart-Shape in the Dust*.

1941: US enters war after Japanese attack on Pearl Harbour. Philip Randolph of the Brotherhood of Sleeping Car Porters organises march on Washington to protest segregation in the military and discrimination in employment. President issues order forbidding racial and religious discrimination in government training programmes and defence industries.

The Harlem Renaissance, also known as the New Negro Movement or a Negro Renaissance, is a period both of cultural consolidation and development in all the arts – music, painting, dance and sculpture as well as the literary genres of poetry, fiction, drama and the essay. It features the powerful voices of writers, academics, activists, and journalists, many of whom were expatriates from the Caribbean. Arthur Schomberg's "The Negro Digs up his Past" and Langston Hughes's "The Negro Artist and the Racial Mountain" characterise concerns about the recovery of black heritage and black identity, achieving a distinctly black aesthetic and dealing with continued racism. Important writers include Angelina Grimke, Alain Locke, Marcus Garvey, Claude McKay, Zora Neale Hurston, Jean Toomer, Langston Hughes and Countee Cullen.

The Communist Movement and affiliations of many African Americans with it, the stock market crash and the Great Depression, World War I, and industrial development (the T-Ford was a symbol of this expansion and the access now possible for a large number of Americans to own a car and acquire mobility in a way that was impossible earlier) – these events were influential for the race as they opened up new realms of thought and greater economic opportunities.

This was also a period when a number of people from the Caribbean came to the US, bringing fresh ideas, styles and habits of thought and an outsider view on the race problem, even as many travelled abroad and connected with political struggles in countries like the USSR, Cuba, and Haiti.

The themes of community, identity and mobility appear in newer ways. With the presence of the Caribbean expatriates the sense of community becomes international/transnational. New notions of blackness and identity are heard and the term "New Negro" (heard first in the 1890s) gains greater currency. The term is distinguished from the "Old Negro" (associated with slavery), and refers to those who have left slavery, emancipation and the disillusionments of Reconstruction behind and are looking forward to a new phase of cultural awakening. The political undertones of the term are melded into the cultural, and many of the processes to shape the New Negro that began in the post-Reconstructionist years are carried forward to find newer expression.

For us as readers in India this phase is interesting as it corresponds to the years of intense activity in the anti-colonial struggle and it is possible to compare the emerging idea of national culture at this time for both nations. The increasing complexity and greater degrees of awareness about distinctiveness as well as efforts to actually work towards such distinctiveness are seen in the literature. It is the period of modernism, the age of Eliot and Pound and Gertrude Stein, of Robert Frost, Wallace Stevens, William Carlos Williams, Carl Sandburg, Ezra Pound and fiction writers like Willa Cather, Sherwood Anderson, Katherine Anne Porter, William Faulkner, playwrights like Eugene O'Neill and Susan Glaspell – a period of intense creativity and critical challenge. Hughes, Sterling Brown, Richard Wright, Countee Cullen and many others were part of this period of ferment. The making of this huge body of writing lent clarity of purpose and showed the way for aesthetic distinctiveness through the mining of African American resources for the shaping of an aesthetics that would be racially exclusive and distinct.

While strict period demarcations are inconvenient because of the role played by older writers from the earlier period who continued to write and influence cultural development, sometimes serving as mentors by example if not through their actual works, and many significant institutions having been founded earlier, or by individuals who began their careers earlier (the Krigwa Little Theatre movement of Du Bois in 1926 is one example), there were certain significant aspects of the location that distinguish this phase. These would be the character of the community's involvement in cultural and political programmes, and the international dimension given by artists arriving from the West Indies. The outpouring of creativity was a countrywide phenomenon and cities like Chicago and Philadelphia saw writers and artists emerging. New York City and the small district known as Harlem, close to Central Park, became a beacon for black writers across the country who converged here to either take up residence in Harlem itself or be part of the cultural activities organised here.

Migration from the South also flooded Chicago and Chicago's South Side, especially, during the period from 1916 to 1920. The Chicago Renaissance ran roughly around the same time as the Harlem Renaissance, developing through organisations like the South Side Writers' Group (SSWG), the South Side Community Art Center (SSCAC), the Chicago School of Sociology, magazines like *New Challenge* and *Negro Story,* the Federal Theater Project, and the federal government's relief projects for artists under the Works Progress Administration (WPA). Richard Wright, Gwendolyn Brooks and Margaret Walker are some writers who we associate with the Chicago Renaissance, and who would eventually go on to become key figures in the modernist literature that we discuss in the next chapter. In fact, Wright's "Blueprint for Negro Writing", published in the fall 1937 issue of the *New Challenge*, was instrumental in distinguishing the Chicago Renaissance from the Harlem Renaissance. And Arna Bontemps claimed that "Chicago was definitely the center of the second phase of Negro literary awakening. Harlem got its renaissance in the middle 'twenties, centering around the *Opportunity* contests and the Fifth Avenue Award Dinners. Ten years later Chicago reenacted it on [the] WPA without finger bowls but with increased power" (cited in Gordon 277). The federal government's funding programmes gave a huge boost to writers in Chicago and elsewhere, freeing them from the white patronage that had characterised the Harlem Renaissance. There were overlaps, with the somewhat older Harlem writers mentoring many of the Chicago writers. Both cities saw writers working on racial themes and elements of black folk culture. In both there was a clear Marxist influence: Harlem writers like Langston Hughes, Claude McKay and Dorothy West "cultivat[e]ing an 'Afro-Marxist cosmopolitanism' that merged black aesthetic and cultural traditions with the Marxist perspective of proletarian art" (Gordon 278).

Literary and cultural activity was also centred in other cities. However, Harlem was in the vanguard, and served as a 'blueprint' for other sites. The location of a fertile creative phase in the district of Harlem is in itself a remarkable event, capturing the imagination of those who came here and all those who would go on to look back on the significance of the period in the cultural life of the community. It was a fortuitous coming together of necessity and chance – as the overcrowded area was abandoned by whites and became available to house black middle class families as well as the many who were migrating in ever larger numbers from the southern states and would go on to constitute an urban working class. While southern blacks had always been moving to the North, escaping slavery in the beginning as well as in the aftermath of the Civil War, during Reconstruction and the years following, now, with the turn of the century, industrial development in the North, the US entry into World War I and jobs falling vacant as a result of white workers signing up in the armed forces, made many more job opportunities available, encouraging blacks from across the country to move.

The transnational dimension of the Harlem Renaissance was made possible by the travel of many of the artists to Europe and Africa and the Caribbean, the expansion of readership of black writing in these places, and the literature from these countries becoming available to readers in the US. New ideas about cultural work – formal innovations, but above all a sense of being set free from the constraints of having to write only about race – came to be adopted. This translated into freedom from the kinds of politics that had accompanied black literary activity from the time of the first written texts. From subversive, guerilla-style resistance work, through the overtly radical and oppositional, aspiring writers now settled into a proud phase of distinctive creative activity.

The romance of Harlem is one of the most engaging aspects of the New Negro Movement, though the literary renaissance was also taking place in other cities like Chicago, Philadelphia, and Washington DC. But Harlem, which "was first a Dutch settlement before it became German, then Irish, then Jewish, then black, and only after a real estate battle followed by white flight", captured the imagination of all those who came here with dreams in their hearts and often little else. "Laborers from the South rubbed elbows with African Americans who had known wealth, independence, and social prestige for generations. Immigrants from the West Indies and Africa encountered black people with entirely different sensibilities and customs" and "all of this mixing provided excellent fodder for African American artists determined to translate the cultural upheaval they saw around them into their art" (Bernard 270).

The nightlife of Harlem attracted all, blacks and whites: "the cabarets, buffet flats, speakeasies, and ballrooms" and the institutions that provided platforms for powerful jazz artists like Duke Ellington, Louis Armstrong, and Bessie Smith, who were an integral part of the Renaissance. These especially included nightclubs like the Cotton Club (which only had a white clientele, while blacks had to sit separately), Connie's Inn and Small's Paradise (Bernard 270). Days were equally busy with activities of institutions like the NAACP headed by Du Bois who edited its mouthpiece, the *Crisis*, the National Urban League headed by Charles S. Johnson who edited its magazine, *Opportunity,* and the Universal Negro Improvement Association (UNIA) of Marcus Garvey who edited its weekly newspaper, the *Negro World*. The labour organisation known as the Brotherhood of Sleeping Car Porters was led by the socialists Chandler Owen and A. Philip Randolph who edited the radical magazine, *Messenger.* These newspapers and magazines offered space for the poems, essays and stories of many of the Harlem writers before they went on to find publishers.

An event mentioned by many commentators was the Civic Club dinner of 1924, sponsored by *Opportunity* magazine and organised by its editor, Charles S. Johnson to felicitate Jessie Fauset for her first novel, *There is Confusion* (1924). This was an occasion for editors, writers and publishers to meet and acknowledge that "a new era in African American art was on the horizon" (Bernard 272). It was also during this dinner that Johnson was asked by the editor of the journal *Survey Graphic* to edit a special issue devoted to African American culture. Johnson invited Alain Locke to help him and the issue titled "Harlem: Mecca of the New Negro" was released in 1925. Locke expanded this into the anthology, *The New Negro*, which featured portraits and sketches as well as literary pieces, and was published a few months after the special issue with an introductory essay on "The New Negro" by Locke.

Opportunity then held a literary-cultural contest. The prize money was put up by the wife of the editor of *Forum* magazine and awards went to Sterling Brown in literature, Roland Hayes in music, E. Franklin Frazier in sociology, Zora Neale Hurston in folklore and Langston Hughes for his poem, "The Weary Blues".

Rudolph Fisher's essay "The Caucasian Storms Harlem" captures a sense of the busy night life of Harlem – his memories of the nightclubs, and their virtual takeover by white patrons that he discovers when he returns following his medical education, are recounted in this essay. He mentions the famous clubs, and performers, the dance and music that was practiced there, and the growing interest among white outsiders. In club after club he discovers that he, or sometimes the group he is with are the only Negroes in the place. What he finds now looks like a significant cultural shift as whites throw themselves wholeheartedly on to the dance floor: "And what do we see? Why, we see them actually playing Negro games. I watch them in that epidemic Negroism, the Charleston. I look on and envy them. They camel, and fish-tail and turkey, they geche and black-bottom and scrunch, they skate and buzzard and mess-around" (Norton 1194).

The race dynamics of this period are evident in the role played by white patrons in promoting black art, supporting and helping, often financially, and giving visibility to artists through prestigious magazines and periodicals as well as through the powerful white presses; but it is also apparent in the distinction made between the Old Negro and the New Negro that divided the older generation of Du Bois and James Weldon Johnson from that of Hughes and Cullen and Toomer. The struggle with identity is represented in many of the writers but it was Locke's emphatic statement about it in his essay on "The New Negro" that gave shape to the complex entity that was being called new.

1

Alain Locke (1886–1954) was uniquely equipped for the role that he gave himself, of a scholar-critic-activist who would help shape what others would write. Born into an elite black family in Philadelphia, he graduated from its Central High School and then went on to study at the universities of Harvard, Oxford and Berlin. He was the first black Rhodes Scholar. On his return to the US in 1912, he joined Howard University to teach English, philosophy and education. Between 1916 and 1917 he completed his doctoral thesis at Harvard and returned to become chair of the Philosophy department at Howard. Locke was the editor of several anthologies: *Plays of Negro Life* (1927 with Montgomery Gregory), *Four Negro Poets* (1927), *The Negro in Art: A Pictorial Record of the Negro Artist and of the Negro Theme in Art* (1940) and *When Peoples Meet, a Study of Race and Culture Contacts* (1942 with Bernhard J. Stern). He played godfather to several of the younger artists like Hughes, Hurston and Cullen besides introducing them to Charlotte Osgood Mason, a wealthy, elderly white woman who supported young artists. He was not himself an artist but through his unflagging enthusiasm and energy in pursuing and discovering writers and anthologising them he performed a necessary service to the nascent movement. In the process he reflected on the identity of the Negro in America, and the new and the old versions of this identity.

In his introductory essay to *The New Negro,* Locke writes,
[t]he Negro today wishes to be known for what he is, even in
his faults and shortcomings, and scorns a craven and precarious
survival at the price of seeming to be what he is not. He resents
being spoken of as a social ward or minor, even by his own, and
to being regarded a chronic patient for the sociological clinic,
the sick man of American Democracy. . . Religion, freedom,
education, money – in turn, he has ardently hoped for and
peculiarly trusted these things; he still believes in them, but
not in blind trust that they alone will solve his life-problem.
(Norton 966)

The resistance and independence that is demonstrated of the New Negro here is seen by Locke in the backdrop of "collective effort" and "race cooperation" and as he said, "[T]his deep feeling of race is at present the mainspring of Negro life" (Norton 966).

In assessments of Locke's role in the Harlem Renaissance Arnold Rampersad, among others, calls *The New Negro* its "definitive text" (87), while Nathan Huggins, author of *The Harlem Renaissance* (1971) writes of Locke that "his energetic championing of the intellectual achievement of Negroes in the 1920s made him the father of the New Negro and the so called Harlem Renaissance" (cited in Rampersad 87).

A similar role of offering encouragement and support was played by **Georgia Douglas Johnson** (1886–1966), who was herself a well-regarded poet, besides writing plays, short stories and four regular newspaper columns. Her poetry collections were *The Heart of a Woman* (1918), *Bronze: A Book of Verse* (1922), *An Autumn Love Cycle* (1928) and *Share My World* (1962), in the second of which she dealt with race themes.

Another influential individual was **Marcus Garvey** (1887–1940) who is usually mentioned in the context of the 'back to Africa' sentiment. Of Jamaican origin, he had early experience with founding labour unions, saw racial exploitation in several places that he visited – he travelled to Costa Rica, Central America and London – and read Washington's *Up from Slavery.* He finally arrived in the Unites States and specifically Harlem, with all his pent-up indignation and anger, in 1916. In 1914 he had already founded the

Universal Negro Improvement Association (UNIA), the title itself expressive of his understanding of the race problem on a global scale. He brought with him a fierce pride in his race that quickly made him popular in Harlem. His inspirational sentiments about race are apparent in declarations like the following in a piece titled, "The Future As I See It":

> I have a vision of the future and I see before me a picture of the redeemed Africa.... Why should I lose hope, why should I give up and take a back place in this age of progress?... Lift up yourselves, men, take yourselves out of the mire and hitch your hopes to the stars.... Let no man pull you down, let no man destroy your ambition, because man is but your companion, your equal; man is your brother; he is not your lord; he is not your sovereign master. (Norton 980)

As we have seen, from the time of the Reconstruction, oppositional views and individuals who have taken on the intellectual currents of their times, have together contributed to the making of complex, multi-dimensional literary-cultural public spheres that have provided impetus and spice to each generation of artists. Garvey's radical stand was at odds with the views of the older generation of literary cultural activists like Du Bois and Johnson and contributed to this fruitful and rich context.

As noted above, a specially enriching aspect of the period was the arrival of several artists of Jamaican origin. One of the most important of these was **Claude McKay** (1889–1948). Born into a peasant family, he grew up listening to his father's stories and learning of the white enslavement of blacks. He had access to several important cultural traditions while still in Jamaica. These included the Ashanti traditions of West Africa from his father, and the Greek and Roman classics, British literature and philosophy from his elder brother with whom he was sent to live while still young. As a teenager, while still with his brother, he served as apprentice to a wheelwright and furniture maker and also worked as a constable in Kingston. In 1907 he met Walter Jekyll, a white British folklorist who encouraged him to write Jamaican dialect poetry and helped him to publish his first two volumes, *Songs of Jamaica* and *Constab Ballads,* that gave expression to two phases of his life, the early years with his parents in Clarendon Parish and the period he spent as a constable in the Kingston police department where he observed the racism still rampant in this British colony. McKay was awarded the Silver Musgrave Medal of the cultural organisation, Institute of Jamaica, for these two poetry collections, becoming the first person of African descent to win it, and he used the prize money to go to the US and join the Tuskegee Institute. But dissatisfied with the regimen of the Institute he left after two months to join Kansas State College where he studied for two years. Walter Jekyll continued to support his studies as also his move to Harlem in 1914. The next five years saw McKay making forays into several professions – failing as a restaurateur, he worked as a porter and dining car waiter on the Pennsylvania Railroad. But in the meantime, he became closely involved with the leftist literary scene in New York, and besides associations with the editors of magazines like *The Liberator*, he published his poems "The Harlem Dancer" and "Invocation" in a 1917 issue of *The Seven Arts*.

His journey towards the goal of becoming a writer is particularly fascinating. There were encounters with some of the prominent white poets and critics and through them he had the opportunity to publish his poetry in the *Crisis* and *Opportunity*. Briefly he also worked on the editorial staff of the *Liberator*. In 1919 he travelled to England, and had his third volume of poems, *Spring in New Hampshire* (1920), published with a preface by I. A. Richards. He became thoroughly immersed in the communist movement, read Marx and wrote regularly for the Communist party newspaper, *Workers' Dreadnoughts*. In 1921 he returned to the US, and his poems came out in a number of magazines, including Garvey's *Negro World*. In 1922 his collection *Harlem Shadows* was published, "virtually inaugurating the Harlem Renaissance" (Gates Jr. and McKay 982). This volume contained the famous and moving "If We Must Die", a poem that was written against the racial violence of 1919 that came to be known as the Red Summer, a period between spring and autumn of that year when white supremacist violence and riots swept through a large number of cities across the country. It evocatively expresses the mood of anger and pride in lines like

"If we must die, let it not be like hogs / . . . Like men we'll face the murderous, cowardly pack, / Pressed to the wall, dying, but fighting back" (Wiley 2, 15). Though this poem emerged from a specific context, it became an iconic rallying point for Allied Forces during WWII and was recited by Winston Churchill in an anti-Nazi speech.

The poems in *Harlem Shadows* depict McKay's enchantment with Harlem, offering many cameos of people, night life, and daytime scenes while depicting America. His poem, "America" is a song of praise to its impressive beauty and its contradictions: "Although she feeds me bread of bitterness / . . . Her vigor flows like tides into my blood" (Wiley 2, 12). "Harlem Shadows" captures the sad nightly routine of a prostitute through the images of, "the halting footsteps", and "tired feet . . . trudging, thinly shod". The weariness is echoed in Langston Hughes's "The Weary Blues", a poem that blends the despair and resilience characteristic of the Blues through "the mellow croon" and "ebony hands of each ivory key", the "lazy sway" of the body on the "rickety stool", playing "that sad raggy tune like a musical fool" (Wiley 2, 213).

In 1923, McKay went to the USSR, addressing the Fourth Congress of the Communist International in Moscow, meeting Trotsky and other Soviet leaders and publishing a poem, "Petrograd: May Day, 1923", in the Soviet newspaper *Pravda*. After this he travelled to France and then to Spain and Morocco and during this period published two novels. *Home to Harlem* (1928) is about a US army deserter Jake Brown who returns to Harlem, meets a prostitute, Felice, who returns the money he pays her, making him fall in love with her, but who then disappears from the novel. Jake then meets a Haitian immigrant Ray who aspires to be a writer, a character who also features in a second novel, *Banjo* (1929). These novels were followed by a collection of short stories, *Gingertown* (1932), and a third novel, *Banana Bottom* (1933). Another novel, *Amiable with Big Teeth,* was recently discovered. McKay wrote a couple of autobiographical works, *A Long Way from Home* that "documents McKay's cosmopolitan attempts at being at home in the world, even as the degrees of separation between him and his native homes increased" (Jarrett, *Representing the Race* 115), and *My Green Hills of Jamaica,* as well as a volume of essays again featuring Harlem, titled *Harlem: Negro Metropolis.*

McKay arrived at a time when jazz was in vogue and beginning to gain nationwide attention. The show *Shuffle Along,* the first African American musical on Broadway, was a path-breaking event, running to 504 performances, with a love story at its centre, jazz dance and music, and black performers in lead roles that broke stereotypes and opened the way to diverse new roles. Black audiences were now able to sit freely and not relegated to the balconies. At the same time, Freud's theories of the unconscious and of repressed desires were popularised by writers like Carl Van Vechten (music critic, portrait photographer and white author of *Nigger Heaven*) and F. Scott Fitzgerald who

[e]spous[ing]ed the notion that the Jazz Age was one great, healthy, acting-out of 'repressed desires.' Like pictures drawn on two transparencies, these two ideas merge rather nicely into a coherent picture of the world: Jazz, being 'primitive' and from the 'dark continent,' was equal to primitive, repressed desires. Jazz was not only carnal and profane, then, but it was 'good medicine,' a kind of voodoo release for the repressed white culture, which had lost touch with its body, soul, earth and roots. (Barros 307–08)

Barros mentions a third influence – "the rise of mass culture generally, through radio, sound recordings, and cinema" that led to a "democratization of culture" (308). McKay represents much of this in his depictions of Harlem in a free flowing, effervescent, no-holds barred style in his novels. *Home to Harlem,* for instance has been called "a voluptuously written book that luxuriates in the sounds, sights, smells, language, and rhythms of the district, swarms with metaphorical equations of jazz with sex, sensuality, animal passion, and the primitive" (Barros 308), with Harlem itself being the main character.

As an outsider who loved the riotous life offered by Harlem, which he documented in several of his works, McKay was also the most eminent of the large number of Caribbeans who came to New York City and to Harlem with fresh ideas about race and art, and with different sources for their culture in the folklore and traditions of the archipelago's black communities. The outsider view, indeed, begins to gain in importance from this period onwards because of the diverse origins of the blacks who were coming to the US. For McKay, Harlem was not just an attractive place, not just a character in his books. It was also a lens to view the life of the black community in the midst of its trials and desires. His novels represented various aspects of Harlem and also offered commentaries on race, on the time, and on its many contradictions.

Another Caribbean outsider was **Eric Walrond** (1898–1966), from Georgetown, British Guiana, who arrived in the US in 1918, having worked as a journalist after his education in Barbados where his mother had moved following his father's desertion of the family. In the US he studied at the City College of New York and then did a year-long creative writing course at Columbia University. His essay, "The New Negro Faces America", published in 1923, strongly criticised some of the major black leaders of the time like Washington, Du Bois and even the popular Garvey for being impractical and out of step with their time. He produced an impressive collection of ten stories, *Tropic Death* (1826). Set in British Guiana, Barbados and the Panama Canal area during the years of the construction of the Panama Canal, the stories in this collection evoke the oppressive heat suggested in the title and features death in all of them, while dealing with themes of power and exploitation in a racist, colonial-industrialised society. Walrond uses a powerfully evocative language (Du Bois in his review mentions his "impressionistic pen" [cited in Owens 97]) as he describes the blazing sun of Barbados (in "Panama Gold"), or the land that has been torched (in "The Palm Torch") – a felicity of description noted by many of his contemporaries – "sun-bright hardness" was Langston Hughes's term (in Owens 99) for his capacity to depict harshness without sentimentality. An example of this refusal to be sentimental is his description of the brutal beating delivered by an American marine in the story "Subjection" where the victim is not described except as "a ram-shackle body" and the "white bludgeon" is depersonalised (Walrond 100).

Walrond's representation of labour migration, as part of the colonial-industrial economy, amongst the several Caribbean islands expands the assumptions of transnational movement beyond the North Atlantic focus that Paul Gilroy prefers in the *Black Atlantic*. *Tropic Death* "adds to our knowledge of black migration narratives by introducing routes of migration that defy a north-south trajectory. Circum-Caribbean migration . . . is as much a part of the modern black experience as the northbound flight from 'cotton, cane, and rice fields' that looms so large in the African American artistic imagination" (Owens 101).

As the body of literature increased and greater awareness about its role in emancipation, in shaping identities and in placing African American historical experience within the larger context of American experience came to be acknowledged, several cultural and literary manifestos were written by prominent artists and activists. These were fundamentally polemical and applicable across literary genres. In a 1926 issue of *The Crisis*, W. E. B. Du Bois wrote the following about plays that would be suitable for Negro theatre:

> The plays of a real Negro theatre must be: 1. About us. That is, they must have plots which reveal real Negro life as it is. 2. By us. That is, they must be written by Negro authors who understand from birth and continual association just what it means to be a Negro today. 3. For us. That is, the theatre must cater primarily to Negro audiences and be supported and sustained by their entertainment and approval. 4. Near us. The theatre must be in a Negro neighborhood near the mass of ordinary Negro people. (135)

Hughes in "The Negro Artist and the Racial Mountain" (published in the 23 June 1926 issue of *The Nation*) similarly takes on the problem of art from the point of view of race, especially the desire, often associated with Countee Cullen and some others, to suppress the Negro and be American. Pointing out that there is a "great field of unused material" and "an inexhaustible supply of themes at hand" for artists to use, he nevertheless acknowledges the rocky terrain and the high mountain of misunderstanding, lack of encouragement, disparagement and hesitation, and argues that "it is the duty of the younger Negro artist . . . to change through the force of his art that old whispering 'I want to be white' hidden in the aspirations of his people, to 'Why should I want to be white? I am a Negro – and beautiful!'" (Wiley 2, 212). Writing of some of the great performers of the folksongs and of dance, he says of his own poems that they are "racial in theme and treatment" with "the meanings and rhythms of jazz". Like many others he too gives his own definition of jazz: "one of the inherent expressions of Negro life in America; the eternal tom-tom beating in the Negro soul – the tom-tom of revolt against weariness in a white world, a world of subway trains, and work, work, work; the tom-tom of joy and laughter, and pain swallowed in a smile" (Wiley 2, 212).

2

Three institutions dominate the political life of the African Americans during this time. These are the Universal Negro Improvement Association (UNIA) of Marcus Garvey which spearheaded the "Back to Africa" movement (though none were actually relocated) and helped disseminate its goals through Garvey's weekly newspaper, *The Negro World*; the Pan African Congress (PAC) of W. E. B. Du Bois which aspired to unify the black world (its first meeting was held in Paris in 1919 and coincided with the Versailles Peace Conference); and The African Blood Brotherhood (ABB), a radical organisation for Pan Africanism founded by Cyril Briggs, an African American journalist of Caribbean origin with strong socialist and communist affiliations, who also founded and edited *The Crusader*, its influential mouthpiece. Meanwhile, continuing to be active were the NAACP with its magazine *Crisis*, edited by Du Bois and which recruited Jessie Fauset as its literary editor from 1919–26, and magazines like *Opportunity*, edited by Charles S. Johnson, and *Messenger*, edited by A. Philip Randolph and Chandler Owen.

International connections fostered by travel and the work of these organisations and their founders and members, who were often expatriate West Indians, gave a new dimension to the transnational nature of the African American experience – and a much wider sense to the theme of community we have been following in this book. Travelogues were a particularly suitable form within this experience. McKay, Hughes and Hurston all wrote travelogues that represented their different interpretations of reawakening exercises.

In the case of Hughes it was the music of Cuba which he came to know intimately from his friendship with Jose Guillen, journalist and editor of a weekly pictorial magazine, *Orbe*. The two men were united by their desire to create a vernacular aesthetics by using the music of the people.

Plays were written by many of the writers because the theatre movement had gained ground and was beginning to provide platforms for different kinds of plays that addressed the era's urgent concerns. The movement also helped many playwrights to break into the predominantly white Broadway. The theatre demonstrates keen awareness of the themes of community and identity in preliminary efforts made to counter the stereotypes that had dogged African American theatre since the start of blackface minstrelsy. The stage was now used to feature and address lynching, migration to the north, family relationships, and the issue of mixed race children including those born to slave mothers from their white masters. It was moulded into a powerful instrument of propaganda and protest as key figures of the period put their weight behind it. In Locke's preference for folk drama which depicted the experiences of black people and Du Bois's for propaganda plays, which made overt projection of political views and protest, it is possible to see the expectations of the theatre that the playwrights fulfilled. Georgia Douglas Johnson, played a role similar to that of Lady Gregory in the nationalist Irish Theatre Movement. The performance culture of early African Americans, always a community experience, now became a much better organised and conscious process with "shared performances of expressive culture" (Stepto 940).

The figure of **Arturo Alfonso Schomburg** (also known as Arthur Schomburg) (1874–1938) exemplifies many of the concerns of this period. He was born in Puerto Rico to a German father and black mother, studied there and only arrived in New York in 1891. He worked as a clerk in a law firm, served as the secretary of the Los Dos Antillas, an organisation for Cuban and Puerto Rican independence, and in 1906 he joined the mail department of the Bankers Trust Company, going on to head their foreign mailing department. While working and supporting a family he simultaneously built up his collection of documents and sketches that recorded the history of the black peoples of the world. This went on to become the famous Schomburg Collection that is today one of the richest repositories of Black material culture from around the world. His primary contribution is as one who recognised the importance of establishing a history for an oppressed people. He was one of the founders of the Negro Society for Historical Research (1911) and served for many years as its secretary-treasurer and librarian. In 1926, through joint efforts by the New York Public Library and the Andrew Carnegie Corporation (which put up the funds), Schomburg's collection of five thousand books, three thousand manuscripts and two thousand etchings and drawings was acquired, and in 1932, Schomburg was made curator of his own collection at the library. The collection contains original texts by many of the key figures of African American history and culture.

Schomburg's essay, "The Negro Digs Up His Past" is a statement of his belief about the "prime social necessity" of history. His declaration that "[T]he American Negro must remake his past in order to make his future" is representative of the many projects undertaken during this period to collect material, make anthologies, record the lives of ex-slaves and shape a distinct culture. In the three conclusions he sees emerging from the increasingly scientific study of the 'Negro's past' a sense of agency is clearly evident. These are, that the Negro has always been part of the struggle for his own freedom, that the group's collective effort has been often ignored, and that the history of the race shows a "record of credible group achievement" (Norton 938). In identifying these elements as necessary to scholarship on the race, Schomburg recognises the feature of African American cultural and political struggle that is most significant in making a distinctive racial identity – that of group, collective, community effort in retrieving and valuing the common past.

An early writer of the Renaissance, **Angelina Weld Grimke** (1880–1958), is now primarily remembered as the author of one of the first plays written by a black woman and successfully performed by blacks – *Rachel*. Grimke, of mixed parentage – her mother was a white woman and her father was the son of a white man and a slave woman, whose paternal aunts acknowledged the relationship and supported him in his education at Harvard – had the advantage of education in some of the best institutions of the time and apparently did not encounter racial discrimination in her growing years. Her play, however, was written as "race propaganda" and "to enlighten the American people" about the "lamentable condition" of the "Colored citizens in this free republic" (Gates Jr. and McKay 943). *Rachel* is a play in three acts about a young black woman who decides not to bring children into the world after she learns that her father and brother were lynched, and after she herself discovers how young black children are treated in schools. It features the racism of the urban north, the psychological effects of race prejudice on young children and of racial discrimination in jobs. The play tells the story of the Lovings, mother and two children, who have fled to the North after the father and a son are lynched. Rachel, the daughter, adopts a young orphan boy and discovers how he as well as a friend's daughter are treated badly by teachers in schools. The play was staged in NAACP anti-lynching rallies. Grimke also wrote poetry which was anthologised in Countee Cullen's *Caroling Dusk* (1927) and Langston Hughes's *The Poetry of the Negro* (1949). She authored short stories such as "Blackness" and "Goldie" in both of which an infant is cut out of the mother's womb by a lynching mob, and "The Closing Door", a tale about opportunities closing and the depression into which the protagonist, Agnes Milton, falls, after her husband is brutally lynched by a mob for not giving right of way on a pavement to a white man. The story ends with Agnes smothering and killing her child as she is traumatised by the thought of the fate that awaits a black child in a white man's world. The metaphor of the closing door is used skillfully as Grimke presents the precarious condition of mothers and their children under racism. "[H]er stories are filled with oppressive atmosphere, and detailed descriptions of scene and time, each with appropriate trappings to evoke gloom and dread" (Duran 44). A recent essay has also sought to connect her lesbianism to lynching by establishing that Grimke saw the black lynched body and the black lesbian body as equally abject (Hammer 2021). One of her critics has noted a blues sentiment in her work as she deals with her identity as woman, black and lesbian, finding in it, "the import, if not the discrete form, of the blues – that musical and poetic cultural form which is the repository for African-American anguish over love, lost love, and political disenfranchisement" (Herron 21).

Jessie Redmon Fauset (1884–1961), the author of poems, short stories, essays and four novels, was the daughter of Reverend Redmon Fauset, a minister in the African Methodist Episcopal Church and his wife, Annie, and had an excellent education, first at public schools in Philadelphia and then on a scholarship at Cornell University from where she graduated in 1905 with a major in classical languages. She went on to teach for a year at the Douglass High School in Baltimore and then at the Dunbar High School in Washington till 1918, before completing an MA in French from the University of Pennsylvania. She joined the *Crisis* around this time and took on the role of literary editor under Du Bois from 1919. Besides writing for the *Crisis*, her seven-year stint at the magazine has also been recognised as important for the Harlem Renaissance because she played the role of facilitator to many young writers like Langston Hughes (whose first poem, "The Negro Speaks of Rivers" appeared in it in 1921), Countee Cullen, Claude McKay and Jean Toomer, and published their works in the magazine. Hughes names Fauset, Alain Locke and James Weldon Johnson in his autobiography, *The Big Sea*, as "the three people who midwifed the so-called New Negro literature into being" (Gutenberg EBook n.p.). She was also instrumental in helping Du Bois develop a children's monthly, *The Brownies' Book* which featured pieces on Africa and current events, as well as on historical personalities like Sojourner Truth. After leaving the *Crisis* she went back to teaching, this time at the DeWitt Clinton High School in New York.

In her novels, Fauset writes of middle class women's aspirations and desire to transcend the limits of gender, class and race through the metaphor of "passing" while also dealing with themes like racial uplift and black solidarity. Her first novel, *There is Confusion* (1924) tells the story of three children, the talented dancer, Joanna Marshall, the exceptionally beautiful but poor Maggie Ellersley, and Peter Bye, who aspires to be a surgeon. Race prejudice and inequality stand as obstacles to their dreams, and Fauset shows the psychological stresses faced especially by women as they struggle to overcome traditional assumptions about women's roles as wives and mothers, by dreaming of careers. However, the novel seems to question these dreams of transcending gender, social class and racial limitations for individual success as it ends in marriage. Her second novel *Plum Bun: A Novel Without a Moral* (1929) takes up the theme of "passing" as a way of ascending out of the physical and cultural limitations of race through the story of the Murrays, and especially their fair-skinned daughter Angela, who in childhood accompanies her equally fair-skinned mother on her pleasure trips around the city, and who quickly develops the desire to leave behind everything her parents had fought for: "[t]he stories which Junius and Mattie told of difficulties overcome, of the arduous learning of trades, of the pitiful scraping together of infinitesimal savings that would have made a latter-day Iliad, but to Angela they were merely a description of a life which she at any cost would avoid living" (Kindle n.p.). The third novel, *The Chinaberry Tree: A Novel of American Life* (1931) continues her interest in black middle class life as it tells the story of two cousins, Laurentine Strange and Melissa Paul through themes such as miscegenation and incest. The fourth novel, *Comedy, American Style* (1933) once again takes up the theme of "passing" through the identity crisis of a fair-skinned Olivia Cary whose distaste about her black heritage affects her children. Her daughter Teresa wishes to be part of her own race, while her son Oliver is neglected by his mother because of his dark skin. All these novels, written during the heyday of modernism, represent the fragmented identities of mixed race individuals and the trauma experienced by them, as they find themselves torn between their African American affiliations and their desire to suppress this aspect and pass as white in order to avail of the advantages of the American success story.

Further interest in racial identity and gender is evident in the work of another woman writer, **Nella Larsen** (1893–1964), the author of novels like *Quicksand* and *Passing*. Larsen's father was of African and Danish West Indian origin and her mother a Dane, who after the death of her husband when Nella was two, remarried one of her own countrymen. Larsen studied at both Fisk University and the University of Copenhagen before joining and completing the nursing programme at the Lincoln School for Nurses in New

York in 1915. Nursing remained her career for several years as she served in succession, as head nurse at the John A. Andrew Hospital and the Nurse Training School at Tuskegee Institute, assistant superintendent of nurses at Lincoln Hospital and then at the New York Department of Health. In 1921 she left nursing and joined the New York Public Library, taking charge of the children's section at its branch in Harlem.

Larsen's first novel is loosely based on her own childhood and tells the story of Helga Crane, the daughter of a Danish immigrant and a West Indian man who left the family soon after Helga's birth. The metaphor of quicksand is cleverly used, as Helga slips from one location to another, from one set of hopes tied to a place and its people to another set, unable to hold on to any one of them, as the novel moves from Helga's experiences in a black southern college in Naxos, to Harlem, then, following disillusionment, to Copenhagen and finally to rural Alabama as the wife of a minister and the mother of five children–a process through which her aspirations to unique selfhood are frustrated.

Passing which takes up this popular theme used so frequently to speak of different kinds of transgressions, is about two women, both light skinned, who discover different ways to deal with the question of their identities. Clare Kendry is married to a racist white man, and moves easily in the white world while Irene Redfield, married to a physician practicing in Harlem, occasionally 'passes'. The two women, who were childhood friends, meet by chance in a tearoom but another two years pass before their lives intersect in a more comprehensive way as Clare arrives uninvited at the Redfield home, wishing for an association with Irene and her family as well as with other blacks as she has begun to find her own deceitful life insupportable. A series of suspicions begin with Irene wondering if Clare is having an affair with her husband and Jack Bellew, Clare's husband beginning to suspect his wife's preference for black company. The novel ends with Clare falling from the window of the sixth floor Redfield apartment and dying and we are left with the vague sense that she may have been pushed. As both women go after what they desire – in Clare's case the pleasures of life in Harlem and in Irene's, protection of her own life as wife and mother – Larsen shows them chafing at restrictions that they have themselves chosen as part of their lives.

Passing in this novel suggests "both the loss of racial identity and the denial of self required of women who conform to restrictive gender roles" (Wall 105). Wall observes the many images of enclosed spaces in the two novels: "[L]ike 'quicksand,' 'passing' is a metaphor of death and desperation, and both central metaphors are supported by images of asphyxiation, suffocation, and claustrophobia" (105).

The problem of passing in Larsen's two novels may be traced to the fact that "the tragic mulatto was the only formulation historically available to portray educated middle-class black women in fiction" but Larsen makes her women subvert this convention (Wall 97). The women "are neither noble nor long-suffering; their plights are not used to symbolize the oppression of blacks, the irrationality of prejudice, or the absurdity of concepts of race generally." They are engaged instead, in exercises of realising selfhood against expectations of appearing ladylike and fantasies of exotic otherness, in which they invariably fail. "The tragedy for these mulattoes is the impossibility of self-definition. Larsen's protagonists assume false identities that ensure social survival but result in psychological suicide" (Wall 98) as happens in the case of Helga, as well as Clare and Irene.

One of the most fascinating figures in African American literary history remains **Zora Neale Hurston** (1891–1960), the author of four novels, two books of folklore, numerous short stories and essays and a number of plays. Born in Alabama, she grew up in Eatonville, Florida, an all-black town where her father was the mayor for three terms and her mother a school teacher. An idyllic childhood was interrupted by the death of her mother in 1904 and the remarriage of her father. After this she had to leave her boarding school and fend for herself, first as a domestic worker in Sanford, Florida, and Memphis, Tennessee, and then as a lady's maid for a travelling Gilbert and Sullivan troupe, before she was again able to get back to educating herself. She joined the Morgan State University and a year later entered Howard University where she helped start the University's newspaper, while continuing to work to support herself, this time as part-time waitress and manicurist. After graduating from the University she entered the literary scene, attending the salons of Georgia Douglas Johnson, publishing poetry and writing short stories. Her first published story was "Drenched in Light" in *Opportunity* in 1924, while another story, "Spunk" was selected by Alain Locke for *The New Negro*. She also came under the patronage of several white benefactors, one of who, Annie Nathan Meyer, procured a scholarship for her to Barnard College. While studying there, she came to the notice of the Columbia University anthropologist, Franz Boas. With his help she got financial support to study southern folklore through the Association for the Study of Negro Life and History. Charlotte Osgood Mason, who was also Langston Hughes's patron, offered her a monthly stipend of 200 dollars with the condition that she should not make her research available to anyone without Mason's permission. Hurston's productive career as a folklorist and anthropologist began, with this support, from Eatonville, which served as a base for her research around the South and the Bahamas. She published a series of articles in *The Journal of American Folklore* (October–December 1931), titled "Hoodoo in America" on the practices and tales connected with obeah, conjure and hoodoo. Her first volume of folklore, *Mules and Men* was published in 1935 and a second, *Tell My Horse*, followed in 1938. In these books she documented various rituals, songs and folk practices, and tales from the areas where she did her fieldwork.

Meanwhile she had begun writing novels and the first, *Jonah's Gourd Vine* had already been published in 1934. This told the story of John Buddy Pearson, a popular preacher who is married to Lucy but is compulsively involved with a bunch of other women, unable to restrain his sexual appetite. As with subsequent books, this novel contains elements of folklore from Hurston's research, including conjuring and hoodoo. Her novel, *Their Eyes Were Watching God* (1937), was written while she was on a field trip to Haiti. This novel tells the story of a light-skinned black woman, Janie Crawford, who goes through three marriages in her search for a sense of independent selfhood. It has been considered a feminist novel and it represents Hurston's own sense of pride and self-worth that withstood all the attacks on her by male contemporaries over what they perceived was her lighthearted approach to race questions. The independent thinking indicated by her attitude is traced by Hurston herself in her essay "What it Feels to be Colored Me", where she recounts how her understanding of race and her sense of self-worth developed during her childhood in the all black town of Eatonville. In his Afterword to *Their Eyes Were Watching God*, Henry Louis Gates Jr. has written of how she integrated folklore into her style, making them into "metaphors, allegories, and performances in her novels, the traditional recurring canonical metaphors of black culture" (250). Hurston's ability to creatively use the material from her research and her employment of black speech is evident in many of her works. She wrote about the uniqueness of black expression and sensibility in her essay "Characteristics of Negro Expression" – the movement of body, the colourful language and the effervescence with which rules of grammar are flouted in the process. Of "the Negro's greatest contribution to language" she lists: "the use of metaphor and simile" as in "sobbing hearted" or "that's a lynch"; "the double-descriptive" as in "little-tee-ninchy (tiny)" or "lady-people"; or "verbal nouns" as in "she features somebody I know" (Norton 1021). She also mentions other unique features like "angularity" used to avoid the simple straight line, "asymmetry" for which she gives examples from Langston Hughes's poetry and from Negro dancing. She writes of the incorporation of culture heroes, many of them from the animal world and especially the trickster heroes like the rabbit. Other characteristics are for her the "absence of the concept of privacy", the use of dialect (and here you can actually perceive the anthropologist at work when she writes of the "clear clipped 'I'" becoming the Negro "Ah" because "a sharp 'I' is very much easier with a thin taut lip than with a full soft lip. Like tightening violin strings" [Norton 1031]).

The 1931 play, *Mule Bone: A Comedy of Negro Life in Three Acts*, written in collaboration with Langston Hughes (and the cause of lifelong acrimony over copyright between them, resulting in the play remaining unpublished till 1990), features the custom of "mule-talking", the verbal duels in the performance routine between Jim and Dave, a two-man song and dance team. The two men quarrel over a woman, Daisy, and a mule bone becomes the weapon with which Jim attacks Dave. Set in Hurston's hometown of Eatonville, the play shows how a small town can be divided by a minor dispute and uses farcical humour for effect. Hurston wrote several other plays that remained unpublished and that are now housed as manuscripts in the Library of Congress. These include a spoof on the "Back to Africa" movement, *Meet the Mamma* (1925) in three acts, each act occurring in a different place – a Harlem nightclub, an ocean liner and the African jungle; two musical comedies, *Spunk* (1935) and *Polk County* (1944) with Dorothy Waring; and four brief sketches.

Barracoon: The Story of the Last Slave (1931) arrived in the midst of the cultural activity of the Harlem Renaissance as a piece of uncomfortable evidence of the African role in sending slaves to America – a fact that would stand as a corrective to the binary of Americans versus Africans or white versus black that has been at the heart of the narrative of African American suffering. Hurston tracked him down and interviewed him over a period of three months and the story he told as the last known slave to come to America on a slave ship was incontrovertible proof about the horrors of the Middle Passage which till then had only been read of in some of the early slave narratives like that of Equiano, or implied in that strange poem by Phillis Wheatley, "On Being Brought from Africa to America." Hurston emerges as someone who held on to her core competencies – her skill as a researcher and her ability to transform this material into subjects for her literary works.

Her autobiography, *Dust Tracks on a Road* came in 1942, but after this her career went on a downslide and she disappeared into virtual anonymity, working as a maid and eventually dying in a welfare home. Her reappearance into the cultural history of those times is a fascinating work of feminist retrieval. Another celebrated author, Alice Walker, undertook this task, positioning her as a significant literary foremother, especially in her *In Search of our Mothers' Gardens*.

Among the most original talents in this time was **Jean Toomer** (1894–1967), whose work *Cane* (1923), difficult to characterise generically, was received with enthusiasm by the younger writers who found in its unique generic mix and evocative stories of black people, a text that matched the literary ideals of modernism. Toomer, born to Nathan Toomer and Nina Pinchback Toomer, grew up in the home of his grandparents in a white neighbourhood in Washington where his mother moved after his father deserted them. His grandfather was a Union soldier during the Civil War and had made a career as a politician, serving as acting governor in Louisiana during Reconstruction. When Toomer was about twelve his mother remarried and took him with her to live in New York, but after her death a few years later he moved back to the home of his grandparents who had meanwhile moved to the black part of town. The issue of race appeared in complex ways to the young Toomer as he made these transitions. He once declared that he had a mixture of "Scotch, Welsh, German, English, French, Dutch, Spanish, and some dark blood" (in Gates Jr. and McKay 1087). After he graduated from high school, he studied at several institutions, worked at different jobs and finally decided to become a writer. It is generally known that the breakthrough in his writing career came out of a four-month stay in Sparta, Georgia, where he had gone to take up the job of an acting superintendent of an all-black school. *Cane* was the result of his experience and observation of Southern life during this period. Toomer was also the author of a one-act play, *Balo,* and another play, *Natalie Mann,* as well as short stories and poems. He practised spiritualism for a period from 1924 under the influence of an Armenian spiritualist, George Gurdjieff, whose theory of Unitism Toomer introduced into Harlem, and wrote about in his long poem, titled *Blue Meridian* (1936). This poem conceptualises the blue man, an integrated identity as American that Toomer always looked for, a fusion of black, white and red-skinned people. He got married twice (both times to white women), and after settling in Pennsylvania following his second marriage, became a Quaker in 1940.

Cane is one of the most important texts of the Harlem Renaissance, one that was recognised as being a truly modernist text in its innovative fragmented style, the blend of literary genres and the collage mode that is strongly reminiscent of T.S. Eliot's

Preludes and *The Waste Land* (Toomer was deeply influenced by Eliot). Toomer used this style to represent race issues. The book is in three sections and is made up of poems, character sketches, short stories and one play, many of which were published separately before they appeared together in *Cane*. The first section based in Georgia in the South, portrays six women – Karintha, a beautiful young girl with "skin [is] like dust on the eastern horizon" who ends up as a prostitute; Becky, the poor white woman who has two mixed race sons and whose existence in her house outside the town is doubtful – the text speculates about her: "if she was there" – and never proved as the house collapses into itself and possibly over the poor Becky; Carma – "nigger woman driving a Georgia chariot down an old dust road" who, because her husband was away most of the time "had others"; Fern, the young woman who drew men to her like moths but was herself untouched by these encounters: "Men were everlastingly bringing her their bodies" but they failed to understand her or their attraction for her; Esther, "near white" who is charmed by the magnificent black known as King Barlo, a vagrant preacher who, Esther decides she loves; and finally Louisa in the story "Blood Burning Moon" whose black and white lovers, Tom and Bob, fight over her before Tom is lynched by a mob. The second part of *Cane* is set in Chicago and Washington D.C., and through a number of prose pieces and poems it evokes the lives of migrant blacks from the South and the disillusionment that they faced when their hopes of a life free of racism and of economic opportunities were frustrated. The third section, Kabnis, was conceived as a play to be performed. It features Ralph Kabnis, a northerner who comes to Georgia and meets a bunch of characters who complicate Toomer's perception of race.

"*Cane* is a productive rewriting of 'race,' allowing for the recognition of multiple authentic African American voices, identifications complicated by class, gender, and geography, and greatly enriched by the significant modulations in narrative address that Toomer undertakes" and each section "records the emergence of a special racial ethos of modern life" (Dow 60). Toomer too wrote about it to the editors of *The Liberator,* calling it "a spiritual fusion analogous to the fact of racial intermingling" (cited in Hutchinson 231).

Critics have also noted the influence of the European avant-garde (Rusch 1991–92, Peckham 2000) especially in his use of "a form that stressed fragmentation and reintegration" to question "the ongoing social revolution in America" (Peckham 276).

While the Harlem Renaissance had many writers of significance and lasting importance there were also others whose radical opinions made them infamous. Of these the one name that crops up immediately is that of **George Samuel Schuyler** (1895–1977) best known for his essay "The Negro-Art Hokum" published in the *Nation* in June 1926 (which also carried Hughes's equally famous rebuttal, "The Negro Artist and the Racial Mountain"), that began with the claim that "Negro art 'made in America' is [as] non-existent" and suggested that there was no distinction between art by white Americans and by "Aframericans", notwithstanding the spirituals, work songs, sorrow song, blues and jazz which were confined to only a small section, "the peasantry of the South" (Norton 1171–74).

Rudolph Fisher (1897–1934), a physician by training (he took his MD from Howard University Medical School), who opened his own practice in Harlem in 1927, wrote fourteen short stories and two novels that feature Harlem street life, besides a critical essay "The Caucasian Storms Harlem", and two scientific articles. His very first short story, "The City of Refuge" was published in the *Atlantic Monthly* and tells of the arrival of a southern migrant, King Solomon Gillis, in Harlem and a series of first impressions: "In Harlem, black was white." "Everybody in Harlem had money." And "cullud policemans!" were seen directing the busy Harlem traffic. Gillis encounters a variety of African Americans, tricksters, confidence men, dope peddlers and other criminals as he moves around in wide-eyed wonder through the streets, bars and nightclubs. Fisher wrote two novels, *The Walls of Jericho* (1928) and *The Conjure Man Dies: A Mystery Tale of Dark Harlem* (1932), a detective novel featuring only black characters and set in Harlem, with a doctor as detective who uses his medical knowledge to help unravel a mysterious murder. The African American detective novel had appeared much earlier with Pauline Hopkins' *Hagar's Daughter* (1901–02) serialised in *The Colored American Magazine* and John Bruce's *The Black Sleuth* (1908–09), serialised in *McGirt's Magazine* where some of the distinctive interventions into the genre become apparent. These include the clear racial identity of the black detectives, and their lives with their families and society, in a departure from the solitary detectives of Conan Doyle or even Poe. The genre would go on to become one of the major forms of popular literature with writers like Chester Himes, Walter Mosley, Valerie Wilson Wesley and many others who invented detectives, placed crime and detection in new sites and conditions, while simultaneously exploring black identity, society, families and relationships.

As we have seen, women played important roles in the Harlem Renaissance. **Dorothy West** (1907–98), who wrote two novels and a number of short stories and was also involved with the magazine *Fire!* with Hughes, Cullen and Thurman, was one such figure. She was the founder of the literary quarterly *Challenge* (which went on to become *New Challenge*) that introduced a number of new writers like Margaret Walker, Richard Wright and Ralph Ellison, and also published Wright's essay, "Blueprint for Negro Writing". Her novel *The Living is Easy* (1948) uses satire "to revise the (male) Great Migration Novel" (Rodgers 161), through the story of Cleo Judson, a migrant from the South who marries a fruit merchant, Bart Judson, twenty years her senior, who is modelled on Dorothy West's father, Isaac Christopher West, known as "Boston's Black Banana King." Cleo is shown as a self-centred woman who left her own family of mother and sisters at the first chance she had and came to Boston. Her constant effort seems to be to use Bart's money to make a life for herself like the black middle class she envies. She gets her sisters and their children to Boston to live with her after persuading Bart to buy a ten-bedroomed house. This gives her an opportunity to exercise an authority that she has always had with her sisters but had missed in her life with Bart. The novel depicts a society where class divisions among the blacks complicate the picture of the North as a haven of equality and opportunity.

Sterling A. Brown (1901–89) was poet, literary and music critic, and literary historian, combining in these roles his sense of pride in the community, a pedagogic responsibility and knowledge of the culture of the African Americans that came alive in his dialect poetry, especially in his first collection, *Southern Road* (1932). Brown was born in Washington D.C. into a life of privilege and opportunity. His father, Sterling Nelson Brown, was a Howard University professor of religion. Brown studied at the Dunbar High School and had Angelina Grimke and Jessie Fauset as his teachers. He went on to Williams College and then to Harvard University for graduate studies in English, and here he read the poetry of Edwin Arlington Robinson, Robert Frost, Carl Sandburg, and Vachel Lindsay. He then took a series of teaching jobs in the South, picking up a knowledge of African American folk traditions and collecting folklore. From these experiences and influences he forged a black dialect style that took it away from the farcical use made in the plantation romances and minstrel shows and re-presented it as an instrument of cultural pride and a means of alternative knowledge. As a popular professor at Howard University for nearly his entire working life, Brown taught many of the next generation of writers and artists, among them Amiri Baraka, besides producing important critical studies of African American literature: *Outline for the Study of the Poetry of American Negroes* (1931), *The Negro in American Fiction* (1937), and *Negro Poetry and Drama* (1937), and an anthology of writings by African Americans accompanied by brief biographies, *The Negro Caravan* (1941). After a considerable gap, in 1975, he published a second volume of poetry, *The Last Ride of Bill and Eleven Narratives*.

Brown's poetry is steeped in the expressive traditions of the African American. In the forms he employs – folk epics and ballads, the 'lie', and sermon – and in the moods he evokes, he relies on the blues tradition and spirit. Many of the poems in *Southern Road* exemplify this mood. One of the finest is 'When de Saints Go Ma'ching Home", a poem of memory and joy and melancholy, based on the well-known black spiritual that was sung by Louis Armstrong and has also been sung by Bruce Springsteen, and for Indian children of a certain generation, part of the musical repertoire in missionary schools. The performer, Big Boy Davis, to whom the poem is dedicated, would "tune up specially for this". As the audience around him would fall silent he would get ready for the song: "Sorrow deep hidden in his voice, a far / And soft light in his strange brown eyes / Alone with his masterchords, his memories". And as he would begin to play his guitar and sing, his gaze would be fixed on the strings, "For he would see / A gorgeous procession" of saints – Ole Deacon Zachary, ole Sis Joe, Ole Elder Peter Johnson, de little brown-skinned chillen, Ole Maumee Annie, Ole Grampa Eli – and all those who "would not be there" and finally he sees his "dear old mudder, / She is in hebben I know" who is proud of her son and ready to go "ma'chin' home" (Wiley 2, 321–24). The poem is in several parts with the first part presenting Big Boy in his musician's role as "his singing re-creates the conditions in which shared performative events may fittingly close" (Stepto 941).

Brown's use of the blues mood and of the folk elements was a strategic response to the challenge that African American traditional culture faced from growing urbanisation and modern education. As one critic has written: "Brown especially feared the loss of folklore, which he believed helped African-American culture renew itself, not only by preserving and strengthening traditions and social practices, but also by serving as a conduit through which individuals devised and communicated new strategies for surviving racial oppression". He understood folklore as "an evolving cultural process that adapts and preserves traditions despite external changes and threats" (Anderson 1023). For Brown the use of the vernacular in all its forms – as source and as mode – was a way of understanding and communicating shared values, and sustaining fellowship and solidarity – necessary elements for a community always in crisis.

Among the most gifted poets of the Harlem Renaissance was **Countée Cullen** (1903–46). While he was born in Louisville, Kentucky, he went to New York to live with Amanda Porter, said to be his grandmother, and after her death, was adopted by the Reverend Frederick Cullen and his wife, and named Countée P. Cullen. He went to the DeWitt Clinton High School in the Bronx, New York City, became closely engaged with the school newspaper and the literary magazine and started writing poetry. In 1922 he entered New York University and during the three years he spent there before graduating, he wrote much of the poetry that went into his three best known volumes. These are *Color* (1925), *Copper Sun* (1927), and *The Ballad of the Brown Girl* (1927). After NYU he joined Harvard University and received an MA in English and French.

The way his three poetry collections were received by critics is an indication of the fracture within the Harlem Renaissance over the kind of subject and style that should be adopted by African Americans. To take just one example, the *New Republic* carried a review by Harry Alan Potamkin of the *Copper Sun* that pointed out that Cullen's "interpretations and manner, his attitude of mind, are drawn, not from the evidences of his personal and intimate life, but from a tradition entirely literary, and, by now, anemic. That his own poems do not lack corpuscle is due to the impact of his nativity" (cited in Hutchinson 239). He is here accused of relying too much on British poetic traditions for inspiration, something that Potamkin also noted of the anthology of African American poetry, *Caroling Dusk,* which Cullen edited. The problem was one of trying to fit "Negro experience" in derivative forms, "what Potamkin regarded as a timidity about truly *appropriating*, challenging, and remaking the English tradition" (Hutchinson 240). The poem, "Yet Do I Marvel" suggests his own awareness of the problem noted by reviewers as it wonders at God's "[I]nscrutable ways" and the "curious thing: To make a poet black, and bid him sing" (Wiley 2, 127). His interest in other themes including his own sexuality is evident in many poems as is his inability to identify fully with his African roots. The poem "Tableau" from *Color,* offers an interracial take on homosexuality: "Locked arm in arm they cross the way, / The black boy and the white" while the "dark folk stare" and the white are "indignant" (Wiley 2, 127). The poem is dedicated to Donald Duff, Cullen's friend and possible lover. A second poem in *Color,* "Heritage", dedicated to Harold Jackman with whom Cullen had a similar relationship, is a series of images of Africa, strung together by the line and sentiment, "What is Africa to me?" (Wiley 2, 128–31).

As noted by Powers, "the politics of race was also the politics of gender and sexuality" (664) and Cullen was judged also for being "effetely comfortable" (Hill et al., 909, cited in Powers 661).

The title of Powers' paper declares that Cullen was "torn between private desire and public responsibility". A poem like "Heritage" seems to suggest that the problem was also of a spirit wrestling with affiliation to Africa and inability to fully surrender to it that must have been the dilemma of many who felt the distance – "three centuries removed". This could translate into the terms of Powers' title in a suggestive shift in the idea of public responsibility as one of identifying with the prevailing idea of a distinctive black aesthetic, expressive, as Langston Hughes declared in "The Negro Artist and the Racial Mountain", of "our individual dark-skinned selves without fear or shame" (Wiley 2, 213). "Heritage" also implies the attraction felt by many, educated in the literary culture of English, for the poetry of the Romantics. Cullen certainly felt this as did Sterling Brown about the forms of ode and sonnet that he used so frequently.

But during this most fertile period of Cullen's creativity, he won awards from magazines like *Poetry, Crisis, Opportunity* and *Palm*, received the Guggenheim Fellowship in 1928, and married Du Bois' daughter, a marriage that lasted only two years. Cullen's next two books, *The Black Christ and Other Poems* (1929), and a novel, *One Way to Heaven* (1932) were not received well. By 1934, his stars seem to have fallen as he was compelled to take a job as a teacher of English and French at the Frederick Douglass Junior High School. His lesser known works include a translation of Euripides, two books for children and an adaptation, with Arna Bontemps, of one of the latter's novels, *God Sends Sunday,* into the musical, *St. Louis Woman.* His poetry endures as among the best from the period in spite of the kind of criticism it received.

With the final writer we discuss in this chapter we come to the most glorious phase of the movement. **Langston Hughes** (1902– 67) was perhaps among the most gifted artists of the Harlem Renaissance, representing in his multiple achievements in several literary genres and in music, the best that emerged out of the creative churning characteristic of the period. He came to be widely known and as many of us in India would have experienced, our introduction to black writing most often came from his poetry, which featured in courses on American literature alongside the canonical white American poets like Whitman or Stevens or Frost, many decades before African American literature entered more comprehensively. Born in Missouri, the separation of his parents left him with his mother while his father moved to Mexico. He grew up in Kansas and Illinois and went to high school in Cleveland, Ohio, after his mother moved there, following remarriage. His lineage was distinguished. His maternal great uncle, John Mercer Langston was a Virginia congressman who was also the founding Dean of the Law School of Howard University. His maternal grandfather was a politician in Kansas during the Reconstruction. After graduating from high school Hughes spent a year with his father who had gone into business in Mexico. In 1921 he returned to New York, joined Columbia University but left after a year. It is from this period that he began to emerge as a key figure in Harlem. His first poem to be published was "The Negro Speaks of Rivers" in the 1921 issue of *Crisis* when Jessie Fauset was literary editor. She encouraged him to publish many more of his poems in the magazine but Hughes also wrote "The Weary Blues" for a contest at *Opportunity* magazine which he won. At this time he came in contact with Carl Van Vechten who helped him to publish his collection, *The Weary Blues,* with Alfred Knopf, in 1926. With this poem and this collection, the blues and jazz aesthetic entered literature in a much more pronounced way than it had earlier. Hughes's deep involvement with and knowledge of music, and his understanding of the uniqueness of African American musical form and sentiment enabled him to use it most effectively in his poetry. Both volumes, *The Weary Blues* and *Fine Clothes for the Jew* (1927) experimented with blues and jazz to transform traditional poetic forms, frequently took recourse to dialect and represented lower class black culture. Reviewers found his no-holds-barred representations especially in *Fine Clothes,* trashy and "[reeking] of the gutter and sewer" and the poems "insanitary, insipid and repulsing" (cited in Gates Jr. and McKay 1252). The negative reception proved to be a spur for his subsequent efforts in determinedly working with basic conditions of black life and the uniqueness of its musical culture ("The Weary Blues" [and several of his other poems] can be heard on YouTube, recited by Hughes himself to the accompaniment of jazz music).

A fine example of the adaptation of such music to literature is the poem "When de Saints go Ma'ching Home" by Sterling Brown discussed above that contains both the narrative and the rhythm of the blues. Hughes's first example of his style, "The Weary Blues" is representative of the mood and the movement – the slow, drowsy, droning tune, the crooning voice and the body "rocking back and forth" as it sets the tone for Hughes and all those others who followed him in using black soul music as a mood for their writings.

Hughes employed the sounds and rhythm of jazz extensively. Jazz can be strident and harsh in its sounds, and in literature it was able to present alternative images of African American selfhood and agency. As Keith D. Leonard has written, Hughes's poem "Jazzonia" "remakes the image of the oversexed, primitive African American falsely conceived by bored and wealthy white bohemians into an empowering ideal of licentious, self-asserted freedom". It expresses joy and sexuality in the "dancing girl" whose racial ancestors are Eve and Cleopatra. And "structurally, Hughes's poem has a refrain that validates this powerful joy" through "[R]epetition with a difference" (Leonard 292–93). Leonard here refers to the lines, "Oh, silver tree! / Oh, shining rivers of the soul!" which appears twice more with slight variations: "Oh, singing tree! / Oh, shining rivers of the soul" and then "Oh, shining tree! / Oh, silver rivers of the soul!" (Wiley 2, 214; also in Leonard 293).

The mood of jazz comes across in Hughes' own words: "jazz to me is one of the inherent expressions of Negro life in America; the eternal tom-tom beating in the Negro soul – the tom-tom of revolt against weariness in a white world, a world of subway trains, and work, work, work; the tom-tom of joy and laughter and pain swallowed in a smile" (Wiley 2, 212). The aural elements of this representation, its repetition of words like "tom-tom", and "work" evoke the sounds of the blues as does its depiction of the opposing emotions of laughter and pain. Hughes's poetry demonstrates what it means to have one creative-expressive form infuse another and merge into it. The writer using jazz music "adopted this new musical idiom predicated on African rhythms, ethnically specific practices of improvisation, black folk language, local urban themes, and the lives of ordinary black people as self-validating substitutes for the Eurocentric literary language, forms, subjects, and themes by which literary value has been determined" (Leonard 287). Leonard writes of "the most powerful implication of the jazz idiom: its hybridity, namely, its complex ability to combine and remake different and sometimes competing cultural materials into everevolving improvisational assertions of black presence" (287).

Hughes's career developed in several directions. He is considered a major scholar of both literature and music, besides being a playwright, novelist and short story writer. Alain Locke introduced him to one of the wealthiest philanthropists of the era, Charlotte Osgood Mason, who steered his career for a while as she did that of Zora Neale Hurston. While under her patronage he wrote his first novel, *Not Without Laughter* (1930) about a young African American boy growing up in Kansas. He travelled in the South during 1931, giving poetry readings. He travelled to Haiti, and then to the Soviet Union, China and Japan, and worked as a newspaper correspondent during the Spanish Civil War. By this time he had also developed strong leftist sympathies and published poems in the left-leaning *New Masses*. When he returned after this period of travel, he wrote his first collection of short stories, *The Ways of White Folks* (1934). The later part of the 1930s was a period of close involvement with theatre. Hughes was a pioneer on Broadway, bringing to it his plays on themes like racial mixing, and working against stereotypes that had developed in the minstrel shows by white performers during the nineteenth century. He wrote eleven plays. The play *Mulatto,* developed from one of his short stories, ran on Broadway for many years.

Hughes's popular stories featuring the comic character, Jesse B. Semple, also called Simple, first appeared in his columns in the *Chicago Defender* and the *New York Post,* and eventually went on to span five volumes. Hughes is also the author of two acclaimed autobiographies, *The Big Sea* (1940) that recounts his life up to the age of twenty-eight and carries a detailed picture of Harlem, and *I Wonder as I Wander* (1956) on his many travels. His scholarly works include *A Pictorial History of the Negro in America* (1956) and the anthologies *The Poetry of the Negro* (1949) and *The Book of Negro Folklore* (1958) with **Arna Wendell Bontemps** (1902–73), another important Harlem figure, a poet who published in *Crisis* and *Opportunity,* wrote several books for children and was the author of three novels, *God Sends Sunday* (1931), *Black Thunder* (1936) and *Drums at Dusk* (1939) – the last two on slave rebellions in Virginia and Haiti.

Hughes remained active till his death, his last volume of poetry, *The Panther and the Lash* (posthumously published in 1967), reflecting his involvement with the Black Power Movement and the Black Panther Party. Several of the writers in fact continued to write and they moved quite naturally into the next era of Modernism.

WORKS CITED

Anderson, David. "Sterling Brown's Southern Strategy: Poetry as Cultural Evolution in Southern Road." *Callaloo.* Vol. 21, No. 4, (Fall 1998). 1023–37. https://muse.jhu.edu/article/5891. Accessed 1 Jan. 2022

Barros, Paul de. "'The Loud Music of Life': Representations of Jazz in the Novels of Claude McKay." *The Antioch Review,* Vol. 57, No. 3, Jazz (Summer, 1999), 306–17. www.jstor.org/stable/4613880. Accessed 27 Jan. 2022.

Bernard, Emily. "The New Negro Movement and the Politics of Art." *The Cambridge History of African American Literature.* Eds. Maryemma Graham and Jerry Ward. Cambridge: Cambridge UP, 2011. 268–87. Kindle (paginated).

Dow, William. "'Always Your Heart': The 'Great Design' of Toomer's 'Cane'." *MELUS*, Vol. 27, No. 4, Varieties of the Ethnic Experience (Winter 2002). 59–88. www.jstor.org/stable/3250620. Accessed 22 Jan. 2022.

Du Bois, W. E. B. "Krigwa Players Little Negro Theatre." *The Crisis.* Vol. 32. July 1926. 134–36.

Duran, Jane. "Angelina Weld Grimke and Racialised Texts." *Literature & Aesthetics.* Vol. 20, No. 2. December 2010. 44–55.

Gates Jr., Henry Louis. "Afterword." *Their Eyes Were Watching God.* http://pdf.allbookshub.com/psychology/their-eyes-were-watching-god.pdf.

Gates Jr., Henry Louis and Nellie Y. McKay. Eds. *The Norton Anthology of African American Literature*. New York and London: W.W. Norton & Company, 1997.
Gordon, Michelle Yvonne. "The Chicago Renaissance." *A Companion to African American Literature*. Ed. Gene Andrew Jarrett. Malden, Oxford, Chichester: Wiley-Blackwell, 2013. 271–85.
Hammer, K. Allison. "Blood at the Root: Cultural Abjection and Thwarted Desire in the Lynching Plays and Poetry of Angelina Weld Grimké." *Frontiers: A Journal of Women Studies*. Vol. 42, No. 1. 2021. 27–57 https://doi.org/10.1353/fro.2021.0005 Accessed 16 Jan. 2022.
Hathaway, Heather. *Caribbean Waves: Relocating Claude McKay and Paule Marshall*. Bloomington and Indianapolis: Indiana UP, 1999.
Herron, Carolivia. *Selected Works of Angelina Weld Grimke*. Ed. and Introd. Oxford and New York: Oxford UP, 1991.
Hill, Patricia Liggins, et al. Eds. *Call and Response: The Riverside Anthology of the African American Literary Tradition*. Boston: Houghton, 1998.
Hughes, Langston. *The Big Sea*. Project Gutenberg Canada EBook. Uploaded 23 July, 2020.
Hutchinson, George. "Jean Toomer and American Racial Discourse." *Texas Studies in Literature and Language*, Vol. 35, No. 2, Anxieties of Identity in American Writing (Summer 1993). 226–50. www.jstor.org/stable/40755010. Accessed 22 Jan. 2022.
Hutchinson, George. *The Harlem Renaissance in Black and White*. Cambridge, Mass and London: The Belknap Press of Harvard UP, 1997.
Jarrett, Gene Andrew. *Representing the Race: A New Political History of African American Literature*. New York and London: New York UP, 2011.
Jarrett, Gene Andrew. Ed. *A Companion to African American Literature*. Malden, Oxford, Chichester: Wiley–Blackwell, 2013.
Jarrett, Gene Andrew. Ed. *The Wiley-Blackwell Anthology of African American Literature*. 2 Vols. Malden, Oxford, Chichester: Wiley–Blackwell, 2014.

Kuenz, Jane. "Modernism, Mass Culture, and the Harlem Renaissance: The Case of Countee Cullen." *Modernism/modernity*, Vol. 14, No. 3, (September 2007), 507–15. https://doi.org/10.1353/mod.2007.0064. Accessed 3 Feb. 2022.

Laarmann, Mario. "'Dwelling-in-Travel': The Politics of Space and Culture in Claude McKay's *Home to Harlem*." *OMNES: The Journal of Multicultural Society*. Vol. 9, No. 1 (2019), 90–109. http://dx.doi.org/10.14431/omnes.2019.01.9.1.90. Accessed 25 Jan. 2022.

Leonard, Keith D. "Jazz and African American Literature." *The Wiley-Blackwell Anthology of African American Literature*. 2 Vols. Jarrett, Gene Andrew. Ed. Malden, Oxford, Chichester: Wiley–Blackwell, 2014. 286–301.

Owens, Imani D. "'Hard Reading': US Empire and Black Modernist Aesthetics in Eric Walrond's *Tropic Death*." *MELUS*, Vol. 41, Issue 4 (December 2016), 96–115 https://doi.org/10.1093/melus/mlw051. Accessed 30 Jan. 2022.

Peckham, Joel B. "Jean Toomer's Cane: Self as Montage and the Drive toward Integration." *American Literature*, Vol. 72, No 2, (June 2000), 275–90. https://muse.jhu.edu/article/1529. Accessed 25 Jan. 2022.

Powers, Peter. "'The Singing Man Who Must be Reckoned With': Private Desire and Public Responsibility in the Poetry of Countée Cullen." *African American Review*, Vol. 34, No. 4 (Winter 2000). 661–78. www.jstor.org/stable/2901424. Accessed 2 Feb. 2022.

Rampersad, Arnold. "The Book That Launched the Harlem Renaissance." *The Journal of Blacks in Higher Education*, No. 38 (Winter 2002–2003), 87–91. www.jstor.org/stable/3134215. Accessed 25 Jan. 2022.

Rodgers, Lawrence R. "Dorothy West's *The Living is Easy* and the Ideal of Southern Folk Community." *African American Review*, Vol. 26, No. 1, Women Writers Issue (Spring 1992). 161–72. www.jstor.org/stable/3042085. Accessed 2 Feb. 2022.

Rusch, Frederik L. "Form, Function, and Creative Tension in Cane: Jean Toomer and the Need for the Avant-Garde." *MELUS*, Vol. 17, No. 4, Black Modernism and Post-Modernism (Winter 1991–Winter 1992), 15–28. www.jstor.com/stable/467265 Accessed 25 Jan. 2022.

Stepto, Robert. "'When de Saint Go Ma'chin' Home': Sterling Brown's Blueprint for a New Negro Poetry." *Callaloo*, Vol. 21, No. 4, Sterling A. Brown: A Special Issue (Autumn 1998), 940–49. www.jstor.org/stable/3299768. Accessed 2 Feb. 2022.

Tidwell, John Edgar and Steven C. Tracy. Eds. *After Winter: The Art and Life of Sterling Brown*. Oxford and New York: Oxford UP, 2009.

Wall, Cheryl A. "Passing for what? Aspects of Identity in Nella Larsen's Novels." *Black American Literature Forum*, Vol. 20, No. 1/2, (Spring–Summer, 1986), 97–111. www.jstor.org/stable/2904554. Accessed 22 Jan. 2022.

Walrond, Eric. *Tropic Death*. 1926. New York: Liverlight, 2013.

CHAPTER 5

Modernism
1940–65

TIMELINE

1941: The US enters the War after the Japanese attack on Pearl Harbour. Protests against racism which had been happening sporadically are seen again in the march to Washington, organised by the Brotherhood of Sleeping Car Porters, to protest segregation in the army and discrimination generally in employment. The march is, however, called off when President Roosevelt issues an order forbidding racial and religious discrimination in government training programmes and defence industries.

1942: Hurston, *Dust Tracks on a Road*; Margaret Walker, *For My People*

1943: First successful "sit-in" demonstration staged by the Congress of Racial Equality (CORE). Race riots in Detroit and Harlem leave over 40 dead.

1944: Melvin B. Tolson, *Rendezvous with America*

1945: Richard Wright, *Black Boy,* Gwendolyn Brooks, *A Street in Bronzeville*

1946: Ann Petry, *The Street*

1947: Tolson named poet laureate of Liberia.

1948: Dorothy West, *The Living is Easy.* President Truman approves desegregation of the military and creates Fair Employment Board.

1950–53: Korean War

1950: Brooks wins Pulitzer Prize for *Annie Allen*. Ralph J. Bunche becomes the first African American to win the Nobel Peace Prize.

1951: Langston Hughes, *Montage of a Dream Deferred*

1952: Ralph Ellison, *Invisible Man*

1953: Tolson, *Libretto for the Republic of Liberia;* Brooks, *Maud Martha;* James Baldwin, *Go Tell it on the Mountain;* Wright, *The Outsider*

1954: In *Brown vs Board of Education*, Supreme Court overturns the *Plessy vs Ferguson* (1896) judgment, ruling segregated schools as unconstitutional.

1955: Baldwin, *Notes of a Native Son;* Rosa Parks arrested for refusing to give her seat on a bus to a white man, inaugurating the bus boycott led by Dr. Martin Luther King. 14-year-old Emmett Till lynched in Mississippi; Supreme Court orders integration of schools; Interstate Commerce Commission orders integration of buses, trains and waiting rooms for interstate travel.

1956: "Southern Manifesto" against school desegregation signed by 101 southern congressmen.

1957: Congress approves Civil Rights Act of 1957; Federal Troops sent to Alabama to enforce school desegregation.

1959: Lorraine Hansberry's *A Raisin in the Sun* is the first Broadway play by an African American woman. Paule Marshall, *Brown Girl, Brownstones*

1960: Sit-in staged by four black students at Woolworth's lunch counter in North Carolina; Student Non-violent Coordinating Committee (SNCC) founded; Congress passes Civil Rights Act of 1960.

1961: Langston Hughes, *The Best of Simple;* Hoyt Fuller revives *Negro Digest;* Le Roi Jones (Amiri Baraka), *Preface to a Twenty Volume Suicide Note; Dutchman;* 13 "freedom riders" sponsored by CORE take bus trip across the South to force integration of terminals.

1962: First production of Adrienne Kennedy's Obie Award-winning play *Funnyhouse of a Negro;* Hayden, *Ballad of Remembrance;* Baldwin, *Another Country*. Riots after Supreme Court orders University of Mississippi to accept James H. Meredith as its first black student; 12,000 federal troops deployed to restore order and ensure Meredith's admission.

1963: Martin Luther King, *Letter from Birmingham Jail*. National support for civil rights movement roused after police attack Alabama demonstration led by King; Civil Rights "March on Washington" attracts 200,000 demonstrators; King delivers *I Have a Dream* speech. President Kennedy assassinated.

1964: Tolson, *Harlem Gallery;* Ellison, *Shadow and Act;* Baraka's *Dutchman* and Adrienne Kennedy's *Funnyhouse of a Negro* win Obie Award (Off-Broadway Theatre Award); Malcolm X founds Organization of Afro-American Unity; 3 civil rights workers murdered in Mississippi by white segregationists, setting off the Mississippi "Freedom Summer"; King wins Nobel Peace Prize; Twenty-fourth Amendment outlawing poll tax used to limit black suffrage; Congress passes Civil Rights Act of 1964 and Economic Opportunity Act; Sidney Poitier wins Academy Award for *Lilies of the Field;* Cassius Clay wins world heavyweight boxing championship, subsequently converts to Islam and changes name to Muhammad Ali.

1965–73: Vietnam War

1965: Malcolm X, *The Autobiography of Malcolm X;* A.B. Spellman, *The Beautiful Days;* King leads march from Selma to Montgomery, Alabama; Malcolm X assassinated in New York City; Watts riot, one of the worst race riots in US history

This brief period of a decade and a half saw African American literature expand in many directions, growing in complexity and responding not just to the political and social crises that continued to emerge but also gaining greater acceptability for the African American as literary creator and literary subject.

America's entry into WW II had several significant implications. Job opportunities increased with the economic expansion demanded by the war effort. Conscription, or mandatory military service for all able Americans brought further employment for large numbers of blacks though the armed forces continued to be segregated. When the US emerged from the war as a political, military and economic superpower, the welfare of its people became a major concern. On the negative side, these years saw the rise of a virulent anti-Communism led by the Republican Senator Joseph McCarthy with artists especially being suspected of affiliations with communists in other countries, and the bogey of communist takeover spreading across the country especially through a section of the media. These developments affected all Americans but African Americans in particular. Despite the opportunities, the realities of segregated educational institutions, restaurants, lunch counters and public transport were evidence of the continuing deep-seated racism of American society. The second wave of migration from the South to the Northern cities, already overburdened by immigrants, brought problems of housing, and a strain on urban facilities. But as blacks moved into the cities of the North, alongside conflicts arising from the forced contiguities at work and residence was the rise of a black, urban street culture – "bop" and "hip talk" – that defined an urban sensibility and saw the city itself becoming the setting for literature.

There were also other factors that were important. These included decolonisation and the independence of countries like Ghana, Nigeria, Senegal and Algeria, the modernist movement in the arts and with it, newer influences, models and ideas, intellectual crosscurrents that were set up as artists moved to and from the Caribbean, Europe and Africa. Another important development was the interest and involvement in Marxism.

Fiction, poetry and drama during these years begin by realistically recording urban experience. Want and poverty, and hard lives lived in the shadow of racist discrimination continued to provide subject matter for literature. Many of the writers who began writing during the Harlem Renaissance remained productive. Hurston's *Dust Tracks on a Road* and a collection of Hughes's Simple stories were published during this time. Hughes continued to write prolifically. There is, therefore, no strict division between this and the earlier period and yet the points of departure were quite clear, especially as articulated in the essays of Wright, Ellison and Baldwin. Writers like Richard Wright, Melvin B. Tolson, Ann Petry, Robert Hayden, Ralph Ellison, Margaret Walker, Gwendolyn Brooks, James Baldwin, and Lorraine Hansberry produced works that expressed various aspects of black aspiration and resistance. Just as there was a many-sided political and cultural effort during the Harlem Renaissance, this period too shows a similar diversity and richness of thinking and writing as older authors produced some of their important works and newer ones emerged. Alain Locke, a central figure in the Harlem Renaissance, published an essay in the *New Challenge,* titled "Spiritual Truancy" where he called the earlier writers "aesthetic wastrels" (63) who failed to address the "people themselves" while attending to a "gallery of faddist negrophiles" (66). The idea of collective work is evident here as it is in Wright's essay "Blueprint", published in the same volume of *New Challenge* (Fall 1937).

Richard Wright's *Native Son* (1940) is a text that defines the period. It inaugurated the genre of the African American protest novel. Written in the naturalist style, it addressed themes of racial inequality, a divided and uneven society and economic deprivation, and proved a pathbreaking work that showed the way for other protest novels like those of Ann Petry, Frank London Brown, William Gardner Smith and William Demby. The protest novel featured the black working class especially in the backdrop of the Depression. But by the 1950s the protest novel gave way to more subtle and nuanced forms of fictional expression that did not always feature black characters or background and frequently addressed non-racial themes. This was an integrationist move that paved the way for newer influences especially from the great Western modernist writers and thinkers like Freud and Marx. The shift can be actually seen in the turn away from realism and naturalism as preferred fictional styles, to the incorporation of more modernist methods of fragmentation as well as the incorporation of jazz and blues. One of the finest examples of this new direction is Ralph Ellison's *Invisible Man* (1952).

Theatre became an important form of expression with Harlem's American Negro Theater and Negro Theater in New York providing an alternative to the largely white Broadway. Harry Belafonte and Sidney Poitier (two names that a certain generation of Indians would recognise immediately from the song "Down the Way when the Nights are Gay" and the film "To Sir with Love" respectively) added a fresh dimension with music and acting. Two playwrights, Louis Peterson and Lorraine Hansberry, broke into Broadway with plays that addressed the race question alongside other, more general, issues of opportunity and self-realisation. Hansberry's play *A Raisin in the Sun* (1959) is considered a watershed event as it focused on the accessibility of the American Dream for African Americans, and was set against the real estate crisis that affected her family and the community in the 1940s.

In poetry Robert Hayden, Margaret Walker and Gwendolyn Brooks take note of the spirit of protest and yet, in their innovations on poetic forms alongside familiarity with poetic tradition, and in their use of African American folk and oral culture, they prove themselves to be quintessential modernists.

The essays of James Baldwin are examples of this other genre that became a political weapon in the hands of emerging intellectuals who evaluated their own roles and that of fellow African American writers in the continuing struggle for civil rights and creative possibility.

Perhaps the most important aspect of literary development in this period was the writing of literary manifestos (a phenomenon that we also saw during the Harlem Renaissance). These manifestos focus on critical evaluation of the work that needed to be done by black artists, identifying sources of inspiration, studying and writing black history and above all reflecting on how the Negro should be represented (as seen in the title and practice at Du Bois's write-in symposium "The Negro in Art: How Shall He Be Portrayed"). Writers addressed the role of literature as an ideological vehicle – with statements that expressed a desire for recognition not merely within the community, but as creative writers irrespective of race. Gwendolyn Brooks's Pulitzer acceptance speech declared that "[t]he Negro poet's most urgent duty, at present, is to polish his technique, his way of presenting his truths and his beauties, that these may be more insinuating, and, therefore, more overwhelming" (Wiley 2, 392). A statement like this is a clear expression of affinity with the modernist spirit of formal innovation.

Newer critical explorations into this period and especially with the questioning of canonicity encouraged by postmodernism has revealed a bunch of writers who charted significantly different paths in their thinking and writing. Placed roughly after the Second World War – a period that is dominated by the likes of Wright, Ellison, Hurston and Amiri Baraka – these other writers dramatically expanded the interests and range of African American writing. They include William Gardner Smith, Leon Forrest, Carlene Hatcher Polite, Robert Hayden and Albert Murray. However, it is with Wright and the immense influence he wielded among his juniors that any account of the literature of this period must begin.

1

Richard Wright (1908–60) had a rocky childhood and youth. Nathan Wright, his tenant farmer father, and Ella Wilson Wright, his schoolteacher mother, were both descendants of slaves. His father deserted the family early in his life and his mother started suffering from a neurological disorder that would trouble her till the end of her life. Poverty sent the children first to the household of their maternal grandmother and then for a while to an orphanage. Eventually the family lived with an aunt and her saloon keeper husband who was later murdered by whites for the sake of his land and business – an incident that appears in the story "Long Black Song" from the collection *Uncle Tom's Children* (1938). Wright's schooling was erratic and he dropped out after the ninth grade to undertake a series of jobs before migrating north, first to Memphis and then to Chicago where he subsequently found employment at the Post Office after clearing the necessary Civil Service examination. He also managed to get access to a library by using the card of a fellow worker, a Roman Catholic, who "being himself an object of hatred", had some sympathy for the Negroes, an episode that is recounted in "The Ethics of Living Jim Crow" (Norton 1395). Wright read extensively in the works of white writers like H.L. Mencken, Theodore Dreiser, Sinclair Lewis, Sherwood Anderson and Alexandre Dumas. He later went on to read Marcel Proust, Henry James and Gertrude Stein. This reading inculcated in him a sense of style, besides opening up new ways of representing society and reality. In 1932 he joined the Communist Party. He left Chicago for New York in 1937 and became editor of the Communist paper, *Daily Worker*. His Marxist sympathies were responsible for the view he took of the world around but it also sometimes led to an element of propaganda in his writing. Nevertheless, it is worth noting that Wright's literary practice of bringing together realism, naturalism, Marxism and Freudianism along with black folk tradition enabled the making of a distinctive and influential style even as it facilitated his criticism of both black and white society. Wright not only opened up opportunities, he set an example of possibilities. He encouraged and supported writers like Baldwin, Walker, and Brooks and also famously critiqued the Harlem Renaissance in his "Blueprint for Negro Writing", an essay that was published in the Fall 1937 issue of the *New Challenge*. This essay is crucial to an understanding of the literary-cultural impulses of this period. After dismissing the previous period for its "humble novels, poems, and plays, prim and decorous ambassadors who went a-begging to white America", he emphasises the need to recognise "a culture of the Negro", which he locates in "the Negro church" and "the folklore of the Negro people." The church was a portal to western culture but it was in the folklore "moulded out of rigorous and inhuman conditions of life that the Negro achieved his most indigenous and complete expression". His characterisation of this folklore summarises the experience of the past and looks forward to future uses of it: "blues, spirituals and folk tales . . .; the whispered words of a black mother to a black daughter on the ways of men; the confidential wisdom of a black father to his black son; the swapping of sex experiences on street corners from boy to boy in the deepest vernacular; work songs sung under blazing suns . . . the channels through which the racial wisdom flowed". He goes on to speak of Negro nationalism, "a Negro way of life in America" that is the result of "lynch rope, bayonet and mob rule". Commenting on the presentation of the life of the Negro people he embraces a galaxy of literary greats that includes Eliot, Stein, Joyce, Proust, Hemingway, Gorky alongside Negro folklore. And on perspective he insists that it is about living fully in one's time: "It means that a Negro writer must create in his readers' minds a relationship between a Negro woman hoeing cotton in the South and the men who loll in swivel chairs in Wall Street and take the fruits of her toil". The capacity to make such a connection is an essential part of the writer's deep understanding of the political, economic and social forces under which his people live. In all of these sections there is evident a sense of togetherness and empathy with his people and with other black writers – "The ideological unity of Negro writers and the alliance of that unity with all the progressive ideas of our day is the primary prerequisite for collective work" (Norton 1380–88). This evaluation, critique and programme represents what Wright perceived as the call of the time.

Gates Jr. and McKay note that Wright "sent 'the word' into battle and stamped his vision of African American culture on this new and necessary era in African American letters". They add that "[D]espite its urban, 'secular' impulses that vision was actually an extension of the didactic, declamatory utterances found in the black sermon and historically linked to the narratives of enslavement". Gates Jr. and McKay make a further significant point that "although Wright defied his grandmother's Seventh Day Adventist religion (as Bigger did the 'old time' religion of his mother in *Native Son*), he was wed no less to the Protestant passions of testifying and truth telling" (Gates Jr. and McKay 1321). Such truth telling and bearing witness is an essential aspect of the theme of protest in African American literature that is not just characteristic of Wright or his followers but a theme that cuts through the entire history. It may be subtle and tacit or in-your-face and overt but it runs through the slave narratives, the oral tales and songs, the poems of Wheatley and Horton and much of subsequent literature, even when the gaze of the writer is turned inward in sharp assessment of his own failure to uplift the race or in his concession to expectations of white society and critics.

While the "Blueprint" offers an agenda for writing, in "The Ethics of Living Jim Crow: An Autobiographical Sketch", Wright records several encounters with white society and the consequent "lesson[s] in how to live as a Negro" (Norton 1388): keep yourself hidden, do not fight against white folks, know your place and stay in it, women, expect to be punished with whip and rape, always agree with white people, avoid certain molestation by staying out of white neighbourhoods, keep smiling through every injustice. As he moved from one job to the next, the strategies of survival became cleverer and more subtle and in the optical company job in Memphis, "Jim Crow education assumed quite a different form .... Here I learned to lie, to steal, to dissemble. I learned to play that dual role which every Negro must play if he wants to eat and live" (Norton 1395). What would appear as invisibility in Ellison's novel is already evident here as the 'place' of the Negro, and the many sites of racism – at workplaces, and in and around neighbourhoods.

The influence of the Chicago School of Urban Sociology has been noted by many critics of the work of Wright and many of his contemporaries. In the year after *Native Son* (1940) appeared, Wright produced *Twelve Million Black Voices: A Folk History of the American Negro,* a text containing photographs and running commentary on the effects of migration on blacks who had come from the South to the North in the hopes of a better life. Wright here notes that if in the South blacks were landless, in the North they are constrained by the poky little one-room apartments they rented, also known as the kitchenette apartments. Urban life only aggravated old problems while introducing many new ones.

Wright was also a significant writer of short stories and novellas. The early collection, *Uncle Tom's Children* (1938), written while he was involved with the Works Progress Administration or WPA Federal Writers Project (established in 1935) contains four novellas – "Big Boy Leaves Home", "Down By the Riverside", "Long Black Song" and "Fire and Cloud". Each of these shows blacks facing mob violence and lynching. "Long Black Song" might be seen as representative in its treatment of the violence meted out by white society. A white salesman forces himself upon the woman Sarah, who is awaiting the return of her husband from a business trip and trying to pacify her distressed child. When Silas does return he is suspicious of her and is determined to whip her to ease the hurt to his pride: "Ah got mah raw-hide whip n Ahm taking yuh t the barn" (Norton 1408) – a scene which while it does not actually materialise, is a reminder of the whipping and sexual domination that female slaves faced in the plantations as well as from their own men, and that is recorded in so many of the slave narratives. Sarah runs out and away from the house with her child and watches from a distance as the white salesman arrives with a friend to hear the decision on the purchase of the clock he was offering at the discount that had aroused Silas's suspicions. Silas attacks him with the whip he is carrying and then shoots him. The salesman's friend jumps back into the car while Silas drags the dead body to the middle of the road. He knows there is no escape from the white mob now and tries to persuade Sarah to leave. He himself refuses to go:

"Ef Ah run erway, Ah ain got nothing. Ef Ah stay n fight, Ah ain got nothing. It don make no difference which way Ah go" (1412). Silas is well aware of what is about to happen: "The white folks ain never gimme a chance! They ain never give no black man a chance!" (1412). As expected the white mob arrives with guns and after a brief exchange of shots they set the house on fire and Silas is burned alive within it. The wide-eyed despair of this novella is Wright's own awareness of all that had remained unchanged.

In a later enlarged edition of this collection, the essay "The Ethics of Living Jim Crow" and a short story "Bright and Morning Star" were added.

Wright's other works include *Eight Men: Short Stories* (published in 1961 after his death), and "The Man Who Lived Underground", a story that appeared in the 1945 collection, *Cross Section*, edited by Edward Seaver. Much of his best work was done before he moved to France in 1946 when the creative source in African American life and speech and song seem to have dried up for him. In the 1950s, Wright travelled widely in Europe and Africa, associated closely with the Negritude movement and its writers like Leopold Senghor and Aime Cesaire, and was able "to see the social and psychological effects of material oppression in global perspective" (Gates Jr. and McKay 1379).

Among the works he is best remembered by are of course *Native Son* (1940) and *Black Boy* (1945). The latter is a version of the slave narrative, an autobiographical account which initially only described his experiences in the South. A second part titled *American Hunger,* on his life in Chicago, published posthumously in 1977, was later incorporated with the first part into one volume and is now available as one book. *Native Son* is in many ways central not just to the collective experience of all blacks but within the corpus of his work. It was adapted for the stage by Wright himself in 1941, had a brief run on Broadway and also toured the country. In style and theme the novel represents his view of what black writing should be. It set the terms of the "protest novel" using realism and naturalism to represent not only the ugly conditions of everyday life on the Chicago South Side but the fear and psychological disintegration of character. It tells the story of the violent young man, Bigger Thomas, who seems to be on a downward spiral he cannot prevent as he commits two murders – one accidental and the second deliberate – and it ends inevitably with his death. The fact of its centrality within the Wright corpus is also attested to by the essay he wrote on the composition of the novel.

Black Boy, "arguably the most important life story from the culture", expresses the anger and bitterness of the post WWII period when African American soldiers, feted and welcomed in Europe, returned to the disillusionments of continuing segregation, voting restrictions, and poorly paid jobs. Many joined resistance groups like the Brotherhood of Sleeping Car Porters, Congress of Racial Equality, and the NAACP (Lowe 341). Gunnar Myrdal's monumental study, *An American Dilemma* (1944) points out how the colour line was sustained and had become entrenched in American society somewhat like the Indian caste system. John Lowe writes that "[T]he new spirit of militancy was stoked by black newspapers such as the *Pittsburg Courier,* the *Chicago Defender,* the *Baltimore African-American* and the *Norfolk Journal and Guide*" as also the work of Myrdal. *Black Boy,* documenting the distress of the Depression years, tells of the young boy growing up in the rural South and his unusual sensitivity not just to violence and suffering that is depicted in the naturalistic style Wright had used in *Native Son,* but also to the natural world. Lowe calls this a *Künstlerroman* (depicting the growth of an artist), much like Joyce's *Portrait of the Artist as a Young Man,* that shows "the gradual unfolding of an unusually sensitive and receptive creativity, one generated by a poetic reception of the natural world and by a horrified reaction to brutality and eruptive force" (Lowe 343).

Wright proved to be a trendsetter for what came to be called the "Wright School", all of whose adherents used realist and naturalist modes to explore the lives of blacks in urban settings. **William Attaway** (1911–86), novelist, short story writer, essayist, and playwright, was a friend of Wright's and was with him on the Federal Writers project. His novel *Blood on the Forge* (1941) depicted the travails of blacks who had migrated from the South to work in the steel mills of the North and who had to compete with white and immigrant labour. **Chester Himes** (1909–84) who was himself active in the labour movement wrote a number of important novels that reflect his concern with the working class. *The Lonely Crusade* (1947) is about a labour organiser who fights against racial discrimination in the unions. Himes is also the author of *If He Hollers Let Him Go* (1945), a novel set during WWII and depicting an educated Northern Negro, pitted against poor, white Southern migrants in a shipyard, who is accused of raping a white woman. Himes had a traumatic childhood and youth. At home there was tension between his parents; his brother lost his sight in an accident, and he himself spent the years between 1929 and 1936 in the Ohio State Penitentiary after having committed armed robbery. His novel *Cast the First Stone* (1952) was based on his experience in prison. In 1953 Himes moved to Paris and began the series of nine Harlem detective novels which include *The Crazy Kill* (1959), *Cotton Comes to Harlem* (1965) and *Blind Man with a Pistol* (1969), featuring two black NYPD detectives, Gravedigger Jones and Coffin Ed Johnson. He also wrote two volumes of autobiography, *The Quality of Hurt* (1972) and *My Life as Absurdity* (1976).

Ann Petry (1908–97) the third significant member of the Wright school started with a degree in pharmacy from the University of Connecticut, and went on to become a journalist in New York City with the *Amsterdam News* (1938–41) and the *People's Voice* of Harlem (1941–44), before studying creative writing at the University of Columbia (1944–46). She is best known for her novel *The Street* (1946) which portrays a woman from the black working class, Lutie Johnson, and her dreams of leaving Harlem and making a different life for herself, but whose poverty and the prevailing racism prevent her from doing so. It records the daily injustices faced by the black single mother trying to realise the American Dream for herself and her son even as it shows disillusionment at the failure to finally achieve it. Besides the urban setting of Harlem, the overcrowding and poor housing, as well as the constant fear of sexual exploitation, Petry's novel is distinguished by the presence of the female protagonist who retaliates for her troubles with violence. The ironies inherent in the failure of the Dream are made apparent in the Benjamin-Franklin-like figure of Junto who, while showing her the possibilities of changing her life, also plots to sexually possess her, and whose henchman she eventually kills. The novel is realist in its depiction of subject matter and is written in a distinctive, naturalist style evident from the opening description, and particularly in the physicality of the account of Lutie's experience of the cold:

> The wind lifted Lutie Johnson's hair away from the back of her neck so that she felt suddenly naked and bald, for her hair had been resting softly and warmly against her skin. She shivered as the cold fingers of the wind touched the back of her neck, explored the sides of her head. It even blew her eyelashes away from her eyes so that her eyeballs were bathed in a rush of coldness and she had to blink in order to read the words on the sign swaying back and forth over her head. (Petry 8–9)

The Street has affiliations with the hardboiled crime thriller (with its cast of seedy characters and unsavoury locales), and in its graphic depiction of harsh living conditions in the Harlem tenements. In its strong feminist impulse, shown in Lutie taking charge of her own sexuality (that might be traced to the theme of vulnerability of the black woman's body from the earliest slave narratives and right through subsequent women's writing, where the body is frequently seen as a source for the precarity of black women's lives), and in the breaking of stereotypes, especially that of the mammy (Lutie is a live-in-maid who works all the time and gets to see her husband and son only a few times every month), the novel makes its radicalism clear. These are all qualities that ensure its continuing place in literary history. Newer work on the gothic and fantastic aspects of the novel (for instance Shockley 2006) shifts away from the realist readings to point out the gothic as a source of Petry's language of terror, and the existence of a trope of "live burial" in metaphorical figures of vampires, monsters and ghosts (Shockley 440).

With her next two novels, *Country Place* (1947) and *The Narrows* (1953), Petry moves into what is often termed an integrationist mode by presenting white characters. *Country Place* tells the story of Johnnie Roane, who returns from military service during WWII to his hometown of Lennox, Connecticut, expecting to resume his life with his wife Glory. The storm which occurs and disrupts the lives of the white community living here is a reference to a real storm that Petry herself had experienced, but it also symbolises the storm in the life of the couple in the form of the secret infidelity of Glory. *The Narrows* is about an educated black man, Link Williams and his tragic love affair with a rich, white woman. Petry began her career by writing short stories: "On Saturday the Siren Sounds at Noon" and "Like a Winding Sheet" (which brought her a literary fellowship) were published in the *Crisis* in 1943 and 1945. Her short stories were collected in *Miss Muriel and Other Stories* (1971). Petry is also the author of four children's books on historical characters, including *Harriet Tubman, Conductor on the Underground Railroad* (1955), and *Tituba of Salem Village* (1964), representing her conviction about the need to remember: "Remember for what a long, long time black people have been in this country, have been part of America; a sturdy, indestructible, wonderful part of America, woven into its heart and into its soul" (Petry from an essay on children's literature cited in Gates Jr. and McKay 1478).

In a 1988 interview given to *MELUS,* Petry spoke of the locales she used in her work, especially in the short stories, her reading of Faulkner and Malamud, the fact of being surrounded by storytellers accounting for the appearance of storyteller characters in her work, and her training in writing at the University of Columbia (Petry and Wilson 1988).

James Baldwin (1924–87) announced himself to his literary peers with the essay "Everybody's Protest Novel". He was a novelist, playwright and brilliant essayist who grew up in Harlem and spent a crucial period, from the age of fourteen to sixteen, serving as a preacher after school hours in a small revivalist church, an experience that is at the heart of his first novel, *Go Tell It on the Mountain* (1953), and in his play on a woman preacher in a Harlem storefront church, *The Amen Corner.* After graduating from high school he held a number of jobs while studying and training himself for a literary career in Greenwich Village, New York. In 1948 he left for Paris, living there for eight years. In 1957 he returned to the US, and joined the Civil Rights Movement. While the theme of black-white relations is central to most of his works, he is also one of the first to explicitly write on same sex relationships. His second novel, *Giovanni's Room* (1956), is the story of an American in Paris, who is trying to come to terms with his homosexuality, even as he wavers between two relationships, one with Hella Lincoln, the other with Giovanni, an Italian bartender. *Another Country* (1962) begins with the suicide of Rufus Scott, a black jazz musician, leaving a bunch of his friends trying to make sense of his death, in the process engaging with their own racial and sexual identities. Baldwin was also the writer of powerful essays that are indictments of American society and institutional racism. He published them in contemporary journals and magazines and most of them are collected in *Notes of a Native Son* (1955), *Nobody Knows My Name* (1961), and *The Fire Next Time* (1963). From 1969, Baldwin began to live alternatively in France and in New York and New England in the United States.

Interesting echoes of the idea of the city have been noted in his work, especially since the 'city on the hill' has been a reference point from the times of Puritan settlement. In his novel it is the play of the earthly and the heavenly cities that Baldwin presents:

> Although the setting of *Go Tell It on the Mountain* is the all too real city of New York, especially Harlem, Baldwin then has based his novel's meaning on one of the richest, most complex of configurations in the history of thought: the idea of the city. In *Go Tell It on the Mountain*, Baldwin juxtaposes two cities, the earthly and the heavenly, and together they help to focus the novel's various themes: father and son, individual and community, the sacred and the profane. Baldwin obviously depends upon Saint Augustine's two cities to give structure to these thematic oppositions. (Scruggs 2)

Baldwin's moving and eloquent essays match Ellison's on black culture. In a comparative analysis of Baldwin and Ellison, Herman Beavers points out that "each understood suffering to be an inimical part of black life. Ellison's and Baldwin's characters are engaged in attempts to fashion for themselves adequate narrative space, to become agents, actors, and subjects" (190).

Ralph Ellison (1914–94) published just the one novel, *Invisible Man*, during his lifetime, but this became a classic and is now considered as one of the great American novels. Ellison, named after Ralph Waldo Emerson, was born in Oklahoma City. His father was a small businessman who died in 1917 and his mother went to work as a domestic to support her family. At the local parsonage where his mother shifted her family, Ralph found a world of books and magazines like *Vanity Fair* and *Literary Digest*. He went to the Frederick Douglass School where he was able to study music and learnt to play several instruments. He heard many jazz musicians and his desire to further cultivate his music led him to join the Tuskegee Institute on a scholarship. Here he received musical training from brilliant teacher-musicians. He also took a course on the English novel and one of his teachers led him to Eliot's *Waste Land*. Studying sculpture opened up another artistic realm (Gates Jr. and McKay 1516). Following this education Ellison moved to New York City and there met Richard Wright, with whose encouragement he started writing short stories, essays and reviews for a number of periodicals. After a stint in the army during WWII, Ellison wrote *Invisible Man*, the story of a young, black man who, even as he joins the fight against white oppression, is ignored by everyone around him. From a college in the south the young man arrives in Harlem and is witness to many forms of racial discrimination. As it details the life of the young man in his encounters with people who do not see him, the novel becomes a reflection on invisibility. In his "Author's Introduction" (written 30 years after the first publication) Ellison writes, "my task was one of revealing the human universals hidden within the plight of one who was both black and American, and not only as a means of conveying my personal vision of possibility, but as a way of dealing with the sheer rhetorical challenge involved in communicating across our barriers of race and religion, class, color and region" (xl).

In order to draw the reader's attention to the "common humanity shared by my character and those who might happen to read of his experience", he writes: "I would have to provide him with something of a worldview, give him a consciousness in which serious philosophical questions could be raised, provide him with a range of diction that could play upon the richness of our readily shared vernacular speech and construct a plot that would bring him in contact with a variety of American types" (xl).

Most importantly, he would have to take note of racial stereotypes, and "reveal the human complexity which stereotypes are intended to conceal" (xl). And he writes about drawing on the culture of the folk tale and the novel while "improvis[e]ing upon my materials in the manner of a jazz musician putting a musical theme through a wild star-burst of metamorphosis" (xli).

In the "Prologue", invisibility is established as an aspect of the viewer's inability to see, "because of a peculiar disposition of the eyes of those with whom I come in contact" (3). In the first face-off with a white man, recounted with the dark humour that is found throughout the book, the nameless narrator realizes that the white man he attacks for calling him an "insulting name" "had not *seen* me". "Then I was amused. Something in this man's thick head had sprung out and beaten him within an inch of his life. I began to laugh at this crazy discovery" (5). This is a unique take on the issue of identity, equally amusing and disturbing, as the white man who would render the black man invisible has now internalised the invisible man as a fearsome spectre of his own mind. Through this assessment of black-white power dynamics Ellison engages with the conditions of African American experience in New York City. The disillusionment that follows the hopeful journey from the racist South and the discovery that the North has evolved much subtler forms of discrimination, is presented in the enmeshing of realistic depictions of society with the surreal presence of the invisible narrator who walks through the narrative with a zany step and a jazz musician's effervescence as he alternately moves us and makes us laugh with his perceptions, his opinions and his reasoning. The hole in the ground that he is systematically lighting up – as the novel begins he has managed to install 1369 filament light bulbs that run on stolen electricity – expresses what he calls "a different sense of time" that invisibility gives him, where you are aware not of the flow but "of its nodes, those points where time stands still or from which it leaps ahead. And you slip into the breaks and look around. That's what you hear vaguely in Louis' music" (8).

Ellison's novel is pervaded by the spirit and the complex emotional states of the blues as it uses puns, speeches and sermons and explores the mood of melancholy through the protagonist. His definition of blues gives a sense of the novel's continuing magic. For him as he said in "Remembering Jimmy", the blues was: "an art of ambiguity, an assertion of the irrepressibly human over-all circumstance" (n.p.). *Invisible Man* expresses this ambiguity, in the way invisibility itself is employed to critique racism.

This novel was followed by two collections of essays, *Shadow and Act* (1964) and *Going to the Territory* (1986). Ellison meanwhile became a popular speaker on Black culture and folklore and taught at several colleges and universities. When he died, he left a second, unfinished novel which was published as *Juneteenth* (1999).

2

A number of powerful poets explored the modernist style and content, among them Robert Hayden, Margaret Walker and Gwendolyn Brooks.

Robert Hayden (1913–82) was born Asa Bundy Sheffey (his surname comes from his foster parents) in a slum neighborhood called Paradise Valley in Detroit, Michigan. Despite poor eyesight he became a voracious reader. He studied at the Detroit Northern High School and at Detroit City College (later Wayne State University). Meanwhile he acted in a Langston Hughes play and worked on the Federal Writers' Project in Detroit, researching local black history and folklore. In 1940 his first collection of poetry, *Heart-Shape in the Dust,* was published. He also got married to concert pianist and composer, Erma Morris. In 1942 he enrolled in the English Literature programme of the University of Michigan and came under the influence of W. H. Auden who was then visiting professor in the English Department. This was the most important of the modernist influences on him (and Hayden was also reading widely in the poetry of Edna St. Vincent Millay, Hart Crane and Carl Sandburg as well as the poetry of the Harlem writers Hughes, Toomer and Cullen). At Michigan he continued to hone his craft, winning prizes for his poetry and also publishing his second collection, *Black Spear* (1942). In 1944 he received his master's degree in English. These early volumes already show Hayden's interest in African American history and capacity to weave it into elegant poetic expression. His other collections include *Figure of Time* (1955), *A Ballad of Remembrance* (1962), *Selected Poems* (1966), *Words in the Mourning Time* (1970), *The Night-Blooming Cereus* (1972), *Angle of Ascent: New and Selected Poems* (1975) and *American Journal* (1978). Much of Hayden's poetry refers to African American history in which he had a lifelong interest, seeing in it the process of evolution of the race. Vilma Raskin Potter writes of his achievement: "The gift of Robert Hayden's poetry is his coherent vision of the black experience in this country as a continuing journey both communal and private. The journey begins in the involuntary suffering of the middle passage and continues across land and into consciousness." And, she adds: "[H]is poems are full of travelers whose imagination transforms the journey" (51). A second area that influenced some of his works is Hayden's engagement with the Baha'i faith, and especially with its idea of a universal civilization.

Among his well-known poems that achieve this amalgam of history and poetry are "Middle Passage", "Frederick Douglass" and "A Letter from Phillis Wheatley London, 1773". "Middle Passage", an early poem, represents the theme of journey across the oceans and on land undertaken by many African Americans. The poem has an unnamed narrator who controls the many European voices – those of shipowners, sick seamen, lawyers and officers – that provide ironic testimony of the middle passage (the use of many voices is a characteristic Hayden style, employed in many poems). Running through the poem is a parody of the song of Ariel from Shakespeare's play *The Tempest,* "Deep in the festering hold thy father lies, / of his bones New England pews are made" (Norton 1504). Towards the end this scene of suffering is changed to that of a trial, in a Connecticut courtroom, of the Amistad rebels and their leader, Cinquez. The "Middle Passage" therefore ends with resistance and resolve. In melding the oceanic journey of the middle passage with more individual journeys, Hayden does what many Black writers have done, showing the community struggle and the individual struggle as mirroring one another.

"Frederick Douglass" is a fourteen-line poem, a sonnet, from *A Ballad of Remembrance* that speaks of freedom as something that is "truly instinct" and must be possible to take for granted, as natural as breathing, like the regular beating of the heart – "diastole, systole" – a "beautiful, needful thing" and the place of Douglass in the struggle to achieve it. The remembering of Douglass has, therefore, to be special, not with the usual memorials but "with the lives grown out of his life", "fleshing his dream" (Norton 1508–09). This poem might be seen as part of a group on historical figures that is scattered across the several volumes. In *Angle of Ascent,* Hayden has written of Sojourner Truth; besides Douglass, *A Ballad* also has a poem on Nat Turner. He went on to write on Malcolm X's transformation into El-hajj-Malik El-Shabazz, in a poem that contains the pithy epigraph "*O masks and metamorphoses of Ahab, Native Son*" that draws on these figures of resistance and resolve.

In the third poem from the collection, *American Journal,* Hayden assumes the voice of Phillis Wheatley, as she writes to her friend Obour of her journey to London in 1773, with the son of the Wheatley family, Nathaniel, in order to seek funds for publishing her book of poems. Hayden makes Wheatley recall the Middle Passage: "I yet have some remembrance of its Horrors", something she never overtly mentions in her poetry. Wheatley's identity as Christian and American is gestured at in a reference to her "Patriot" duty even as racial inferiority is ironically referred to when she tells Obour that at a dinner where she is made much of and her poetry moves many in the audience to tears, she has her meal separately from the rest, like "captive Royalty". The poem ends with a young chimney sweep, covered in soot asking her if she too swept chimneys, a query that amuses her but not Nathaniel (Norton 1514–15). Hayden takes apart the psychological underpinnings of slavery with precision – in the many ironies of Wheatley's apparently innocent perception of her visit, her interactions with those who would be her patrons, and especially in the position of Nathaniel who is shown as a peddler displaying a performance that will bring in money from the audience.

History, explorations and journeys, resistance and striving are repeated themes in Hayden's poetry. The African American experience is represented for what it is but it also often becomes a model or metaphor for other struggles. This is evident in a poem like "For a Young Artist", that is developed from Gabriel Garcia Marquez's famous short story, "A Very Old Man with Enormous Wings" and shows the miserable state of living in a pigsty from where the man eventually succeeds in pulling himself up into the sky (we might recall the folktale, discussed in Chapter 1, "All God's Chillen Had Wings"). As one critic of Hayden has written: "What one sees, smells, and touches in his poetry is the human imagination *searching* for something else besides the muck of history or of one's own foul rag and bone shop" (Zebrun 22 original emphasis).

A similar command over material and technique is demonstrated by another poet of this time, **Gwendolyn Brooks** (1917–2000). Distinguished by positions like that of poetry consultant to the Library of Congress, and poet laureate of Illinois State, besides becoming the first black author to win the Pulitzer Prize, Brooks was deeply immersed in the political life of her time even as she kept step with the best of the poets. Brooks's parents, her janitor father and her schoolteacher/pianist mother encouraged the gifted child to read and write and her first poem, "Eventide" was published when she turned thirteen. She wrote poetry without interruption, finished junior college, attended many poetry writing workshops and polished her skills. She also worked for the NAACP. Her first collection was *A Street in Bronzeville* (1945), followed in 1949 by *Annie Allen* – both volumes containing poems that presented pictures of the poor African Americans in the Bronzeville district of the city of Chicago.

The one novel she wrote, *Maud Martha* (1953), uses the typical modernist style of fragmented pictures and collage to portray a character who suffers from racial prejudice directed at her by both whites and lighter skinned blacks. Critics suggest that sometime around the late 1960s a dramatic change is evident in Brooks' work, especially in *In the Mecca* (1968). One of her early biographers, George E. Kent noted her ability to speak across a span of time, from the 1940s to the 1960s. In a review in *The New York Times* of 7 January 1973, Toni Cade Bambara writes of her work at this time, that there is "a new movement and energy, intensity, richness, power of statement and a new stripped lean, compressed style. A change of style prompted by a change of mind" (Web n.p.).

The more overt literary politics that Brooks began to practice with this newer consciousness of wanting to support black literature and writers, is probably best manifested in her turn to Black publishing houses for her works written after 1968. She published several of her collections of poetry from the Broadside Press of Dudley Randall. These include *Riot* (1969), *Family Pictures* (1970), *Aloneness* (1971), *Aurora* (1972), and *Beckonings* (1975), as well as the first volume of her autobiography, *Report from Part One* (1972). Among other publishing houses that she patronised was the Third World Press of Haki L. Madhubuti.

Margaret Walker (1915–98) has two works that are unique in their reflection of African American history, character and aspirations. One is the collection of twenty-six ballads, sonnets and free verse poems titled *For My People* (1942), which won her the Yale Series of Younger Poets Award; and the second is the historical novel *Jubilee* (1966) which turned the popular plantation romance, *Gone With the Wind* on its head, demolishing the stereotypes of black people, especially the mammy figure, used in that novel, by presenting a black heroine and the story of a slave family during the Civil War. Both these works came out of Walker's family environment, the tales told to her by her grandmother, especially about her great-grandmother who was a slave, and her own research into the history of slavery and the African American people. Margaret Walker was born into a family where her father, a Methodist minister directed her reading of the classics, of the philosophy of Spinoza and Schopenhauer and of the Bible, while her mother, a musician, played ragtime and read the Bible and the poetry of Dunbar and Shakespeare to her daughter. Biblical echoes are often heard in her poetry. While she was still a child other influences included poetry readings by James Weldon Johnson and Langston Hughes. Later at university her reading also included the poetry of Whitman, Randall Jarrell, Eliot and Pound.

Walker graduated from Northwestern University in 1935 and joined the Federal Writers' Project in Chicago, where she associated closely with Richard Wright for about three years. This was a fruitful association with Wright reading and critiquing her poetry while Walker helped with revisions of some of his work and with the research for *Native Son*. In 1949, she joined Jackson State University as a faculty member. In 1968 she founded the Institute for the Study of the History, Life and Culture of Black People at the University. Her second volume of poetry, *Prophets for a New Day* (1970) presented Civil Rights Movement leaders as prophets, while in the next volume, *October Journey* (1973), she presents poems on Harriet Tubman, Gwendolyn Brooks, her father and other people known to her or who she revered. Other works include *How I Wrote Jubilee* (1972), *A Poetic Equation: Conversations between Nikki Giovanni and Margaret Walker* (1974). She also wrote a critical study, *Richard Wright: Daemonic Genius* (1988); *This is My Century: New and Collected Poems by Margaret Walker* (1989); *How I Wrote Jubilee and Other Essays on Life and Literature* (1990), and *On Being Female, Black and Free: Essays by Margaret Walker, 1932–1992* (1997).

The title poem of her first volume, "For My People" is a synopsis of the life experiences of suffering and slavery, of being cheated and defeated at every turn, the efforts to emerge from these conditions and the hope and beauty at the heart of all the ugliness. Stephen Vincent Benet in his introduction to the volume, spoke of Walker's poetry as "controlled intensity of emotion and language that, even when most modern, has something of the surge of biblical poetry" (cited in Graham 40). That "surge" is clearly audible in the cadences of this poem. In the twenty-six poems of the volume

> [t]he sacred and the profane merge as the reader grasps the profound and subtle significance of racial memory. Each poem becomes part of a collective memory narrative as told through a black vernacular matrix which emphasizes the flow and rhythm of the myths, folk tales, legends, ballads and narratives as well as free verse forms, sonnets, odes, and elegies. Structurally, the volume emulates the call and response pattern inherent in traditional African American expression. (Graham 40)

The volume explores historical episodes, folk tales and folk figures, and personal memories, and finally emphasises the importance of struggle in the face of the life described in the earlier poems. This is illustrated in the final stanza of the title poem, where the voice rises to a climactic declaration of a "new earth" and calls for courage and freedom and healing (Norton 1573).

Walker's one published novel *Jubilee* is set in Georgia and Alabama during the Civil War. Its heroine Vyry is modelled on the author's great-grandmother whose stories she had heard from her own grandmother. Vyry is one of the fifteen children of the owner of Shady Oaks Plantation, John Morris Dutton, and his slave Sis Hetta who he raped regularly. The novel opens with Sis Hetta on her deathbed. The child is then passed on from Mammy Sukey to Aunt Sally, the cook, from whom she learns cooking and who she eventually replaces when Aunt Sally is sold away. Vyry meets and is attracted to Randall Ware, a blacksmith and free black with his own shop, who comes to the plantation to do some work. She has two children with Ware but is unable to escape to join him after he moves to the North. She remains on the plantation through the Civil War, through the death of the master, his son and the mistress, the departure of most of the slaves and the coming of the Union Army. This is when another character enters the novel. Innis Brown who saves Vyry from an assault, falls in love with her and asks her to move to Alabama with him. They set up house but face a series of disasters, with their first home being washed away by a flood, and the second being burnt down by the Ku Klux Klan. Finally, they settle in a town where the white residents express a need for Vyry's skills as a midwife. Vyry and Brown have two children, Ware returns to take away his son Jim and finally Vyry and Brown settle into peaceful family life. The end is idyllic as Vyry after a period of rumination atop a hill, returns to her farm, calling the chickens home.

In a later collection of essays, *How I Wrote Jubilee,* Walker described the research she did for this novel, besides writing about the life of an artist as a woman and an African American. The book also contains essays on several writers including Richard Wright and Du Bois.

In theatre, the prominent name was that of **Lorraine Hansberry** (1930–65). She was born in Chicago into a prominent middle class family that was active in politics, academics and business, with her father being a real estate broker, her mother a schoolteacher and her uncle a professor of African history at Howard University. She came into contact with prominent cultural figures like Paul Robeson, Duke Ellington and the novelist, Walter White, developed an interest in black liberation struggles through her uncle and experienced the socio-political struggles of the African American people through her family's challenge to segregated housing in Chicago. She studied at the University of Wisconsin (1948–50), and then attended the Art Institute of Chicago and Roosevelt University. After moving to New York, she also studied at the New School for Social Research. She was active in the various protests held during this time, and it was while on a march that she met Robert Nemiroff, who went on to become a theatre producer and songwriter and whom she married in 1953. By 1957 Hansberry was beginning to come out as a lesbian, and writing on homophobia and the challenges and objections to feminism. In 1962 the marriage ended in divorce but Nemiroff remained a collaborator, and became her literary executor after her death from cancer, compiling all her autobiographical writings, letters and unpublished plays.

Besides *A Raisin in the Sun*, Hansberry wrote two other plays, and left several unfinished ones. *The Sign in Sidney Brustein's Window* (produced 1964) is, as she described it, about "the nature of commitment" which according to her was "one of the leading problems before my generation here: what to identify with, what to become involved in; what to take a stand on; what, if you will, to believe in at all" (cited in Gates Jr. and McKay 1727). *The Arrival of Mr. Todog* which remained unpublished at the time of her death, was a satire on Beckett's *Waiting for Godot* and its popularity among American intellectuals. Hansberry also wrote the commentary for *The Movement: Documentary of a Struggle for Equality* (1964), a book prepared by the Student Non-Violent Coordinating Committee (SNCC), containing hundreds of photographs from the Civil Rights Movement with particularly vivid photographs of lynchings and beatings of civil rights demonstrators.

The events of her most famous play *Raisin,* are loosely based on experiences from the real estate business of her father. Carl Hansberry was called the "kitchenette king" as he subdivided and resold to African Americans, large homes that white owners were leaving to settle in the suburbs. He himself bought a house in the white neighborhood of Washington Park subdivision on Chicago's South Side and moved his family there in 1938 in the face of violent protests – an incident that became exemplary in the struggle for integrated housing when the Supreme Court decided in his favour in the famous *Hansberry vs Lee* case of 1940.

A Raisin in the Sun remains one of the most powerful plays written by an African American. It appeared, at the height of the Civil Rights era. Besides the desegregation of housing, there were also other landmark events surrounding it – the Supreme Court decision on school desegregation five years earlier, the Montgomery Bus Boycott four years earlier and the student sit-in movement just after it. Gates Jr. and McKay cite Amiri Baraka's description of it as the "quintessential civil rights drama" (1726), and its influence extended to the African American theatre of the 1960s. It was made into a film by Columbia Pictures with a screenplay by Hansberry herself.

The play's title is taken from Langston Hughes' poem, "A Raisin in the Sun", and the events in it and its overall mood are drawn from the poem's opening lines: "What happens to a dream deferred?" It captures the dreams of the Younger family – mother, daughter, daughter-in-law, son and grandson – as they live in extreme hardship but aspire for better times. The play's action is structured around the cheque for 10,000 dollars that Mama, Lena Younger, receives as her dead husband's gratuity, an amount on which Walter and Beneatha, brother and sister, peg their hopes – one for an investment in a liquor business and the other for a medical education. Mama however, goes out and pays the deposit on a house in a white neighbourhood, Clybourne Park, and gives the rest of the money to Walter, with a part to be put away for her daughter's medical school fees and the remaining to be invested by Walter in his business. Inevitably, this money is lost, while a representative from Clybourne Park, Lindner, comes with a purchase offer for the house so that the all-white neighbourhood is not adulterated by the presence of a black family. In a speech that sums up the opposition that blacks had to face as the movement for integration proceeded, Lindner says: "[t]he overwhelming majority of our people out there feel that people get along better, take more of a common interest in the life of the community, when they share a common background". And he communicates the opinion of the white residents that "Negro families are happier when they live in their own communities" (Norton 1772). Walter on behalf of the family turns down the offer and orders Lindner out of the house.

In Act III, for a while it seems that the family will bargain for a good price for the house but in the climactic final moments Walter, finally in sync with the long-seated desire of his family and rising to the occasion in a speech of deep emotion turns down the offer:

> What I am telling you is that we called you over here to tell you that we are very proud and that this is – this is my son, who makes the sixth generation of our family in this country, and that we have all thought about your offer and we have decided to move into our house because my father – my father – he earned it . . . we will try to be good neighbors. That's all we got to say. (Norton 1788)

The family is overwhelmed by what the play itself, in a subsequent stage direction, calls "the nobility of the past moment" even as they get busy with preparations for the move (1788).

Besides realistic depictions of family life, the bickering between brother and sister over Beneatha's career, and with Ruth playing peacemaker for the family, there are moving lines on love and relationships, and on the psychology of different characters. Mama's response to Beneatha's contempt for her brother's weakness is the wisdom acquired from intense suffering and hardship: "Child, when do you think is the time to love somebody the most, when they done good and made things easy for everybody? . . . It's when he's at his lowest and can't believe in hisself 'cause the world done whipped him so" (Norton 1786–87).

After she won the New York Drama Critics' Circle Award for *A Raisin in the Sun* (1959), Hansberry was asked for her views on the Nation of Islam by one of the makers of the documentary *The Hate That Hate Produced* on Malcolm X and the NOI. She replied: "Let's not equalize the oppressed with the oppressor . . . My position is that we have a great deal to be angry about, furious about. You know it's 1959 and they are still lynching Negroes in America?" (Wiley 2, 599).

Even as the play captures the individual experience, it resonates with many other concerns that were challenging the community. These include integration, the always looming spectre of racial violence, the stereotype of the Mammy which both Ruth and Lena represent and counter, the scope of transnational black identities, and the affiliations with African freedom struggles against colonialism. The last is gestured at through the attractive figure of Asagai, the Nigerian student and intellectual who courts Beneatha and offers an alternative vision of life for blacks, even as the family and especially Mama would much prefer that Beneatha marry George Murchison who belongs to a rich African American family.

Hansberry's political awareness and her strongly leftist leanings are evident in this play as is her attention to the appropriate form necessary for the rendering of protest and redemptive vision in her own understanding of realism as appropriate for evoking not only that which *is* but that which is *possible* (in Gates Jr. and McKay 1726). The play's continuous relevance in the history of struggle is attested to by its production history (see for instance Wilkerson [1986] for an anniversary estimate).

The literature produced during this period touched upon the life of the community with deep insight and sharpness, revealing the many emotional scars that were still embedded in its individual and collective consciousness, as well as a simmering discontent that developed into raging anger during the next period we track, when the Black Arts Movement set itself on a course of militant protest and confrontation, finding in these heightened emotional states, both theme and style.

Works Cited

Baldwin, James. *Go Tell It On the Mountain.* London: Michael Joseph Ltd, 1954. https://ia801601.us.archive.org/13/items/in.ernet.dli.2015.184884/2015.184884.Go-Tell-It-On-The-Mountain.pdf. Accessed 20 Nov. 2021.

Bambara, Toni Cade. "Report from Part One." *The New York Times* (Jan 7, 1973). n.p. nytimes.com/1973/01/07/archives/report-from-part-one-by-gwendolyn-brooks-prefaces-by-don-I-lee-and.html. Accessed 22 Aug. 2022.

Beavers, Herman. "Finding Common Ground: Ralph Ellison and James Baldwin." *Cambridge Companion to the African American Novel.* Ed Maryemma Graham. New York: Cambridge UP, 2004. 189–202.

Egejuru, Phanuel and Robert Elliot Fox. "An Interview with Margaret Walker." *Callaloo,* No. 6 (May, 1979). 29–35. https://www.jstor.org/stable/3043889. Accessed 22 Aug. 2022.

Ellison, Ralph. "Author's Introduction." *Invisible Man.* (1981 edn.). London: Penguin, 2001. xxv–xli.

———. "Remembering Jimmy." *The Saturday Review* XLI. (July 12, 1958). 36–37. *The Saturday Review Archives.* https://www.unz.com/print/SaturdayRev-1958jul12-00036/. Accessed 22 Aug. 2022.

———. "The Blues." *The New York Review.* (Feb 6, 1964). n.p. https://www.nybooks.com/articles/1964/02/06/the-blues/. Accessed 22 Aug. 2022.

———. *Invisible Man.* (1952). London: Penguin, 2001

Gates Jr., Henry Louis and Nellie McKay. Eds. *The Norton Anthology of African American Literature.* New York and London: W.W. Norton & Company, 1997.

Graham, Maryemma. "Margaret Walker: Fully a Poet, Fully a Woman (1915–1998)." *The Black Scholar.* Vol. 29, No. 23 (1999). 37–46 DOI: 10.1080/00064246.1999.11430961.

Jarrett, Gene Andrew. Ed. *The Wiley-Blackwell Anthology of African American Literature.* 2 Vols. Malden, Oxford, Chichester: Wiley-Blackwell, 2014.

Kent, George E. *A Life of Gwendolyn Brooks.* Lexington: UP of Kentucky, 1990.

Locke, Alain. "Spiritual Truancy." In *The Critical Temper of Alain Locke: A Selection of His Essays on Art and Culture.* Ed. Jeffrey C. Stewart. New York: Garland, 1983. 63–66.

Lowe, John. "Writing the American Story, 1945–1952." *The Cambridge History of African American Literature.* Eds. Maryemma Graham and Jerry Ward. Cambridge: Cambridge UP, 2008. 341–55. Kindle EBook (paginated).

Myrdal, Gunnar. *An American Dilemma: The Negro Problem and Modern Democracy.* 2 vols. New York: Harper and Bros., 1944.

Petry, Ann. Interview with Mark K. Wilson. "Ann Petry. The New England Connection." *MELUS.* Vol. 15, No. 2, Sp Issue. Varieties of Ethnic Criticism (Summer 1988). 71–84 https://www.jstor.org/stable/466973. Accessed 19 Nov. 2021.

———. *The Street.* London: Michael Joseph Ltd, 1947. https://ia601609.us.archive.org/11/items/in.ernet.dli.2015.247848/2015.247848.The-Street_text.pdf. Accessed 20 Nov. 2021

Potter, Vilma Raskin. "A Remembrance for Robert Hayden: 1913-1980." *MELUS.* Vol. 8, No. 1. Tension and Form. (Spring 1981). 51–55. https://www.jstor.org/stable/467369. Accessed 12 May 2021.

Scruggs, Charles "The Tale of Two Cities in James Baldwin's *Go Tell it on the Mountain.*" *American Literature.* Vol. 52, No. 1 (March 1980). 1–17. https://www.jstor.org/stable/2925184. Accessed 20 Nov. 2021.

Shockley, Evie. "Buried Alive: Gothic Homelessness, Black Women's Sexuality, and (Living) Death in Ann Petry's *The Street.*" *African American Review.* Vol. 40, No. 3 (Fall 2006). 439–60. https://www.jstor.org/stable/40027383. Accessed. 20 Nov. 2021.

Wilkerson, Margaret. "*A Raisin in the Sun:* Anniversary of an American Classic." *Theatre Journal.* Vol. 38, No. 4, Sp. Issue: Theatre of Color. (Dec 1986). 441–52.

Zebrun, Gary. "In the Darkness a Wellspring of Plangency: The Poetry of Robert Hayden." *Obsidian* (1975–1982). Vol. 8, No. 1. A Robert Hayden Special Issue (Spring 1982). 22–26.

CHAPTER 6

Pride and Anger
The Black Arts Era: 1965–75

TIMELINE

1965: Black Arts Movement started by Amiri Baraka in Harlem following the assassination of Malcolm X.

1966: Black Panther Party and National Organization for Women founded; Senator Edward W. Brooke becomes first elected black senator since Reconstruction. "Black Power" concept is adopted by CORE and Student Non-violent Coordinating Committee (SNCC).

1967: Haki R. Madhubuti: *Think Black;* Ishmael Reed: *The Free-Lance Pallbearers;* Martin Luther King announces opposition to Vietnam War; Worst race riot in US history in Detroit kills 43. Thurgood Marshall becomes first black Supreme Court justice; Supreme Court overturns law against interracial marriage.

1968: Etheridge Knight: *Poems from Prison*; Nikki Giovanni: *Black Feeling*; Eldridge Cleaver: *Soul on Ice*; Quincy Troupe's anthology: *Watts Poets: A Book of New Poetry and Essays*; Caroline Rodgers: *Paper Soul*; Earnest Gaines: *Bloodline*; Audre Lorde: *The First Cities*; June Jordan: *Who Look at Me*; Alice Walker: *Once: Poems*. Martin Luther King assassinated in Memphis, Senator Robert Kennedy assassinated in Los Angeles. Shirley Chisolm becomes the first black woman elected to the US Congress.

1969: Sonia Sanchez: *homecoming*; Jayne Cortez: *Pisstained Stairs and the Monkey Man's Wares*; Lucille Clifton: *Good Times*; Al Young: *Dancing: Poems*; anti-war demonstrations in Washington.

1970: Charles Gordon wins Pulitzer Prize for *No Place to be Somebody;* Mari Evans: *I am a Black Woman*; Maya Angelou: *I Know Why the Caged Bird Sings*; Toni Morrison: *The Bluest Eye*; Michael S. Harper: *Dear John, Dear Coltrane*; Toni Cade Bambara edits *The Black Woman*.

1971: Addison Gayle: *The Black Aesthetic*; Angelou: *Just Give Me a Cool Drink of Water 'fore I Diiie*; Gaines: *Autobiography of Miss Jane Pittman*

1972: Reed: *Mumbo Jumbo*. Congress passes Equal Rights Amendment; Chisholm runs for President.
1973: Etheridge Knight: *Belly Song and Other Poems*; Morrison: *Sula*
1974: Charles Johnson: *Oxherding Tale*; Albert Murray: *Train Whistle Guitar*
1975: Ntozake Shange's play *for colored girls who have considered suicide/when the rainbow is enuf* becomes second play by an African American on Broadway. Sherley Anne Williams: *Peacock Poems*; Gayl Jones: *Corregidora*

In 1963, a review of Gwendolyn Brooks' *Selected Poems* by Louis Simpson, carried a couple of sentences that summarise the kind of perception that prevailed among white readers and critics of black writing: "I am not sure it is possible for a Negro to write well without making us aware he is a Negro. On the other hand, if being a Negro is the only subject, the writing is not important" (cited in Sullivan 27). The Black Arts period is a mere decade in the history of African American literature. But it is a decade of exceptional productivity, and cultural and political activism through art. It is when the idea of black pride came to dominate the work of artists and writers as never before. It is a ferocious, angry time, when radical and often militant views were expressed by writers who were all cultural activists, and believed that the idea of a black aesthetic was a vital political stand, necessary to take stock of the past, remember it and discover ways to express it, deal with it and show the world an art that was founded on the most horrific experiences of slavery and continuing racism, but that expressed agony and racial pride in equal measure. Black Arts poets used Black language and speech and the music of jazz, and freely experimented with punctuation, grammatical norms and spellings to best represent the cadences of black speech. This can be seen in the poetry in long extended vowel sounds, or jarring consonants (much like the effects of jazz), while the notion of Black Power appeared in the images of strength, and in representations of black women figures who are strong and resolute and beautiful. It was a period of political turmoil. The Civil Rights Movement was at its peak, led by Martin Luther King who adopted the nonviolent protest methods of Mahatma Gandhi, and it involved marches, bus boycotts and sit-ins. A number of African countries, like Ghana, Senegal, Ivory Coast and Kenya achieved their freedom from years of colonial rule.

At the same time American society became much more conservative as if in response to the waves of black protest and calls for equality. The teachings of Malcolm X (who followed in the wake of Marcus Garvey and his 'back to Africa' doctrine, spent time in prison and came under the influence of the Nation of Islam leader, Elijah Muhammad, but subsequently parted ways from him and formed the Organization of Afro-American Unity) coincided with the anger and accompanying nationalist desire to separate from white society and constitute all-black communities, an idea already being articulated by Baraka and others. As Baraka put it, "Malcolm X put words to the volcanic torrent of anger and frustration many of us felt with the civil rights movement" (*Baraka Reader* 496, cited in Zygmonski 149). The logical step to realising the nationalist goal was the integration of African Americans into a community and as Larry Neal observed in his essay on the Movement, the artist was not separate from the community. The notion of community itself was continuing to expand. In an essay on "The Writer and Black Liberation" (1968), John Oliver Killens argued for the development of connections with "the worldwide revolution of people of color against colonialism and white racism" (266). Anger and pride are expressed through the wide use of the discordant sounds of jazz and in the prosodic elements of black speech and music; while writers also drew on the sermons, the songs and other forms that depended on the communication between a performer and an audience, to bring their writing closer to readers. Stephen Henderson in an important study, *Understanding the New Black Poetry* (1972) points out some distinctive verbal innovations: "(1) virtuoso naming and enumerating; (2) jazzy rhythmic effects; (3) virtuoso free-rhyming; (4) hyperbolic imagery; (5) metaphysical imagery; (6) understatement; (7) compressed and cryptic imagery; (8) worrying the line" (cited in Bolden 533). He sums up aspects that were already in use in earlier poetry – especially during the Harlem Renaissance in the poetry of Hughes – and that would be further refined by later writers, with each generation making its unique experiments with the sounds, rhythms and characteristic styles that had emerged out of the long history of music, dance and storytelling. Many of the ideas of racial pride had already been expressed by early-twentieth-century intellectuals like Du Bois and the activist Marcus Garvey but now there was a much wider practice of artistic resistance as writers explored different ways to articulate different forms of it.

As with other periods a number of enabling factors account for the emergence of writers, ideologies and unique literary practices. Publishing houses and presses, magazines and periodicals, the founding of drama and dance troupes, writing circles and writers workshops, bookstores, and cultural centres all contributed to the energy of the Black Arts Movement (BAM). Throughout the period activities clustered around these different focal points helped forge artistic relationships, brought audiences, readerships and artists together, provided a training ground and sounding board, and kept alive a revolutionary, rousing, dissenting art that was yet founded on the oral, folk, performative elements of African American culture. Poetry and drama flourished, radical artistic manifestos came to be written and the moods of blues and jazz touched everyone. Artists and writers crossed generic boundaries and wrote and performed in multiple genres. One of the most significant things was a deep consciousness of what the black writer must do, an approach and philosophy expressed in several manifestos, but perhaps nowhere more trenchantly than in Amiri Baraka's "The Myth of a Negro Literature" (an address given at the American Society for African Culture on 14 March 1962, that was later published in *The Saturday Review* in April 1963). In this piece, while noting the "mediocrity" of most Negro writing and the occasional foray into "high art", Baraka makes the point that, "[A] Negro literature, to be a legitimate product of the Negro experience in America, must get at that experience . . . in its most ruthless identity", transforming the very negatives that defined them for the whites into their strengths – "The Negro could not ever become white and that was his strength". Because the Negro "could not participate in the dominant tenor of the white man's culture . . . he had to make use of other resources, whether African, sub-cultural, or hermetic."

"And this is the only way for the Negro artist to provide his version of America – from that no-man's-land outside the mainstream. A no-man's land, a black country, completely invisible to white America". This series of statements is equally an assessment and a programme, and describes what most artists actually did. Baraka asserts the need for difference, and the importance of the marginal, oppositional and outsider stand. The basic sentiment of the piece appears in the concluding sentence where Baraka declares that: "as long as the Negro writer contents himself with the imitation of the useless ugly inelegance of the stunted middle-class mind, academic or popular, and refuses to look around him and 'tell it like it is' – he will be a failure, and . . . not even a significant failure" (Wiley 2, 619–20).

What Baraka says seems to define the literature that would appear as black writers creatively interpreted what it meant to be black, powerful and different and "forever, outside that culture" (Wiley 2, 620). James T. Stewart whose essay "The Development of the Black Revolutionary Artist" (first published in the anthology *Fire!*) calls for distinctive black artistic forms and a rejection of white models, points to the need for understanding a different "cosmology", citing "temples made of mud that vanish in the rainy seasons" and exquisite drawings of the great Japanese artists that are then engraved on newssheets and sold cheap to people often to be used for "wrapping fish" that are then rescued by the white researcher and given their real value. In his impatient response to such assumptions of ignorance, Stewart writes of alternative orders of creativity: "We know, all non-whites know, that man cannot create *a* forever, but he can create forever. But he can only create if he creates as change. Creation is itself perpetuation and change is being" (Stewart 4). This "estrangement" from "white Western civilization" would enable the black revolutionary artist "to make new definitions founded on his own culture – on definite black values" (10). The date of commencement for this phase of creative activity is said to be 1965, a year when Malcolm X was assassinated, Baraka started the Black Arts Repertory and School, and the Broadside Press was established by Dudley Randall.

A number of factors were responsible for the unique character of this period that featured the Civil Rights Movement, The Black Arts Movement, the Black Power Movement, the resources offered by Africa where writers like Sonia Sanchez, Baraka, Larry Neal, Hoyt Fuller and others travelled, the personality of Malcolm X and the Nation of Islam (compelled into existence by the denial of full citizenship rights to African Americans), and the influence of the New Left movement. It is a time of considerable political upheaval and ideologically driven, ethnic cultural movements like the Chicano Arts Movement (inaugurated by Rudolf Anaya's 1972 bildungsroman, *Bless Me, Ultima*), and the Native American Renaissance (marked by N. Scott Momaday's 1968 novel *House Made of Dawn*). Gene Andrew Jarrett who makes these connections also notes the influence of postmodernism during these years in breaking the boundaries between genres (he mentions the blurring of autobiography and fiction), and offering enabling styles and techniques. He writes: "[t]he era was a fruitful one for authors seeking to reveal yet overcome the traditional ways in which race, ethnicity, gender, and region alternately or collectively relegated underrepresented experiences to the margins of society" (Wiley 2, 611). And yet as other critics have noted, rather than being avant-garde, the Black Arts Movement "embraced aspects of popular culture and conventional literary structure within their transformative work" with Baraka's *Dutchman* providing a good example in its "linear tragic narrative consisting of the introduction of characters, the staging of central conflict, and the death of the protagonist – in order to express the political philosophies of the artistic movement" (Zygmonski 149).

1

The first significant challenge was to create conditions that would facilitate the kind of writing thought to be necessary and most expressive of the anger, aspirations and understanding of the place of the African American in contemporary America. Many writers started doing some of their important writing during this period with these goals in mind and made significant contribution to its spirit of racial pride and radical politics. One of these was **Hoyt Fuller** (1923–81), a Wayne State University graduate in literature and journalism, who as editor of *Negro Digest* which he renamed the *Black World* (and after this journal was discontinued, became a founder, with black activists, of the *First World*), demonstrated the importance of the press for the promotion and articulation of changing views about the African American struggle. He wrote prolifically on what he saw as Western erasures of black art and black progress and in his periodicals published poems, essays and short stories by new authors, among whom were Mari Evans, Etheridge Knight and Alice Walker. In *Journey to Africa* he counters the white American search for origins in Europe with the argument for African American origins in Africa. He supported the cultural work done by the Organization for Black American Culture, and organised several pan-African festivals in both the US and Africa. This vigorous life-long engagement with popularising black art and artists and establishing its distinctiveness is expressed in the polemical essay "Towards a Black Aesthetic". Arguing for a phase beyond the cultural revolution of Frantz Fanon, he writes of the "young writers of the black ghetto" who "have set out in search of a black aesthetic, a system of isolating and evaluating the works of black people which reflect the special character and imperatives of black experience" (Norton 1814). He mentions a workshop sponsored by the Organization of Black American Culture of Chicago, which he founded, where "writers are deliberately striving to invest their work with the distinctive styles, and rhythms and colors of the ghetto" as well as the music of some of the jazz musicians of the day. And he argues for the need to capture the black "style" marked by a sense of "Cool" and embodied in movement and speech, that lends subtlety and technique to the writing (1815).

Fuller was one of an important group of writer-activists who called for a distinctive black aesthetic and whose manifestos, anthologies and literary works contributed to the special significance of this period in cultural history. **Larry Neal** (1937–81) who wrote an essay titled "The Black Arts Movement" (originally published in a special issue of *The Drama Review* edited by the playwright Ed Bullins), aligns the concept of "Black Arts" with that of "Black Power" – seeing both as nationalistic. "One is concerned with the relationship between art and politics; the other with the art of politics" (Norton 1960), but both understand the need to challenge the western view of the world and art. Neal further declares: "the motive behind the Black aesthetic is the destruction of the white thing, the destruction of white ideas, and white ways of looking at the world. The new aesthetic is mostly predicated on an Ethics which asks the question: whose vision of the world is finally more meaningful, ours or the white oppressors? What is truth?" (Norton 1960).

These are basic questions that, according to him, earlier black intellectuals failed to ask. For Neal, the "Black Arts Movement is an ethical movement" and involves a destruction of the Euro-American cultural sensibility "before the Black creative artist can have a meaningful role in the transformation of society" (Norton 1961–62).

Other writings that similarly expressed the need for a distinctive Black aesthetic include Addison Gayle's "Introduction" to the anthology *The Black Aesthetic,* Baraka's poem "Black Art", and Maulana Karenga's essay "Black Art: Mute Matter Given Force and Function." **Maulana Karenga** (b. 1941), a prominent scholar and activist, known for his work on Afrocentric theory and for his position on the inclusion of ancient Egyptian studies within black studies, reinforces the idea of art and culture as tools of revolution or "revolutionary machinery". Using a rhetoric of violence he writes, "Black art must expose the enemy, praise the people and support the revolution. It must be like LeRoi Jones' poems that are assassins' poems, poems that kill and shoot guns . . . The second characteristic of Black art is that it must be collective" (Norton 1973). In conclusion, urging a movement out of the past into the present and the future, he writes, "Let our art remind us of our distaste for the enemy, our love for each other, and our commitment to the revolutionary struggle" (Norton 1977). A reference to Leopold Senghor (co-founder of the Negritude movement in the 1930s) suggests the association of this aesthetic with a larger African culture and strengthens the resolve to fight and overthrow the demeaning, exclusionist aesthetic of the Euro-American.

Addison Gayle (1932–91) who wrote extensively on the Black Aesthetic, compiled and edited critical and theoretical writings on it, and taught English for twenty-five years at the Bernard M. Baruch College of the City University of New York, mentions that most critics note two common themes in black art: "anger" ("as old as the first utterances by black men on American soil") and "black nationalism" that has been there at least since the National Negro Convention of 1836. In his Introduction to *The Black Aesthetic,* a collection of essays by several writers which Gayle edited, he quotes Hoyt Fuller's statement – "The Negro revolt is as palpable in letters as it is in the streets" – and suggests that the revolt is actually a "war" waged by black artists against an oppressive society. Unlike the earlier black artist whose war was against the South, these new artists are fully aware of the pervasive nature of racism equally in the North as in the South, with the Northerner being duplicitous and more "sagacious and dishonest" in knowing how to "'keep the nigger in his place'" (Norton 1872–73). Against earlier assumptions, Gayle sets the central question of his Introduction and of the collection itself: "How far has the work gone in transforming an American Negro into an African-American or black man?" As a credo for black criticism, he says: "unique art derived from unique cultural experiences mandates unique critical tools for evaluation" (Norton 1876). *The Black Aesthetic* appeared in 1971. In sections on theory, music, poetry, drama and fiction, it featured writings by LeRoi Jones, Hoyt Fuller, Sarah Webster Fabio, Don L. Lee (Haki Madhubuti), Larry Neal and Dudley Randall. It also reprinted essays by Du Bois, Langston Hughes and Richard Wright and "thus underscored the intergenerational links among black writers" (Smethurst and Rambsy II 406).

The idea of a black aesthetic and its articulation is also seen in another path-breaking volume, *Black Fire: An Anthology of Afro-American Writing* (1968), edited by LeRoi Jones (Amiri Baraka) and Larry Neal. *Black Fire* appeared at the height of the protests of the Civil Rights movement and its contributors "seemed to embody the spirit of rebellion and revolution that engulfed cities across the nation as black people rioted in response to the assassination of Martin Luther King on April 4, 1968" (Smethurst and Rambsy II 405).

Its contributors included Sonia Sanchez, Ed Bullins, Julia Fields (b. 1938), Henry Dumas (1934–68), Harold Cruse (1916–2005), Lorenzo Thomas (1944–2005), Lance Jeffers (1919–85) and many others, all linked by "a common mission" (Smethurst and Rambsy 405). Smethurst and Rambsy note that between 1965 and 1976, more than a hundred anthologies appeared of which at least sixty were of verse. Among these are Houston Baker's *Black Literature in America* (1971), Dudley Randall's *The Black Poets* (1971), Richard Barksdale and Keneth Kinnamon's *Black Writers of America: A Comprehensive Anthology* (1972) and Stephen Henderson's *The New Black Poetry: Black Speech and Black Music as Poetic References* (1973). Other volumes include *Black Voices, Soulscript, The Black Woman, Jump Bad, Black Spirits* and *Giant Talk*. These anthologies established a tradition of black writing by featuring early writers alongside contemporary ones and helped create a canon. They contributed to the idea of a black nation and a distinct black culture that was conscious of its moorings, its history and a style founded on the circumstances of black life. Along with the anthologies were magazines and journals like *The Black Scholar, Liberator, Soulbook,* and *The Journal of Black Poetry,* all of which helped to circulate and disseminate ideas and writings on Black Art. While one of the most important publishing houses was Broadside Press founded by Dudley Randall which, in the period between 1965 and the mid-1970s, published over four hundred poets in more than a hundred books and recordings (it was originally founded to publish broadsides, cloth books and recordings for easy circulation), there were many others like Lotus Press, Jihad Productions (Baraka), and Third World Press which played significant roles in bringing writers to their readers. Publishing indeed was one of the most important agents of cultural transformation. An example is the influential publication *For Malcolm* (1967) that brought together tributes to Malcolm X after his assassination.

2

As many of these anthologies demonstrate, poetry was the genre that was most evocative of the revolutionary spirit of this age.

Gates Jr. and McKay, in their Introduction to this phase of African American literature in the Norton Anthology, write of poetry, that it was "ideally suited to the felt immediacy of struggle". Black Arts writers drew on the "African-American vernacular resonances of sermons, popular music, and black mass 'speech'" as well as jazz, blues, African praise poetry, and the oral performative style of the African *griot* (1797), all of which enabled powerful expressions suited to the requirements of struggle, the sense of nationhood and cultural distinctiveness. Amy Abugo Ongiri writes: "The Black Arts Movement dreamed of creating an artistic tradition that not only celebrated the cultural impulses of the African American Community but also became a natural part of the constructing and maintaining of that community" (Ongiri in Zygmonski 150).

Fiction was a relatively insignificant form during this decade, with only a few authors like Henry Dumas (who wrote short stories focusing on Africa), John A. Williams (author of the novel, *The Man Who Cried I Am,* on disillusionment with revolutions) and James Allan McPherson (author of short story collections like *Hue and Cry* and *Elbow Room* depicting racial prejudice and the work and lives of ordinary blacks) practicing it. Rather, it was poetry and drama that helped the formation of communities through performances that brought writers in close touch with their audiences, and had artists working with several media to bring alive their works. One example of such multiple art forms used together is the creation by members of Chicago's OBAC Visual Arts Workshop of the mural, *The Wall of Respect,* in 1967. This included Baraka's poem "SOS", and was made up of photographs and portraits of black political and cultural figures. As the mural took shape, poets, actors, and musicians performed alongside. Once it was done, the site of the mural became a spot for political and art events (Smethurst 308). Smethurst also gives the example of Baraka and other poets who "often performed with a band":

> When Baraka performed a poem like 'It's Nation Time' with a band and making wild James Brown-style vocalizations, was it poetry, music or a political address? Even when declaiming without accompaniment, Baraka, Sanchez, Amus Mor, and

Haki Madhubuti would interpolate songs, saxophone riffs, shouts and moans, as well as drums or whatever was handy in order to merge poetry and music. (308)

Visual effects of this generic mix were also achieved on the page as writers like Baraka, Sonia Sanchez, Askia Toure and David Henderson "played with typography, lineation, space, and punctuation to approximate the form and feeling of R&B (Rhythm and Blues), soul, and the new jazz" (Smethurst 308). While this can be best experienced through the look of the poem on the page, and by reading poems in their entirety, one representative text is from *A Blues Book for a Blue Black Magic Woman* by **Sonia Sanchez** (b. 1934). In "Part One: Introduction (Queens of the Universe)" Sanchez writes of black women who have been called "foxes", "whores", "sisters", "Queens", who have been a "combination of all these words" but who can now "discard" many of them.

The verse-paragraph demonstrates these labels as "vulgarity splattering us" – a visual and aural evocation of the way an abusive word falls on body and mind. And the use of the slash: past/history – enables reference to both an individual past and racial history – individual remembrance as a community act. The slash is used many times as are extended vowel sounds – "woooomen – mooooOOVE" in the line below where the swaying body, a queenly, graceful and savvy gait is represented – the queenliness equally evoking an "in your face" attitude and an underlying melancholy:

> and what/how
> we must mooooOOOVE to as the only QUEENS
> OF THE UNIVERSE to sustain/keep our sanity (Wiley
> 2, 673–79)

A blues feeling of sadness and melancholy turning to resolve, courage and forbearance is the overall effect of the poem. When performed, with the words drawn out and the tone of voice lending emotion, the impact would be increased. But even seen and read on the page it creates the effect of the human voice and sounds and enunciations that are distinctive of black speech: words that are uniquely visual and aural – "savvvVVVE, maaaAANN, looovve/livvvVVE, musssSST" – (Sanchez herself can be heard on YouTube reciting her poetry).

The savvy female figure that Sanchez depicts here is also seen in other writing. It appears for instance in the poem, "Phenomenal Woman" by Maya Angelou (discussed in the next chapter) in the
> reach of my arms,
> The span of my hips,
> The stride of my step,
> The curl of my lips, (Young 384–386)

a "phenomenal woman" who is cool and sassy, whose entrance brings men to their feet and whose "head's not bowed". The walk is an interesting aspect of many of these representations – "I walk like I've got oil wells / Pumping in my living room" (Angelou "Still I Rise") as is the image evoked by the word "cool".

Sonia Sanchez, poet, essayist, children's writer, short story writer, dramatist, and radical academic who steered the black studies programme at San Francisco State College and the Afro-American Studies programme at Amherst College, was born Wilsonia Benita Driver in Birmingham, Alabama. On her mother's death when she was a year old, she went to live for six years with her paternal grandmother before moving, after her death, to Harlem to live with her father, a musician and teacher. It was here that she started writing poetry. She attended Hunter College and graduated from there with a degree in political science in 1955. She also attended New York University to study poetry with Louise Bogan. She worked during this period for the Congress of Racial Equality. When she joined the Black Arts Movement and began her association with Baraka and Larry Neal she began to write and perform her poetry, "in[voke]ing the vocal intonations of Africa and African America in performance, moving audiences to call-response interaction that can make the rafters of the largest auditoriums ring" (Gates Jr. and McKay 1901).

Sanchez's poetry collections are *Homecoming* (1969), and *We a BaddDDD People* (1970). She uses jazz and rap style and rhythm and represents the radical black spirit of the time. Among her plays produced around this time are *Sister Son/ji* (on racial identity), and *The Bronx is Next* (on the politics of violence in revolutions). Sanchez was particularly conscious about the education of black children and her poems and stories for children reflect this concern.

Her books for children include *It's A New Day: Poems for Young Brothas and Sistuhs* (1971), *The Adventures of Fathead, Smallhead, and Squarehead* (1973) and *Sound Investment: Short Stories for Young Readers* (1980).

Nikki Giovanni (b. 1943) is the author of poems like "Nikki-Rosa" where she contrasts the impressions of "hard childhood" and inconveniences, with "Black love" and black community and "For Saundra" where she weighs the possibilities of different kinds of writing – "a poem that rhymes", a "green tree poem" and a "blue sky poem" before concluding that she shouldn't write at all but "clean my gun / and check my kerosene supply". The sentiments expressed here are typical of her early poetry in the collections *Black Feeling, Black Talk* (1968), *Black Judgment* (1968) and *Re: Creation* (1970), when she was vocal about a militant response to white oppression, recording instances of it and advocating a true representation of black life and emotions beyond the racial stereotypes circulating among whites. A sense of the unique and yet shared feeling that was rising in this period is seen in her poem "Black Power" with its image of the panther that pounces on the white policeman with a "tremendous growl" (all three poems in Young 443–45). Giovanni has also written love poems, and poems for children.

Carolyn M. Rodgers (1945–2010) represented African American lives and speech in sharp, often obscene and violent language in collections like *Paper Soul* (1968) and *Songs of a Blackbird* (1969), both published by Third World Press of which she was one of the founders. With an MA in English from the University of Chicago and training in creative writing workshops conducted by Gwendolyn Brooks and the Organization of Black American Culture, she produced a volume of writing that includes *how I got ovah: New and Selected Poems* (1975), *The Heart as Ever Green: Poems* (1978) and *Mor,* where she developed a "vernacular speech-act theory" (cited in Bolden 532).

Mari Evans (1923–2017) whose poems about loss and courage in the face of adversity give her the status of a blues philosopher, was also an educator and musician, and was active in theatre and media production. Her television show, The Black Experience (telecast in the 1960s and early 1970s by WTTV in Indianapolis), "attempted to answer the question posed by some anonymous poet: 'Who will show me myself'" (Evans quoted in Gates Jr. and McKay 1807). She is also the author of children's books, plays, and poetry. Among her collections of poetry are *Where is All the Music* (1968), *I Am a Black Woman* (1970), *Nightstar 1973-1978* (1981), *A Dark and Splendid Mass* (1992) and *Continuum: New and Selected Poems* (2007, expanded 2015). Her second book of poems, *I Am a Black Woman* (1970), sees slavery and oppression of the blacks as part of a global oppression of people of colour and a key reference point is the American neo-colonialist venture in Vietnam. The title poem of the collection, "I Am a Black Woman", represents a blues aesthetic, as it moves through three stanzas from the "sweet arpeggio of tears" to a quick history of the coloured people from the Middle Passage, life on the plantation, Nat Turner's rebellion and execution, WWII and the Korean War, and finally to the last stanza and its figure of the black woman "tall as a cypress / strong ... impervious / indestructible" who says "Look / on me and be / renewed" (Norton 1808). Evans edited an influential anthology of criticism, *Black Women Writers (1950-1980): A Critical Evaluation* (1984), and published a collection of her own essays, *Clarity as Concept: A Poet's Perspective* (2006). Her poem, "Speak the Truth to the People" is a call to free the mind of blacks from fantasy and untruth and to "identify the enemy" which are seen as prerequisites for "other things" and especially "To BUILD", the repetition of which emphasises the goal, which is eventually "To BUILD a strong black nation" (monksandmannequins.com). Evans here presents the essentials of collective work, throwing off the shackles of the past and offering a programme for the future.

Each of the poets who established themselves with an affiliation to the idea of the black aesthetic were influential, each in her/his own unique way. One of the most striking figures in this company was **Etheridge Knight** (1931–85). Knight had a chequered career, with a lifelong addiction to drugs, a childhood and youth spent with older men, soaking up the atmosphere of bars, juke joints and poker establishments, a period of about four years in the US Army, and an eight-year prison term for robbery. But these experiences also proved to be valuable artistic resources. He honed his skills with performances of "black toasts", which improvise, exaggerate and often take tangents from an event, a dynamic and creative approach to a tale that is reminiscent of many Indian performance traditions, founded as it was on the oral and folk traditions of African American ancestry but adapted to the moment. Gates Jr. and McKay in their note on Knight, describe these toasts as "long, rhyming, humorous verbal performances that require extraordinary memory and deft oratorical ability" (1866). The toasts "prefigured rapping in hip hop culture" but with origins in the period of slavery, they are "poetic narratives that often feature rough and rowdy characters who inspire fear in blacks as well as whites" (Bolden 535). Knight's youthful experiences in the form were furthered in prison where he recited poetry to his fellow inmates in an exercise that lifted their spirits (they would eventually revolt against prison authorities in the 1970s), but also refined his own style. His poetry collection *Belly Song and Other Poems* (1973) contains many examples of his use of the form. In "Hard Rock Returns to Prison from the Hospital for the Criminally Insane", the character named Hard Rock is fearless and is shown in conflict with white prisoners and the guards. "The Idea of Ancestry", written during his eight-year prison term, reflects on family and generational connections, especially with the historical reality of the fracture of families, broken and denied by slavery. As he imagines the "47 black faces" on the walls of his prison cell he moves back and forth in time to finally come back to the "gray stone wall" of his prison cell that is at the same time "the western wall" of "He Sees Through Stone". The prison walls represent the obstacles to freedom of thought and expression that is a reality not just for the prisoners, but for the black person in a society that imposes western values as norms for art and life. The prison which recurs in the poems of this collection becomes a powerful metaphor that evokes loss of freedom and what that implies on a much wider scale. "For Black Poets Who Think of Suicide", with its twice-repeated sentence "Black poets should live", urges black poets to be different, to write for black people and to "die as trumpets", an instrument of celebration and militancy, or resistance and triumph. (The theme of suicide is, in fact, seen in works by many other writers. Examples would be Baraka's "Preface to a Twenty Volume Suicide Note" or

Shange's "for colored girls who have considered suicide/when the rainbow is enuf".) It is also a reflection of the tendency to suicide among young black people as also thoughts of suicide in the minds of many as a response to injustices and inequalities. Poetry of this kind is found to be healing and sustaining: Dudley Randall of the Broadside Press writes of it thus: "Poetry has always been with us. It has always been a sustenance, a teacher, an inspiration, and a joy. In the present circumstances, it helps in the search for black identity, reinforces black pride and black unity, and in helping to create the soul, the consciousness, and the conscience of black folk" (in Sullivan 29. The archives of the Broadside Press may also be seen at Special Collections Research Centre https://quod.lib.umich.edu/s/sclead/umich-scl-broadside?view=text).

Jayne Cortez (1934–2012), author and performer, wrote politically charged poetry, was co-founder of the Watts Repertory Theatre (in 1964) and also set up her own publishing house, Bola Press, in 1972. She is best known for striking performances of her own poems, and she travelled and read her poetry in the Caribbean, Latin America, Africa and Europe. In her performances she combined blues and jazz styles and was accompanied in many of these by her son, Denardo Coleman, a drummer who was part of her band, the *Firespitters*. Recorded albums of her works include *There It Is* (1982), and *Maintain Control* (1986), *Everywhere Drums* (1990) and *Taking the Blues Back Home* (1996). Among her poetry collections are *Pisstained Stairs and the Monkey Man's Wares* (1969), *Festivals and Funerals* (1971), *Scarifications* (1973), *Firespitter* (1977) and *Jazz Fan Looks Back* (2002). Her poem "How Long Has Trane Been Gone" is a tribute to the jazz saxophonist, John Coltrane (1926-1967) where she also calls for the memorialisation of Black People.

In his editor's introduction to a recent anthology, *African American Poetry: 250 Years of Struggle and Song* (2020), Kevin Young writes of the innovative embodiment of music in "the music of the page", citing June Jordan's description of it as "'vertical rhythm'", as the poem "not only trips down the page, but springs across it", inaugurating a "new sound" that was also "a reimagining of ancestry", with Sanchez, Baraka, Madhubuti and Cortez inspiring subsequent performance poetry, sound poetry and slam poetry (liii–liv).

The emergence of so many writers whose goal was to use culture as a political weapon had its beginnings in expressions of racial pride by W. E. B. Du Bois (in his poem "The Song of the Smoke") and Marcus Garvey (through the Universal Negro Improvement Association and African Communities League) among others. But there were other compelling factors. For instance, the assassination of Malcolm X in 1965 was the direct inspiration for the establishment, by Amiri Baraka, of the Black Arts Repertory Theatre/School (BARTS) in Harlem. It produced plays, organised poetry readings and held classes in the arts for young people of the community, giving currency to the term "Black Arts".

3

The consciousness of being engaged in a special endeavor is evident in the many texts of this brief period that reflect, deliberate and express various facets of black identity while demonstrating the weight of and the need for collective will and action. This spirit was also evident in the "outdoor art exhibitions that would move each night to a different spot in Harlem, live music in parks and playgrounds, poetry readings, and trucks with removable stages for plays" (Zygmonski 145). As Baraka wrote of BARTS: "When we got our regular programs going, concerts, readings, plays in the downstairs auditorium we made by tearing down a couple of walls, black artists flowed through those doors. Some for single performances, some for longer relationships, some to absorb what it all was. We were trying to grow together" (*Baraka Reader* 369, in Zygmonski 145).

Alongside poetry, theatre was the site that provided scope and space for articulating the black aesthetic. Many who visited Africa came back with "new styles of dress, movement and song to incorporate into performative black American poetry and the new black drama" (Gates Jr. and McKay 1801). Baraka and Bullins were among the pre-eminent playwrights and theatre activists who created a unique dramaturgy for the Black Arts movement which the dramatist Paul Carter Harrison named the "drama of Nommo", the word Nommo invoking "West African philosophical and aesthetic concerns with the power of the spoken word" (Gates Jr. and McKay 1801).

Drama and theatre helped in building audience and writer relationships that further fostered the goal of community building. Theatre and writing groups across the country disseminated the idea of cultural nationalism and collective struggle.

Amiri Baraka (1934–2014), poet, playwright, essayist, cultural leader and activist, also known in the early part of his life and career as Everett Leroy Jones or simply LeRoi Jones, towers over this period. He was born in Newark, New Jersey, attended Howard University for a brief while, and then joined the Air Force but was "dishonorably discharged" for writing what was perceived as Communist-leaning pieces. He then moved to Greenwich Village, married a Jewish woman and started a press where he published the works of the Beat writers, Allen Ginsberg, Jack Kerouac and Frank O'Hara, with whom he found many affinities. But disillusionment at what he felt were their apolitical stands came soon after a visit to Cuba in 1960 and exposure to the revolutionary leadership of Fidel Castro. In 1963 he published *Blues People: Negro Music in White America* on blues and jazz, and jazz musicians John Coltrane, Ornette Coleman and Sun Ra. In 1964 his play *Dutchman* premiered, followed in the same year by three short plays, *The Slave, The Toilet* and *Baptism,* launching his career as a playwright and establishing his Black Nationalist credentials. *Dutchman* is a one-act play with two scenes. It is about two people – a young black man Clay, and an older white woman, Lula – who meet on a train and engage in verbal sparring that is full of obscenities, racial and sexual provocations and a veiled anger that climaxes with a slap across the face to Lula by Clay, and his murder at her hands in full view of the other passengers who appear in the second scene. It was declared by critics to be "an explosion of hatred rather than a play" and a "mélange of sardonic images and undisciplined filth" but they also noted the arrival of "a promising, unsettling talent" (*New York Times* critic Howard Taubman cited in Zygmonski 139). The rage that was seen as an essential aspect of Black Art is represented in the monologue by Clay at the end after he is enraged enough to slap her: "Let me be who I feel like being. Uncle Tom. Thomas. Whoever. It's none of your business. You don't know anything except what's there for you to see. An act . . . And I sit here, in this buttoned-up suit, to keep myself from cutting all your throats" (Norton 1893). The sparring between Clay and Lula is disturbing, with Lula's effort to rouse Clay – "Clay, you got to break out. Don't sit there dying the way they want you to die. Get up" – apparently representing the call to action of the Black Power Movement, put into the mouth of a white woman. But Clay is set up by Lula as feminised, emasculated and almost programmed for the death so commonly shown as the fate of the black man, which Aimee Zygmonski calls "the inevitability-of-black-death trope" appearing as "slavery and lynching, the stereotypical sacrifice of blacks for their master or companions . . . in fiction, short stories and plays." She mentions Morrison's *Song of Solomon,* August Wilson's *Fences,* and Suzan-Lori Parks' *The Death of the Last Black Man in the Whole Entire World* as examples of this trope which appears in black literature from the 1800s to the present (143).

The *Dutchman* was performed in street corners and in theatres. It received an Obie award for best play and remains exemplary for the Black Arts Movement. This play and Baraka himself had already become an important figure during the previous era but it was with his role in the BAM, his statements about the need for an art that could attack, as he put it in the poem "Black Art", with "assassin poems", and especially in his leadership role in the black theatre, that he came to dominate the art scene during this decade.

In his essay "The Revolutionary Theatre" published in the magazine *Black Dialogue,* Baraka declared passionately that it "must Accuse and Attack because it is a theatre of Victims. It looks at the sky with the victims' eyes, and moves the victims to look at the strength in their minds and their bodies" (Norton 1900–02).

While BARTS gave new direction to black arts, it was plagued with financial difficulties and Baraka's departure from Harlem for Newark virtually sounded its death knell. Baraka set up Spirit House in Newark along the lines of BARTS, married a black woman, Sylvia

Robinson (he had earlier divorced his first wife) and continued his work on community art with revolutionary, nationalist goals.

The work of **Adrienne Kennedy** (b. 1931) is political and subversive in ways that are significantly different from that of Baraka and many others of the BAM. She was born Adrienne Lita Hawkins to an African American father and white mother and she frequently visited the estate of her maternal grandfather, a peach farmer in Montezuma, Georgia. Montezuma's residents were of largely British origin and here she was exposed to European culture and music, and watched a production of Tennessee Williams' play, *The Glass Menagerie,* besides reading the work of African American writers, mostly of the Harlem Renaissance. She writes of these influences on her literary sensibility in her memoir *People Who Led to My Plays* (1987). She studied education for her BA at Ohio State University from where she graduated in 1953. Then she attended Columbia University and also studied drama in theatre programmes like Edward Albee's Theatre Workshop in New York City.

Adrienne Kennedy wrote plays, short stories, memoirs and essays that examine racial categories and questions of female identity. Her best known play, *Funnyhouse of a Negro,* which won the Obie award in 1964, uses expressionism to portray "black self-hatred and communal disunity" (Carpenter 176) through the psyche of the central character, Sarah, a light-skinned African American with frizzy hair, also known as Negro. It is a one-act play, set in New York, that begins with a woman, Mama, in a white nightgown and wild open hair moving across the stage in a trance, carrying a bald head in front of her, establishing the symbolism of falling hair as a unifying theme in the life of characters who appear or are spoken of. Four of the characters, Queen Victoria, Duchess of Hapsburg, a hunchbacked, yellow-skinned Jesus and Patrice Lumumba (Congolese freedom fighter and first Prime Minister of independent Congo, who was assassinated in 1961), are Sarah's different selves or "one of herselves". The racial mix and Sarah's identification with these figures is offered as a way of entering the discourse on blackness which is seen as the desired political and aesthetic goal. The declaration of Larry Neal that "[T]he motive behind the Black aesthetic is the destruction of the white thing, the destruction of white ideas, and white ideas of looking at the world" (Norton 1961), is represented skillfully by Kennedy through the running theme of whiteness and blackness in the play, in the historically white figures like the two royals, and in her inversion of blackface minstrelsy through the strategic use of whiteface. In her stage directions, which are elaborate and detailed about the appearance of characters, she emphasises the use of pale and dark colour and lighting, with dramatic flashes of red. The two royals for instance are clearly visualised: "They look exactly alike and will wear masks or be made up to appear a whitish yellow. It is an alabaster face, the skin drawn tightly over the high cheekbones, great dark eyes that seem gouged out of the head, a high forehead, a full red mouth and a head of frizzy hair" (Wiley 2, 639). The visuals of frizzy hair throughout the play set alongside the equally strong visual impact of whiteness are a "persistent reminder of the real body beneath the mask . . . emphasizing the fabricated nature of [our] racial identities" especially through "enactments of white, rather than black representation" (Carpenter 177). The play moves cleverly between notions of white domination and personal lives of individual characters in its deconstruction of racial identity and notions of white superiority. The queen and the duchess are psychologically unstable and mere puppets – facts that are drawn from their lives – while Sarah, the Negro, is equally torn as she moves about in an apartment filled with photographs of castles, and statues of these two figures who have become her alter egos. The visual messages that the play sends to its audience offer a complicated texture, where whiteness and blackness as signs of desirability, power, powerlessness and suffering are all constructed.

Jarrett in his introduction to Kennedy's work writes of her plays that they are "non-linear, surreal, expressionist, and suffused with charged metaphors" (Wiley 2, 637). The falling hair, bald head and white faces, the head of Lumumba "split in two with blood and tissue in eyes" as the stage directions inform (Kennedy, Wiley 2, 641), are as shocking as the white costumes stained with blood worn by the girl students in another play, *A Lesson in Dead Language* (1968). The symbolism is effective precisely because it is not always absolutely clear what is being suggested. It remains open ended and therefore, suggests a number of possibilities. In *Funnyhouse* for instance, Sarah, also called the Negro, has as her other selves, two white European women, one yellow skinned character, and the Congolese Lumumba, complicating racial and gender identity, while suggesting through the psychic distress of Sarah, the deep and lacerating wounds of all black people and especially of the women of the race. Interestingly, by having Sarah identify with two powerful white women, the play extends its sympathy to women of all races – an extension of the idea of community that had begun primarily as an intra-racial phenomenon. In another of her striking one-act plays, *The Owl Answers* (1965), Kennedy explores religion, and specifically Catholicism, with its impact on the female characters, but also continues her exploration of mixed race inheritances with references to St Peter's Basilica and St Paul's Cathedral as well as the cult of the Virgin Mary. The selves/alter egos and multiple identifications that were present in *Funnyhouse* are again seen here. The main characters are SHE who is CLARA PASSMORE who is the VIRGIN MARY who is the BASTARD who is the OWL, the BASTARD's BLACK MOTHER who is the REVEREND's WIFE who is ANNE BOLEYN, and GODDAM FATHER who is the RICHEST WHITE MAN IN THE TOWN who is the DEAD WHITE FATHER who is REVEREND PASSMORE (capitals used in original). The settings are many places at the same time, the subway is the chapel is the hotel room in Harlem is the Tower of London. SHE dreams of acquiring a heritage even as she is pulled between black and white racial identities. At the start she is visiting London with her adoptive white father, the Reverend Passmore, who suddenly dies while they are at the Tower of London and whose funeral in St Paul's Cathedral she is not allowed to attend because she cannot convince anyone that the white man is her father. She is put into the Tower by Chaucer, Shakespeare and William the Conqueror. Written up and presented with skilful use of expressionist techniques, the whiteface subversions of *Funnyhouse* are also achieved in *The Owl Answers* with the black and white masks and light changes that support the presentation of multiple selves.

Of particular interest is the bird imagery which recurs throughout her work. *Funnyhouse* too features owls that "seem to represent a world other than the blackness that Sarah, and especially her mother, despised." But they have further and deeper connotations in *The Owl Answers*, "one equated with whoredom, with non-belief, and with death" (McDonough 396). There is reference to the source in Kennedy's autobiography that McDonough cites. Kennedy mentions a time in Ghana:

> The owls in the Leees outside the Achimota Guest House were close and at night, because we slept under gigantic mosquito nets, I felt enclosed in their sound. In the mornings I would try to find the owls in the trees but could never see them. Yet, at night in the shuttered room, under the huge white canopied nets, the owls sounded as if they were in the very center of the room. (in McDonough 396)

Distinguishing the "rebellion in cultural/political registers" of *Funnyhouse* from the riposte that is offered in *The Owl Answers*, one critic points to how Kennedy "deftly dramatizes the sexual economy of racism or colonial governance that constructs blacks as hypersexual and culturally deficient; promises seeming social acceptance to those blacks knowledgeable of dominant culture; and yet preserves the power of white heterosexual, elite men to exercise control over everyone designated unlike them" (Richards 240).

The articulation of an aesthetic that was "about overthrow and survival" made these artists "cultural revolutionaries, intent on reorienting (and in many cases, destroying) current American cultural practices that were white-centered and middle and upper class-focused" (Zygmonski 150). Once this period of extreme radicalism was over, many of the writers moved on to a quieter kind of writing, a more assured sense of identity without the anger that is so characteristic of this period. In the coming decades writers would go on to innovate, explore black history anew, recover writers, use the aesthetic potential of postmodernism and remake old forms.

WORKS CITED

Bolden, Tony. "Cultural resistance and Avant-Garde Aesthetics: African American Poetry from 1970 to the Present." *The Cambridge History of African American Literature*. Eds. Maryemma Graham and Jerry Ward. Cambridge: Cambridge UP, 2011. 532–65. Kindle EBook (paginated).

Bracey Jr., John H, Sonia Sanchez and James Smethurst. Eds. *SOS—Calling All Black People: A Black Arts Movement Reader*. U of Massachusetts P, 2014.

Carpenter, Faedra Chatard. "Spectacles of Whiteness from Adrienne Kennedy to Suzan-Lori Parks." *The Cambridge Companion to African American Theatre*. Ed. Harvey Young. New York: Cambridge UP, 2013.

Ceynowa, Andrzej. "The Dramatic Structure of *Dutchman*." *Black American Literature Forum*, Vol. 17, No. 2 (1983). 18.

Erickson, Peter. "The Love Poetry of June Jordan." *Callaloo*. No. 26 (Winter,1986). 221–34. http://www.jstor.com/stable/2931089. Accessed 12 Jan. 2022.

Gates Jr., Henry Louis and Nellie McKay. Eds. *The Norton Anthology of African American Literature*. New York and London: W.W. Norton & Company, 1997.

Jarrett, Gene Andrew. Ed. *The Wiley-Blackwell Anthology of African American Literature*. 2 Vols. Malden, Oxford, Chichester: Wiley–Blackwell, 2014.

Killens, John Oliver. "The Writer and Black Liberation." *Black America 1968: The Year of Awakening*. Ed. Patricia Romero. Washington, DC: United Publications Corporation, 1969. 265–71.

McDonough, Carla J. "God and the Owls: The Sacred and the Profane in Adrienne Kennedy's *The Owl Answers*." *Modern Drama*, Vol. 40, No. 3 (Fall 1997). 385–402. https://doi.org/10.1353/mdr.1997.0050. Accessed 5 Mar. 2022.

Rambsy II, Howard. *The Black Arts Enterprise and the Production of African American Poetry*. Ann Arbor: U of Michigan P, 2013.

Richards, Sandra L. "African Diaspora Drama." *The Cambridge Companion to African American Theatre*. Ed. Harvey Young. New York: Cambridge UP, 2013.

Saloy, Mona Lisa. "The African American Toast Tradition." https://www.louisianafolklife.org/LT/Articles_Essays/creole_art_toast_tradition.html. Accessed 22 Aug. 2022.

Smethurst, James E. "The Black Arts Movement." *A Companion to African American Literature*. Ed. Gene Andrew Jarrett. Chichester, Malden, Oxford: Wiley-Blackwell, 2013. 302–14.

Smethurst, James E. and Howard Rambsy II. "Reform and Revolution, 1965-1976: The Black Aesthetic at Work." *The Cambridge History of African American Literature*. Eds. Maryemma Graham and Jerry Ward. Cambridge: Cambridge UP, 2011. 405–50. Kindle EBook (paginated).

Stewart, James T. "The Development of the Black Revolutionary Artist." 3–10. https://blogs.cofc.edu pdf. Accessed 20 Feb. 2022.

Sullivan, James D. *On the Walls and in the Streets: American Poetry Broadsides from the 1960s*. Urbana and Chicago: U of Illinois P, 1997.

Taubman, Howard. "The Theater: 'Dutchman'." *New York Times*, March 25, 1964. 46.

Young, Kevin. Ed. *African American Poetry: 250 Years of Struggle and Song*. New York: Library of America, 2020.

Zygmonski, Aimee. "Amiri Baraka and the Black Arts Movement." *The Cambridge Companion to African American Theatre*. Ed. Harvey Young. New York: Cambridge UP, 2013. 137–54.

CHAPTER 7

New Directions
The Contemporary Period: 1975 to the Present

TIMELINE

1970: The film, *Watermelon Man*, a comedy about a white man who, one morning, wakes up black, released. The Marin County courthouse incident sparked by racial discriminations in the criminal justice system occurs. Leftist UCLA philosophy professor and activist, Angela Davis arrested (and later acquitted) on the charge that the weapons used belonged to her. Charles Gordon wins the Pulitzer for *No Place to be Somebody* (1969). Angelou publishes *I Know Why the Caged Bird Sings,* Michael Harper publishes *Dear John, Dear Coltrane;* Morrison, *The Bluest Eye,* and Bambara edits *The Black Woman.*

1971: Ernest Gaines' novel of the Reconstruction, *The Autobiography of Miss Jane Pittman* published. Supreme Court rules that the closure of swimming pools in Mississippi to avoid desegregation is legal.

1972: Ishmael Reed publishes *Mumbo Jumbo.* The 40-year long Tuskegee syphilis experiment undertaken by the US Public Health service to find out how long it takes syphilis to kill sufferers, involving 399 black men ends.

1973: A breakaway group from the New York based National Black Feminist Organization, called the Combahee River Collective of lesbian socialist black feminists is formed in Boston and is active till 1980.

1974: Salsa Soul Sisters, Third World Wimmin Inc Collective, an organization of lesbians, womanists and women of colour, formed in New York City. Charles Johnson publishes *Oxherding Tale* and Albert Murray, *Train-Whistle Guitar.*

1975: Ntozake Shange's *for colored girls who have considered suicide when the rainbow is enuf* becomes second play by an African American woman, after *Raisin in the Sun,* to be performed on Broadway. Sherley Anne Williams's *Peacock Poems* published.

1976: Black History Month is founded by Professor Carter Woodson and his Association for the Study of Afro-American Life and History.

Alex Haley's *Roots* wins the Pulitzer Prize. Etheridge Kennedy's *A Movie Star Has to Star in Black and White* is produced. Octavia Butler's *Patternmaster* published.

1977: *Roots* made into a popular TV series. Rita Dove's *Ten Poems* published.

1978: James Alan McPherson wins the Pulitzer Prize for *Elbow Room*. Ntozake Shange *Nappy Edges*. Supreme Court rejects quotas for college admissions

1982: Michael Jackson's bestselling album, *Thriller,* released.

1983: Alice Walker gets the Pulitzer Prize for *The Color Purple*

1984: *The Cosby Show,* a sitcom featuring Bill Cosby, on the life of an upper middle class African American family in Brooklyn, begins.

1986: Greg Tate publishes "Cult-Nats Meets Freaky-Deke: The Return of the Black Aesthetic" in the *Village Voice* which along with Trey Ellis's "The New Black Aesthetic" became manifestos of what came to be known as post-soul aesthetics.

1988: The film, *Mississippi Burning* on the murders of three civil rights activists, released. Morrison wins the Pulitzer Prize for *Beloved,* published in 1987.

1989: The television mini-series *The Women of Brewster's Place* based on Gloria Naylor's novel and starring Oprah Winfrey, Robin Givens among others is directed by Donna Deitch. Several of Jamaica Kincaid's short stories are published in different issues of *The New Yorker.*

1990: The Gulf War begins. Charles Johnson's *Middle Passage* is published and the author is awarded the National Book Award for Fiction for it.

1991: The USSR is officially disbanded signalling the end of the Cold War. Tim O'Brien's *The Things They Carried* published.

1992: Derek Walcott receives the Nobel Prize for Literature. Rioting in Los Angeles after the four police officers who brutally beat up Rodney King and were filmed in the act by a bystander, were acquitted. Toni Cade Bambara's *Gorilla, My Love* published as also Rita Dove's *Through the Ivory Gate.* Alice Walker's *Possessing the Secret of Joy,* and Terry McMillan's *Waiting to Exhale* all appear on *The New York Times* bestseller list.

1993: Maya Angelou reads "On the Pulse of Morning" at the inauguration ceremony of Bill Clinton as President. Rita Dove appointed Poet Laureate of US. Kevin Young's *Most Way Home* (published later in 1995) is selected as a National Poetry Series

Winner. Ernest J. Gaines's *A Lesson Before Dying* is published by Alfred Knopf Publishers and it wins the National Book Critics Circle Award for Fiction. Toni Morrison wins the Nobel Prize for literature.

1994: Yusef Komunyakaa wins Pulitzer Prize for Poetry and the Kingsley Tufts Poetry Award for *Neon Vernacular* which was published in 1993. Suzan-Lori Parks's *The America Play and Other Works* published. Alice Walker's *The Complete Stories,* and Edwidge Danticat's *Breath, Eyes, Memory* are published.

1996: George Walker becomes the first African American to win a Pulitzer Prize for Music for "Lilies for Soprano or Tenor and Orchestra," based on a poem by Walt Whitman.

1997: Tiger Woods wins the Masters Tournament in Augusta, Georgia, becoming at 21, the youngest golfer ever and the first African American to win the title. African American women participate in the Million Woman March in Philadelphia, focusing on health care, education, and self-help. President Bill Clinton makes a formal apology to black men who were made to take part in the U.S. Public Health Service Tuskegee Syphilis experiment.

1999: Serena Williams wins the U.S. Open Women's Singles Tennis Championship in Flushing Meadows, becoming the first African American woman to do so since Althea Gibson won it in 1958.

2005: Hurricane Katrina hits the Gulf Coast, taking around 1,700 lives, a majority from Louisiana especially the African American dominated New Orleans.

2008: On November 4, Barack Obama of Illinois, the only sitting African American US Senator, is elected President of the United States and is sworn in as the 44th President of the United States on January 20, 2009.

2010: Obamacare passed by Congress and signed into law by the President.

2011: 9/11 or the September 11 attacks – a series of airline hijackings and suicide attacks, one of which brought down the Twin Towers of the World Trade Center in New York, killing 2750 people.

2012: Barack Obama is re-elected President of the United States for a second term. Trayvon Martin, a teenager, is shot fatally by the 28-year-old Hispanic American, George Zimmerman in Florida. Zimmerman was later acquitted of all charges in 2013.

2013: Black Lives Matter hashtag founded by activists Alicia Garza, Patrisse Cullors and Opal Tometi following the not-guilty verdict for Zimmerman.

2015: A white supremacist and neo Nazi, Dylann Roof, takes the lives of nine African American people at a Bible study gathering at Emanuel African Methodist Episcopal Church in Charleston, South Carolina. This would become known as the Charleston Church Shooting. Dylann Roof was convicted of 33 counts of hate crime and murder charges and is currently serving nine consecutive life sentences without the possibility of parole.
2016: Smithsonian National African American History Museum opens. NFL Quarterback Colin Kaepernick kneels for the national anthem drawing nationwide attention to police violence.
2017: Amanda Gorman is named the youngest National Youth Poet Laureate.
2020: 26-year-old Breonna Taylor gunned down in her own home by police officers on suspicion of drug dealing. 25-year-old Ahmaud Arbery shot and killed by three white men while jogging in Brunswick, Georgia. George Floyd dies at the hands of police officer Derek Chauvin who is later found guilty and sentenced to 22.5 years in 2021.

The Black Power Movement and the Black Arts Movement of previous years put racism firmly on the social and political map of the United States, influencing subsequent generations of writers who responded to the nationalist emphasis of these movements in different ways. By this time anti-colonial struggles across the world exposed the connections between colonialism and racism, and helped develop transnational political and cultural affinities. The early years of the twentieth century had already seen questioning about the subjects, styles and readership of black writing. During the 1970s and after, there are newer aesthetic engagements, "fusing aesthetics with political theory and social responsibility" (Bolden 532), as there is serious scholarly study of history and culture at universities in specialised African Studies programmes. New issues and themes take centre-stage, as homosexuality, alternative black experiences, especially with the continuing arrival of immigrants from the Caribbean and from countries in Africa, and the emergence of writers with roots in the South as well as in the North, make the understanding of black experience and history much more complex and many-dimensional. There is free movement of ideas and sensibilities as authors range over historical and geographical diversities, connecting the sites of slavery and oppression in the US to African locations and histories. As John Oliver Killens wrote in his 1968 essay, "The Writer and Black Liberation", black writing would only be relevant if it recognised that it "is part and parcel of the worldwide revolution of people of color against colonialism and white racism" (266). This transnational perspective transformed the writing and the reception of black literature.

But perhaps the most stunning development from this point onwards is the emergence of women writers of exceptional ability and brilliance, beginning with Toni Morrison (with *The Bluest Eye* [1970]), and going on to a black women's literary renaissance. Female protagonists, new locations, reviewing of the past and new racial relationships saw the evolution of neo-slave narratives, science fiction, fantasy fiction and epistolary novels. The travails of male heroes in novels like *Native Son* and *Invisible Man* now came to be countered by a long line of women characters like Sethe (*Beloved*) and Celie (*The Color Purple*) and their unique forms of resistance bringing forth women's experiences that had been ignored; or Dana (in the science fiction, neo-slave narrative, *Kindred*) who rewrites her family's history as she is transported back in time to the slave past.

Gates Jr. and McKay in their Introduction to the literature of this period in the Norton Anthology mention a number of trends that distinguish it. These are:

(1) the remapping of African American cultural and social history, much of which had been neglected, distorted, or hidden; (2) the exploration of African American folk forms; (3) the attention to African American women as writers both creative and scholarly, an attention demanded by their presence in every literary genre; (4) the acknowledgment of the multiplicity of African American identities; and (5) the increased participation of African Americans in framing the study of American literature. (2012)

Such trends that are based on reviews of the past also show up in the post-Civil Rights era with what has come to be called a post-soul aesthetic that involves "a range of aesthetic responses (satire, self-reflexivity, and a diverse range of allusions or intertexts), to the specifically African American experience of post-1960s postmodernity" (Lordi n.p.). Most of the writers discussed in this chapter employ postmodernist techniques to review black history and experience.

1

Writers like Maya Angelou, Paule Marshall, Toni Morrison, Sherley Ann Williams, Alice Walker, August Wilson, June Jordan, Jamaica Kincaid, Octavia Butler, and Yusef Komunyakaa produced a rich body of writing, transforming old forms like the slave narrative and the gothic, evolving new forms, addressing contemporary challenges to the African American, while commenting on issues beyond race. Popular forms of the novel like science fiction, detective fiction, romances and children's fiction offer occasions for fresh interpretations of African American life and identity. (These appear on the scene as a result of a number of significant changes that include new publishers, their willingness to cater to a wider taste and the not infrequent making of movies based on the bestsellers).

Maya Angelou (1928–2014), best known for her autobiography, *I Know Why the Caged Bird Sings* (1970), was actor, dancer, singer, and composer, besides being a journalist, writer, teacher and civil rights activist. In her writings that included several volumes of poetry and a number of volumes of autobiography, she dealt with different kinds of experiences drawn from her observation of sexual and racial oppression during her childhood with her paternal grandmother in Arkansas. When she was about eight years old, she was raped and she spoke about it to the family, after which her uncles murdered the rapist. These traumatic events saw her withdrawing into complete silence for five years. But the mute child watched and absorbed everything around her and started reading works by both black and white writers like Langston Hughes and Du Bois, and Shakespeare, Dickens and Poe, before emerging to become one of the most influential voices of her time – holding important administrative positions (she served on presidential committees for Presidents Gerald Ford and Jimmy Carter) and teaching posts (she was professor of American Studies at Wake University). She was the recipient of many awards and honours, the most prominent among them being the National Medal of Arts (from President Bill Clinton in 2000) and the Presidential Medal of Freedom (from Barack Obama in 2010).

Her poetry offers testaments to endurance and resolve, themes that are movingly represented in "Still I Rise" (written in 1978) where, despite being trod on and lied about in history, "still, like dust, I'll rise" establishing the base for the "rise" of "sassiness", "haughtiness", "sexiness" against organised efforts to break and shoot and kill, and through "pain" and "hate", rising "Into a daybreak that's wondrously clear" (Norton 2039–40). Her evocation of the past is graphic and searing – as in "Out of the huts of history's shame / I rise" from "Still I Rise" that refers to the slave quarters on plantations, or in the poem "Arkansas" where "Old crimes like moss pend / from poplar trees" (Norton 2040), evoking the grisly sights/sites of many lynchings.

She wrote several autobiographies beginning with *I Know Why the Caged Bird Sings* (exploring a new voice in each one. She explains her repeated use of the form as an opportunity to explore the past each time in a new voice: "I liked the form – the literary form – and by the time I started *Gather Together* I had gone back and reread Frederick Douglass' slave narrative. Anyway, I love the idea of the slave narrative, using the first person singular, really meaning always the third person plural" (Neubauer and Angelou 286).

The point she makes here, that the first person singular voice in the literature of the African American is also always a collective voice, is significant, especially since the connection she makes is between autobiography and the slave narrative. The changing voice is also commented upon. In *Gather Together* she aspires to render the voice of herself as a young girl, "eratic, sporadic, fractured" while in *Singin' and Swingin'* the voice is "sassy" (287). Neubauer in the interview referred to above, comments on the two voices at work in the different books – the ironic voice of the writer who is in the present allowing/enabling the autobiographical presence and voice from the past to come through.

Of her peculiar process of remembrance which, as her interviewer notes, makes the past "both treasure-chest and defense", she says that there is no particular "pattern" to her remembrance: "But when I remember it, I will remember everything about it. Everything. The outside noises, the odors in the room, the way my clothes were feeling – everything" (289).

The period of muteness which she lightly touches on in *I Know Why the Caged Bird Sings,* and her subsequent recovery, the learning of other languages and her reading, all enrich her perspective and the way she recalls and renders her life with each new work, selecting incidents from the past and permitting them to emerge – "the greens, the reds and the light coming through the window" (289). The chapter from *Caged Bird,* on Mrs. Flowers, "the lady who threw me my first life line" (Norton 2040) shows this method as small details of her life and the people who were in it at that time, coming back in clear jewel tones. For example, Mrs. Flowers's smile – "A slow widening of her thin black lips to show even, small white teeth, then the slow effortless closing. When she chose to smile on me, I always wanted to thank her. The action was so graceful and inclusively benign" (2041) – illustrates the manner in which incidents and people come back to her, "sweet-milk fresh in my memory", in clear, compelling images or not at all, and it equally well represents what she says about the way the autobiography allows her to work with two voices, the current voice presenting the voice of that time in the past, enabling its emotion to come through as strongly as the incidents and the people that affected her. Mrs. Flowers in her memory is "[L]ike women in English novels who walked the moors . . . [who] sat in front of roaring fireplaces, drinking tea incessantly from silver trays full of scones and crumpets. Women who walked over the 'heath' and read morocco-bound books and had two last names" (2041). In this picture that is both real and imagined she shows how the form works and how it also establishes cultural difference by setting the lives of English women from literature alongside that ironic, parenthetical admission of ignorance – "whatever they were" – securing for Mrs. Flowers the stature that she retained in Angelou's memory, making her "proud to be a Negro, just by being herself" (2042).

If Angelou gave a special charge to the autobiography and autobiographical thinking as a simultaneously individual and collective exercise, **Paule Marshall** (1929–2019) stepped into these early phases of the black women's literary Renaissance with her first novel, *Brown Girl, Brownstones* (1959), featuring a female protagonist and opening a window for writers like Alice Walker, the playwright Ntozake Shange, and many others. She set several other trends for later writers, including the establishment of connections amongst black writers from other parts of the world through her travels in the Caribbean and Brazil. Born to Ada and Samuel Burke, immigrants from Barbados, the West Indian-American experience forms the subject and backdrop of much of her writing. She wrote three more novels after the first one – *The Chosen Place, The Timeless People* (1969), *Praisesong for the Widow* (1983), and *Daughters* (1991); a collection of four novellas, *Soul Clap Hands and Sing* (1961) and many short stories. The first of the novels, *Brown Girl, Brownstones,* that tells the story of Selina Boyce, is based on her own experience as a young West Indian in America who went back to the Barbados and lived there between 1938 and 1939, and visited several times in later years. The novel is about Selina's life in a family where the mother wishes to buy the brownstone house in which they are tenants, and the father wants to return home to Barbados. This basic conflict captures the longing for the past and the possibilities of the future that was fundamental to the immigrant experience. The tones of Caribbean speech find representation in this first book and her rendition of black voices became a characteristic and distinct feature of her writing. Marshall evolved ways to represent the past, enabling the portrayal of alternative African lives that went on to become a rich literary resource. In her frequently anthologised short story, "Reena", the narrator writes of how "the people of my past" come back to her: "Whenever I encounter them at the funeral or wake, the wedding or christening – those ceremonies by which the past reaffirms its hold – my guard drops and memories banished to the rear of the mind rush forward to rout the present" (Norton 2052). Through the character of Reena, emphatic, strong and sharp, and the story of her graduation from college, Marshall presents her observations of what it meant for her people to move out of the conditions which had tied generations down to the lowest strata of life:

> My mother was so proud she complained about everything: her seat, the heat, the speaker; and my father just sat there long after everybody had left, too awed to move. God it meant so much to them. It was as if I had made up for the generations his people had picked cotton in Georgia and my mother's family had cut cane in the West Indies. It frightened me. (Norton 2059)

There are equally sharp insights into the attitudes of whites – "how come white folks is so *hard*?" – the smiles that "looked almost genuine" (2059) and the white boyfriend Bob who displayed her to his parents as an "instrument of his revenge" against them (2058).

In the essay, "The Making of a Writer: From the Poets in the Kitchen", she writes of growing up listening to her mother and her mother's friends as they gathered in the kitchen of their brownstone house and gossiped about their friends and neighbours and discussed world affairs with equal enthusiasm over coffee. For the young girl sitting quietly in a corner, the content and the style of those conversations were eye-opening, especially "[T]he insight, irony, wit and humor they brought to their stories and discussions and their poet's inventiveness and daring with language". These women had transformed the English they had learnt in schools in Barbados into an idiom, bringing in rhythm, sound and accent and a colourful "raft of metaphors, parables, Biblical quotations, sayings and the like" (Norton 2076). One particular effect was their use of the antonym with a word, "the linking of opposites" as in "beautiful-ugly" of which Marshall speculates that "my mother and her friends were expressing what they believed to be a fundamental dualism in life: the idea that a thing is at the same time its opposite". This was for them, not a Manichean dualism, but a completion, where "soully-gal," their favorite form of address for one another was just that: "soul: spirit; gal: the body, flesh, the visible self" (Norton 2077). Marshall goes on to write about other influences – white and black writers – but the first influence remains the most important – the group of women from "the wordshop of the kitchen" who "taught me my first lessons in the narrative art . . . trained my ear . . . set a standard of excellence" (2079).

Audre Lorde (1934–92) of African American and West Indian origins – her mother was from the Caribbean island of Grenada – understood the role of the black writer as one that would pull together the collective experiences of blacks from Africa, the Caribbean and the US. In her account of the making of the poet "Poetry is Not a Luxury", she writes of a special "quality of light by which we scrutinize our lives" and of "poetry as illumination" and "distillation of experience", and a "vital necessity." Making the distinction between white and black ways of thinking and approaching life, she writes: "the white fathers told us: I think, therefore I am. The Black mother within each of us – the poet – whispers in our dreams: I feel, therefore I can be free." (Norton 2210–11). The difference expressed here, is a key idea in her work – in her poetry and in the many essays she wrote. As Gates Jr. and McKay write about her: "The emphasis on difference . . . was fueled by her belief that she must claim her many identities – 'black, lesbian, feminist, mother, lover, poet'" and they suggest that her "reevaluation of the meaning of difference was a major theoretical contribution to the study of race, gender, and sexuality" (2203). Several experiences of her childhood and youth proved crucial to her development as a writer. She did not learn to speak until she was five and even then spoke only with difficulty. She studied at Catholic schools in New York and then entered Hunter College in 1951, supported herself with several jobs, and graduated only in 1959. In between for a year, in 1954, she went to the National University of Mexico. She took a degree in library science from Columbia University in 1961 and worked as a librarian for several schools in New York. Around this time she married a white, gay man, Edwin Rollins with whom she had two children. They divorced in 1970. In 1972, Lorde found her long-time partner, Frances Clayton.

Lorde had been a poet since she was twelve, using poetry to get over her speech difficulties. She went on to produce several volumes of poetry – *The First Cities* (1968) that announces her themes of blackness in nuanced, rich poems; *Cables to Rage* (1970), that contained poems about marriage and bearing and nurturing children, and announced her homosexuality; and *The Black Unicorn* (1978), where she made use of African mythology, religion and art in poems that explored dark states of mind out of which there is recovery and healing. Her other collections include *From a Land Where Other People Live* (1972), *New York Head Shop and Museum* (1974), and *Coal* (1976).

One of the best known of Lorde's poems, "Coal", from the collection bearing that name, celebrates blackness and the ideology of the Black Power movement. "I / Is the total black, being spoken / From the earth's inside". Coal becomes "diamond" in the next couple of lines, both speech and the essence of being emerging, opening from harsh experiences, paid for by the one speaking with pain and love, words that are like "stapled wagers" or that live in the throat, "breeding like adders" and diamond like, that flash and cut. One critic has written of the poem's use of coal and diamond as symbolising the power play of black and white speech:

> [t]he contingent nature of the poem's celebratory Black essence becomes a political strategy in the interests of the moment that repudiates any sacral primacy . . . the tropes in the poem battle each other inasmuch as they share a strategic homogeneity of vision; coal and diamond, the one staple black fuel and the other privileged white jewel, undermine even as they affirm each other's positions as controlling/speaking symbols. (Dhairyam 232)

The ambiguity suggested by the poet in the diamond emerging from the coal seems to deny the racial binary as the word comes like the diamond out into the open from the "earth's inside". The striking aspect of her poetry is her ability to give a sharp edge to her writing through the minutiae of some experience that is startlingly used – a quality that appears in "Coal"– the stub of an "ill-pulled tooth" for instance or in another poem, "Now That I Am Forever with Child", where the carrying of a child is sensuously depicted showing it to be full of wonder; an experience that stays permanently with her as her own, unforgettable, felt bodily experience, and yet, that can equally well suggest the sexual exploitation of black women in a long history of bearing the children of their white masters. Another poem, "Power", about the shooting by police of a ten-year-old black child, had its genesis in the immediate fury and helplessness that she felt after the event and that she expressed in her journal. From her brush with breast cancer and a mastectomy, came *The Cancer Journals* (1980) and after the reappearance of cancer in the liver and her recourse to alternative treatments like homoeopathy and self-hypnosis, she wrote *A Burst of Light* (1988), reflecting on her struggle with the disease and impending death. Her experience of life with cancer and determination to speak and write about it was an elaboration on the theme of difference and community with which she engaged all her life.

In 1984 she published *Zami: A New Spelling of My Name* (1984) which the publishers called a biomythography for its blend of autobiography, myth, fiction and poetry, perhaps to explain its capacious form that was evolved to contain her multiple identities. The text has two generic sources, the African American slave narrative and the lesbian coming-out story. One critic, Monica B. Pearl, who makes this association, argues that it is the latter form's equal assertion of individuality and community that *Zami* represents. She cites Bonnie Zimmerman to claim that Lorde's text reveals "an ongoing tension between the ideas of unity and community and those of diversity and individuality" especially with regard to the notion of women's community (299). As Lorde herself says at the end of this work, "Zami" is a "Carriacou name for women who work together as friends and lovers" (223). In Pearl's reading, the trope of "home", fundamental to both genres is used in *Zami* as a quest for community or belonging with others like herself (299) family, sisters, lesbians, blacks – a quest that re-presents the theme of community with fresh understanding in this time of multiple identities.

Zami is a new spelling of her name, weaving into this act the assumption of literacy and through it a literate identity in the slave narrative, and the assuming of lesbian identity in the coming-out story. The text recounts Lorde's life up to her 20s and features the many women who played defining roles in her life, beginning with her mother whose strong presence was an important element of her childhood – a woman who insisted that the little girl keep her bedroom door open because she believed the craving for solitude was unnatural (the feelings that this discipline evoked is perhaps what she means in the poem "Sister Outsider": "Now you have made loneliness / holy and useful") – and who she rebelled against in later years; and climaxing with her relationship with a black woman from the South, Afrekete, who matches her own self-assurance and love of independence. *Zami* also records some of the darker aspects of her life, the suicide of a friend, and an illegal abortion and betrayals, and offers glimpses of New York's lesbian subculture in its bars where these women who had come out, met and cherished their togetherness even as they struggled to be acknowledged for what they were.

Lorde was the author of an influential collection, *Sister Outsider: Essays and Speeches* (1984) that contains some of her most important theoretical engagements with feminism, lesbianism and blackness, and with the craft of the writer. Some of the pieces for which she is best known appear in this volume. Among them are "Poetry is Not a Luxury" briefly discussed above; "The Transformation of Silence into Language and Action" which gestures at her own childhood period of muteness out of which her skills in observation and her poetry began; and "The Master's Tools Will Never Dismantle the Master's House" which was an address at a Humanities conference at New York University, where she speaks of difference and feminist theory and particularly of the neglect of the consciousness of lesbian and Third World women. It is here that she makes important statements about art and difference: "Within the interdependence of mutual (nondominant) differences lies that security which enables us to descend into the chaos of knowledge and return with true visions of the future . . . Difference is that raw and powerful connection from which our personal power is forged" (Wiley 2, 765). To stand outside, to stand alone are ways to transform difference into strengths – "*For the master's tools will never dismantle the master's house*" (Wiley 2, 765; emphasis in original). And the woman has to "*reach down into that deep place of knowledge inside herself*", the courage of this confrontation with what is within then becoming the "illumination" that enables the personal to become the political (Wiley 2, 766; emphases in original).

In another paper delivered at the Copeland Colloquium at Amherst College that finds a place in *Sister Outsider*, "Age, Race, Class, and Sex: Women Redefining Difference", Lorde again takes up difference and the many forms of otherness into which she is categorised, and makes an emphatic, conclusive statement about the details within each life that can be utilised to express difference. What divides women from one another is the "reluctance to recognize those differences and to deal effectively with the distortions which have resulted from the ignoring and misnaming of those differences" (Wiley 2, 771).

June Jordan (1936–2002) was a poet, playwright, essayist and writer of books for children. Of Jamaican origin, her poetry shows a keen interest in identity and lived experience, and like others who came from the Caribbean island nations, she was aware of the need for collaboration amongst all marginalised peoples of the world. She was an activist, involved in some of the major movements of her time: for civil rights, for women's rights and for sexual freedom. Born in Harlem to Jamaican immigrants, she studied at Barnard College and Chicago University, and went on to teach at Yale, State University of New York at Stony Brook, and University of California–Berkeley (where she was professor of African American Studies and founder-director of the Poetry for the People programme). After a broken marriage to a white man, with whom she had a son, Jordan began working and writing. Her first volume of poems, *Who Look at Me* (1969) is actually a single long poem on the representation of Black Americans and contains prints as illustration. She ran workshops for children of Black and Puerto Rican families, encouraged the use of Black English and put together a volume of her pupils' writings as *The Voice of the Children*. Her other books for children are the novel, *His Own Where* (1971), *Dry Victories* (1972), *New Life, New Room* (1975), and *Kimako's Story* (1981) inspired by the daughter of friend and fellow writer, Alice Walker. The autobiographical *Soldier: A Poet's Childhood* (2000) explores her relationship with her father who was something of a tyrant and often beat her, but who pushed her to excel.

Besides this keen interest in teaching and forming and catering to the literary tastes of children, Jordan wrote a number of other kinds of works. In 1970 she edited the collection, *Soulscript: Afro-American Poetry*. Her essays on topics like racism, education, Black English, and the 9/11 terrorist attack, focus on the inequalities of American society. In an interview to Alternative Radio just before her death, she spoke of the role of the poet as working to "deserve the trust of people":

> And the task of a poet of color, a black poet . . . is to rally the spirit of your folks . . . I have to get myself together and figure out an angle, a perspective, that is an offering, that other folks can use to pick themselves up, to rally and to continue or, even better, to jump higher, to reach more extensively in solidarity with even more varieties of people to accomplish something. I feel that it's a spirit task. (Interview to Alternative Radio)

The men and women who came to the US from the Caribbean made a signal contribution to the idea of community and identity that marks African American literature. They expanded the idea of blackness to include all people of colour and brought a fresh perspective to questions of gender, race and colonisation. Many among them, and especially feminist theorists like Audre Lorde, went on to contribute to the growing idea of an African American woman's renaissance. **Jamaica Kincaid** (b. 1949) is one among this important assembly. Born Elaine Potter Richardson in colonial Antigua, she felt loved and privileged as a child but was violently displaced from parental affection when her three brothers were born, taken out of school at thirteen to nurse a sick stepfather, and sent to the US as an au pair girl to earn money for the family. But once out of Antigua she cut herself off from her family and started saving money for herself from the various jobs she took one after another. She moved to New York City, attended community college to complete her high school education and took photography courses. Meanwhile she started writing poetry and pieces for *The Village Voice* and *Ingenue,* in one issue of which (1973) her interview, "When I was Seventeen" appeared. This was the year when she changed her name to Jamaica Kincaid. She also began a foray into journalism, assisting George Trow in researching stories for his column in *The New Yorker,* published a piece on the West Indian Day Parade in the same magazine at the behest of William

Shawn, one of its editors. Her short story, "Girl" was published by the magazine in 1978 and was the first of several. These were later collected to form her first book, *At the Bottom of the River* (1983). "Girl" inaugurates the theme of identity and self-formation that Kincaid would go on to explore in subsequent texts. This story is narrated by a mother who instructs her daughter in all that a good Antiguan woman should know:

> This is how you sweep a corner; this is how you sweep a whole house; this is how you sweep a yard; this is how you smile to someone you don't like too much; this is how you smile to someone you don't like at all; this is how you smile to someone you like completely; this is how you set a table for tea . . . (Web n.p.)

The interjections by the girl are treated with contempt by the mother. At one point when the mother instructs her on how to buy fresh bread by squeezing it for softness, the girl responds with the doubt that the baker may not let her near the bread. The mother's reply, caustic and unsympathetic, expresses surprise that the girl might indeed become the kind of woman who bakers will not allow near their bread, suggesting the rule-bound life that the girl must learn to live by, and that Kincaid addressed comprehensively through the recurring figure of the mother who represents the obstacles to full realization of distinct womanhood in many of her works.

One critic has written of this kind of regulation: "the daughter's education is in subservience to the culture's negative definition of womanhood. Her only power comes in manipulation of appearances and in avoiding evil forces. She cannot be self-defining or assertive" (Byerman 97).

Kincaid's second novel, *Annie John* (1985), on the life of a young girl in Antigua, is loosely modelled on her own life, and captures, in separate episodes, the crucial period of her own unhappy experiences between the ages of 10 and 17. From an idyllic childhood as the centre of her parents' affection, with her mother chewing up food for her, bathing her, and mother and daughter dressing identically, her mother pushes her away when she is twelve, with the injunction that the child cannot always be an image of her mother and must instead find her own way. Annie turns to a couple of friends but eventually realises that she must find her own identity as an adult. The novel culminates in Annie leaving to study in England. The mother in these works stands as a symbol of what needs to be outgrown and escaped – family and the island culture – in order to move into adulthood and a sense of separate self. The novel is a *bildungsroman* distinguished by the race, geography and culture of the island nation. Motherhood and identity are themes that Kincaid explores in other novels, like *Lucy* (1990), and *The Autobiography of My Mother* (1996), a novel set in Dominica and with a 70-year-old woman as its narrator. As works like these show, Kincaid regularly blurs generic boundaries, blending fiction, personal memories and history, as she draws up critical pictures of colonial domination and destruction of native cultures from her Antiguan/West Indian experience, even as she notes the continuing racism in America. She also wrote an account of her brother's battle with AIDS in *My Brother* (1997). The book that has remained as her most well-known critique of colonialism, postcolonialism and associated ills like corruption and economic exploitation in the West Indies is *A Small Place* (1988), written after her first visit to Antigua since she left it at seventeen. This work, expressive of anger at the persistence of colonial legacies of corruption, and of tourism as a new form of colonialism, offers a postcolonial critique that is appropriate for all postcolonial regimes where the structures of power remain unchanged even after independence. The following passage describing Antigua is characteristic of her angry style. She writes of its settlement:

> [b]y human rubbish from Europe, who used enslaved but noble and exalted human beings from Africa (all masters of every stripe are rubbish, and all slaves of every stripe are noble and exalted; there can be no question about this) to satisfy their desire for wealth and power, to feel better about their own miserable existence, so that they could be less lonely and empty – a European disease. (80)

Kincaid has also been an avid gardener and has written a number of books like *My Garden* (2000) and *Among Flowers: A Walk in the Himalaya* (2005) that explore what Susie O'Brien calls "the complex connections between local human/nature interactions and the world-shaping force of colonialism" (170). Kincaid's garden writing began as a column in *The New Yorker*. "As much about garden writing as they are about gardens, the essays in Kincaid's suggestively titled *My Garden* (Book) document the gaps between imagination and reality, and the precarious structures that seek to bridge them" (O'Brien 170). When the second work came out in 2005 Kincaid spoke of the distribution of plants and seeds in different places and mentioned Joseph Banks, colonial era botanist and explorer who, she says, was largely responsible for the plants reaching places that they were not native to, and she makes some "characteristically very fierce comments" (Warner 53) on plunder and power as she writes of the English garden. The garden books are one more site where she examines power, politics and colonialism, and as she herself works in her own garden or goes for that seed-gathering walk in the Himalayas, she reflects on what it means to garden, the memory of her mother growing things in the garden, what it has meant to impose the order of the garden and landscaping on colonised spaces, how naming things has been an act of appropriation, especially in processes of naming and claiming, and renaming and reclaiming – a fact that is familiar to us in India when places are renamed or a local name for something starts to be reused.

Amidst writing of great variety and formal experimentation that tackled the race issue in new ways, the work of **Octavia Butler** (1947–2006), the first African American woman writer of science fiction/speculative fiction who brought issues of race and identity into the genre is exceptional. As Jarrett has written of her, "Butler's work helped set a template in speculative fiction for future African American, female and other socially marginalized writers" (Wiley 2, 778). Born Octavia Estelle Butler in Pasadena, California, she lived with her mother and grandmother (her father died when she was very young) in a strictly Baptist household, was diagnosed with dyslexia, but read voraciously in science fiction, especially the novels of Ursula Le Guin and magazines like *Amazing, Fantasy and Science Fiction* and *Galaxy*. She studied at Pasadena City College, completed a writing course at the University of California, Los Angeles, and also trained for a year at a mentoring workshop for young African American and Latino writers run by the Screenwriters Guild of America. Here she came under the influence of science fiction writer Harlan Ellison and under his tutelage she started writing. Through him she also attended the Clarion Science Fiction and Fantasy Writers' Workshop and met another prolific science fiction writer, Samuel Delany. Under these influences her writing career began with two short stories, "Crossover" and "Childfinder". In 1976, with the publishing of *Patternmaster* she launched her five-volume series that includes *Mind of My Mind* (1977), *Survivor* (1978), *Wild Seed* (1980) and *Clay's Ark* (1984), dealing with issues of race superiority, racial mixture and African traditions. In the first book of the series, *Patternmaster*, she tells the tale of two brothers who seek the throne of their father. The series follows the story of the progeny of two shape-shifting protagonists, Doro and Anyanwu (introduced in *Wild Seed*), who move easily in and out of their bodies. Doro wears the bodies of people like clothing and discards them in his programme of selective breeding, while Anyanwu changes the shape of her body to mimic humans and animals, irrespective of race, gender or age. The *pattern* that connects the series comes from this "telepathic matrix that connect all the children of Doro and Anyanwu" (Hampton 246). In an obituary for Butler, Hampton writes,

> Through her characters and narratives, readers are better able to explore the meaning of various identities such as race, sex, and gender. These terms are seen for what they are, arbitrary markers designed to give stability to that which is unstable and ambiguous. Science fiction is the window Butler used to open the imagination of readers about the problematic of the body. (247)

The focus on the body as the site of modification, suffering, excess and power is seen in all Butler's works as she blends the genres of science fiction, history and the slave narrative. The novel *Kindred*, considered as a neo-slave narrative achieves this quite wonderfully, subverting racial identity through the story of a black woman, married to a white man, who travels back in time to save her white, slave-owning ancestor. *Lilith's Brood,* also known as the *Xenogenesis* trilogy, came out during the 1980s. The books in this series, *Dawn* (1987), *Adulthood Rites* (1988) and *Imago* (1989), follow the story of a woman of colour, Lilith Iyapo, a matriarch who wishes to produce hybrid offspring to create a fitter race, and the Oankali gene traders of an alien race who travel through space seeking difference for survival. This becomes the common aim – the importance of difference as survival strategy – and the three novels feature the progeny resulting from the genetic intervention. The Oankali arrive on earth after it has been destroyed by a nuclear war and Lilith is the first human they awaken. The series also features a xenophobic race, known as the Resisters, who oppose the Oankali design of genetic mixing.

The third series that Butler authored, the Parable series, is a set of two novels, *Parable of the Sower* (1993) and its sequel, *Parable of the Talents* (1999). The first features Lauren Olamina, who Butler describes as "hyperempathic", able to feel the pleasure and pain of others, and who works to establish a religion for sustainable and safe life on earth. The second features Lauren and her daughter Asha Vere living in a hypernationalist America where the religion of Earthseed itself becomes a target of zenophobia. Butler's last novel, *Fledgling* (2006), published posthumously, is a vampire story where a part human, part vampire character called Shori is simultaneously a 53-year-old member of the Ina species and a 10-year-old African American. The Ina and human relationships are mutually sustaining (unlike in the common vampire story), as the venom of the Ina boosts human immunity while the blood of the human sustains them. This theme of species collaboration and hybridity is crucial to the rethinking Butler has engaged in throughout her work, as she offered new versions of identity and re-addressed the race question – particularly in this novel through the dark skin of Shori that is better adapted to sunlight than white skin.

One interpretation of the science fiction novels of Butler and Delany suggests that they feature two notions of power that find manifestation in non-consensual and consensual slavery, the critique emerging especially for the situations of sexual exploitation. The critic argues that "we find in Butler a compelling and elegant critique of non-consensual socio-economic slavery" but that Butler "raises the possibility of a liberating, egalitarian, consensual form of erotic slavery" (Call 279). This is especially evident in the relationship between Doro and Anyanwu where both are enslaved to one another by their mutual desire. Anyanwu enjoys Doro's caresses just as Doro discovers after thousands of years as absolute master that he is dependent on Anyanwu for sexual pleasure.

The discussion of science fiction as offering an alternative form of fictional-historical engagement would hardly be complete without the huge body of work of **Samuel Delany** (b. 1942), African American gay writer who is also considered to be one of its most important theorists. Delany was born in Harlem to Samuel Ray Delany Sr., who was the proprietor of the Levy & Delany Funeral Home in Harlem's Seventh Avenue, and Margaret Delany who worked in the New York Public Library. His father's two sisters were civil rights activists with one of them also earning a doctorate in dental surgery from Columbia University. Their lives were immortalised first in 1993, in a *New York Times* biography, *Having Our Say,* and then by Samuel Delany himself in his novella *Atlantis: Model 1924* (1995), as the characters Elsie and Corry. This environment nurtured his natural gifts in both science (he attended the Bronx High School of Science) and art as he went on to become a writer, musician, filmmaker and radio broadcaster. In 1961, he met and married Marilyn Hacker, a young and talented Jewish poet, whose intellectual companionship remained with him for years even after they separated in 1975 and divorced in 1980. He began his prolific career as a writer of science fiction with *The Jewels of Aptor* (1962), followed by *The Fall of the Towers* trilogy – *Out of the Dead City* (1963), *The Towers of Toron* (1964), and *City of a Thousand Suns* (1965). After this came *The Ballad of Beta – 2* (1965), about an archaeology student who tries to discover what would happen to the Star Folk by trying to interpret some song fragments; *Babel – 17* (1966), which features alien linguistic weapons sought to be countered by Earth with the help of a poet; *The Einstein Intersection* (1967) featuring the Great Migration and its hero Lo Lobey who uses his flute as a weapon; and *Nova* (1968), about a black starship captain who is on a quest across the galaxy to find fire, and with strong echoes of *Moby Dick,* in its assorted crew that includes a novelist, and the Mouse who wields a unique instrument, the sensory-syrynx that can double up as a weapon. Critics note Delany's role in bringing about "a shift in the kind of 'science' in which science fiction could engage – from the natural sciences to the social sciences" (Tucker 367). Delany's work after 1968 has made use of new material and explored new social and sexual relationships. This is perhaps best seen in the massive novel, *Dhalgren* (1975), running to 800 plus pages, where the fictional American midwestern city of Bellona is hit by an inexplicable, traumatic event – Delany himself has said that you could pick the event, it could be anything from a race riot to a plane crash ("'To Pull the Veil Away': Samuel R. Delany on *Dhalgren*" by Mark Gunnery. Dec 21, 2020. 1.33 pm EST, wypr.org). The result is a city where nothing works anymore and people are listless and lost. Delany speaks of the world around that prompted the writing of this novel in 1975 – shootings and race riots, large areas of the cities he moved in falling into disrepair, and different kinds of marginalised groups moving into them; the latter appear in the novel as the Scorpions. The present-day resonances of these novels are among their most rewarding characteristics. Commenting on the use of the notion of Apocalypse, Delany says that "apocalypse is not about something collapsing. It's about something being revealed" (wypr.org). The salutary effect is what these novels achieve as they become commentaries on slavery, racism, and stereotyping, by featuring black characters in new roles and reimagining societies. Delany went on to write the four volume, "sword and sorcery" (a fantasy genre containing magic, romance and battles) series, *Nevèrÿon*, where besides representing slavery, he also presented queer sexuality. The subversive quality of the series is seen in its vague location that could be "Asian or African, Mesopotamian or Mediterranean" and that "implicitly critiques the Eurocentrism of typical fantasy and sword-and-sorcery tales" (Tucker 368).

The late arrival of African American science fiction has been accounted for in different ways, the most obvious of which has been the alienation of a large majority of the African Americans from technological culture or what is often characterised as the digital divide. The emergence of "Afrofuturism" (the term is attributed to Mark Dery who interviewed Samuel Delany and several other sci-fi writers) shows that there *are* stories "to tell about the relationship between people of African descent and technological culture, one in which . . . science fiction plays an important role" (in Tucker 360). Delany's work shows this new way of addressing anew the history of slavery – in Gorgik the Liberator of the *Nevèrÿon* series who wants to end slavery in the eponymous site, and explores alternative social and sexual relationships. Delany went on to write a number of texts that explore sexuality, like the graphic novel (a genre in which he has written several books), *Bread and Wine* (1999), as well as *Phallos* (2004) and *Dark Reflections* (2008). His work with all these multiple interests is seen as contributing to and showing the connections between African American Studies, Gay and Lesbian Studies, and critical theory. Like Octavia Butler and other sci-fi writers who would follow, Delany's large body of work offers new possibilities of what the idea of community might mean as the world around changes, and creates challenging new identities for the African American individual.

Delany and Butler showed the way for a new generation of African American Science fiction writers by refashioning the predominantly white genre. Among those who have followed their example are Tananarive Due, Steven Barnes, Nalo Hopkinson, and Walter Mosley. Of these, **Nalo Hopkinson** (1960) is particularly accomplished in drawing on her multiple Caribbean locations – Jamaica, Guyana and Trinidad – to fashion characters and settings. She mixes the usual science fiction conventions of technology and urban setting with Caribbean dialects, references to Caribbean writers and popular and folk legends and stories. Her works include *Brown Girl in the Ring* (1998), *Midnight Robber* (2000), *The New Moon's Arms* (2007), a number of edited collections, *Whispers from the Cotton Tree Root: Caribbean Fabulist Fiction* (2000), *Mojo: Conjure Stories* (2003) and another novel, *The Salt Roads* (2005) that has been described as "a pan-Africanist womanist parable, linking the stories of black women across centuries and continents" (Tucker 373).

The African American name that is most easily recognised by readers worldwide is that of **Toni Morrison** (1931–2019), winner of the Nobel Prize for Literature in 1993. In her multiple roles as editor, theorist of race and writing, and writer of some of the most luminous novels on race, slavery and memory, the figure of Morrison looms large over the African American literary world. Born Chloe Anthony Wofford in Lorain, Ohio, to parents who were migrants from the South, and who created a rich and sustaining home environment for their children through their own immersion in black culture and folklore, Morrison attended Howard University where she studied English and Classics and where she also took courses with Alain Locke. It was around this time that she changed her name from Chloe to Toni. She graduated from Howard in 1953 and went on to Cornell University for an MA in English. Here as part of the requirements of the course she wrote a dissertation on the works of William Faulkner and Virginia Woolf. She taught briefly at Texas Southern University and then at Howard for several years. In between she married Harold Morrison, a Jamaican architect, had two sons but divorced in 1964, and went back to live with her parents in Lorain, taking her sons with her. A year and a half later she stepped into a new career as textbook editor with Random House in Syracuse, New York, and moved up to a senior editor position in 1968 with the same publisher in New York City. Like many other African American writers before and during this time, one of her roles was to use her position as editor to help publish the works of many emerging writers. Meanwhile, the writing that she had begun as a refuge from her unsatisfactory marriage, and continued during the years following her divorce, resulted in her first novel, *The Bluest Eye* (1970), inaugurating her rich and influential career as a novelist who evolved her own style of magic realism, blending African American folklore and locations, to explore slave and race history in its gender and class dimensions, through the lives and psyche of several powerfully-drawn, African American female protagonists.

The Bluest Eye is set in Lorain in 1940–41 and tells the story of a young eleven-year-old girl, Pecola Breedlove who longs for the "bluest eye" through which to gain social acceptance, as she is forced to live with the MacTeers, one of the three families (the other two being Pecola's own homeless one and the white Fishers) represented in the novel. The text is structured as four sections named for the four seasons, beginning with Autumn and each section is divided into chapters with titles taken from a popular children's series of the 1940s, about a white middle class family. The narrative follows Pecola as she faces multiple abuses – beatings, rape, verbal abuse and cruel tricks – and eventually goes to Soaphead Church, who claims to be able to interpret dreams and perform miracles, to get a pair of blue eyes. In the final section, "Summer", Pecola has become pregnant after the rape by her father and has lost her mind. Fragmented, and with shifting narrative perspective (between omniscient and first person), the novel established the style that Morrison would go on to use in subsequent novels, even as it explored the internalisation of racism and its effects on the self-perception of individuals.

Morrison's next work was a collaborative one that resulted in *The Black Book* (1974), a collection of around five hundred documents and pictorial representations from African American history that included sketches of Africans by slave traders from the seventeenth century, slave auction notices from the nineteenth century, sheet music for work songs and freedom chants from the twentieth century, photographs of war heroes in uniform, antebellum era reward posters for capturing runaway slaves, besides recipes, newspaper clippings, images of lynchings and cross burnings, transcripts from fugitive slave trials, proclamations by Frederick Douglass and other abolitionists, and patents registered by black inventors – a blend of uplifting and tragic images and texts that forms a compelling record of the past.

Morrison went on to write several other novels, blending folklore, history, and individual stories and often using the form of the bildungsroman to follow the growth or dissolution of protagonists over a period of time. *Sula* (1973) is a story of friendship between two women, Sula and Nel, set against a community in Medallion, Ohio, that is angry and frustrated as a result of the racism around them. *Song of Solomon* (1977), is about the spiritual recovery of Macon Dead, one of her few male protagonists, through the support and example provided by his aunt Pilate, told through a blend of realism and fantasy. *Tar Baby* (1981) examines the relationship of two people from different classes. *Love* (2003) is about the granddaughter and the widow of a hotelier, Bill Cosey, who hate each other but live together in the dead man's mansion. *A Mercy* (2008), is based on the 1680s slave trade. *Home* (2011) features a young black veteran of the Korean War who returns to an America still caught in the grip of racial hatred. *God Help the Child* (2014) the only one of her novels set in the twenty-first century, features a dark-skinned young woman and her fair-skinned mother who abuses her because of her skin-colour – continuing Morrison's interest in mother-daughter relationships while exploring the obsession with skin colour that cuts across racial boundaries and that also appeared in earlier works as 'passing'.

Beloved (1987), *Jazz* (1992), and *Paradise* (1997) constitute a trilogy that covers a historical period from the mid-nineteenth century to the 1970s. *Beloved,* the first in the series, tells the story of three generations of women and their memories of the Middle Passage and slavery in Kentucky, of escape, and families, all structured around the central episode of the killing of a child by her mother, that is drawn from one of the newspaper accounts Morrison came across when she was collecting material for *The Black Book*. *Jazz* is set in 1920s Harlem and refocuses on post-Civil War South and post-Reconstruction migration through the memories of a woman who is bringing up a mixed-race child, but it is also one of the finest literary equivalents of jazz as style and mood. *Paradise,* set in Oklahoma in the 1970s after the Civil Rights Movement, shows many of Morrison's literary influences, especially that of Faulkner (on whom she wrote her MA dissertation) and Virginia Woolf, in a layered narrative through which she interweaves personal and collective history. The trilogy is characterised by themes of family and social and sexual relationships that Morrison explores in most of her work. One of her critics has identified these themes as "[T]he dysfunctional family, the oppressive nature of class, and the domination of black women by black men" which Morrison uses as "lenses through which African American history is reinterpreted" (Peach 235).

Morrison also wrote two plays. *Dreaming of Emmett* (first staged in 1986) was based on the killing of the fourteen-year-old Emmett Till by a group of white men, and shows the young boy returning as an adult seeking vengeance. The second was *Desdemona* (first staged in 2011), a feminist adaptation in which Morrison invents an African nurse for Desdemona, taking a cue from a line in the original play referring to Barbary, Desdemona's mother's maid.

She wrote a number of children's books with her son Slade, picture books in a mix of free verse and rhyme that include *The Big Box, The Book of Mean People, Who's Got Game? The Ant or the Grasshopper (*a retelling of the Aesop's fable in a modernised urban setting, also often printed with two others, *The Lion and the Mouse* and *The Poppy and the Snake), Penny Butter Fudge,* and *Please Louise.*

In her only short story, "Recitatif" (published originally in the 1983 anthology *Confirmations: An Anthology of African American Women*, edited by Amiri and Amina Baraka), Morrison keeps the racial identity of the two girls, Twyla and Roberta, ambiguous, experimenting instead on writing a narrative without using racial codes, as she said in *Playing in the Dark* (xi). The story traces the journey, over three decades, of these two girls, from their youth to adulthood, subverting the race issue by focusing on how race, class, appearance and food habits can all be identity markers. There is also the shadowy remembered figure of Maggie, the kitchen help who is abused and beaten by the "gar girls", and who is recalled as "the Maggie thing" (Wiley 2, 830), and "that business about Maggie" (Wiley 2, 831) that troubles both characters because of their foggy memories of the incident and their own feared involvement in it. This tension makes the ending, with its last line "What the hell happened to Maggie?" (Wiley 2, 834), a telling comment on how deeply scarring the memory of violence can be, especially when one is involved in it.

Alice Walker (b. 1944) writes in several genres and is one of the most influential writers to emerge from the 1970s and 80s. She is the author of several novels, volumes of poetry, a number of short story collections, and essays. She has also written books for children. She was born in Eatonton, Georgia, where her mother, Minnie Lou Grant worked as a domestic but also created a beautiful garden that enriched the lives of her children and herself, and provided the example that Alice Walker would go on to refer to in her writings, of black women who transformed the constraints and cruelties of their lives through the everyday work of gardening, cooking, and quilting, while remembering and retelling. If the kitchen was the forge in which Audre Lorde honed her poetic skills, her mother's garden was Alice Walker's first and strongest creative and spiritual resource. This garden is immortalised in the title essay of the volume, *In Search of Our Mother's Gardens: The Legacy of Southern Black Women* (1974), where gardening is synonymous with art and creativity. The other interesting aspect of this volume is Walker's inauguration of a style that blends the personal anecdote with literary allusions and criticism. The title essay refers to her mother in her garden, to literary history through the question of how Phillis Wheatley and other early black women came to writing, and to Virginia Woolf's *A Room of One's Own,* citing the comment that "genius of a sort" must have existed among women (Norton 2380–87). Walker's method of bringing earlier writers into her essay – Woolf and Hurston in this essay, and others throughout the collection – is what has been called "signifying" by Henry Louis Gates – signifying on another writer is to engage in repetition along with difference – a way of paying tribute through the repetition, but also critiquing and showing limitations. The performative aspect of Walker's writing in these essays allows her to achieve several goals. As one critic declares of this characteristic, "Walker presents herself as a somewhat fictionalized character, inhabiting certain roles in each narrative. This turn to performance not only moves beyond self-absorption as it attends to audience reception, but it also implies a fluid and changing notion of subjectivity that avoids gendered dichotomies, resists claims to authenticity, and problematizes an identity politics" (McMillan 112).

An accident when she was eight left the young Alice blinded in one eye, leaving her traumatised and making her withdraw into a world of her own where her only solace were her books and the poetry she began to write. Her sharecropper parents kept her in school despite many hardships and she graduated in 1961, earned a scholarship to Spelman College in Atlanta, Georgia, but left after a couple of years to join Sarah Lawrence College in New York City, from where she graduated in 1965. Coming into adulthood in the heady years of the Civil Rights Movement, she participated in its activities and her first volume of poetry, *Once* (1968), came out of this turbulence. During this time she met and married Jewish civil rights attorney, Melvyn Levanthal, a marriage that drew criticism from all quarters even as it was considered a crime in Jackson, Mississippi, where the couple had moved. They had one daughter but the marriage ended in 1977. Meanwhile several of Walker's books were published in quick succession – *Five Poems* (1972), *In Love and Trouble: Stories of Black Women* (1973), and *Revolutionary Petunias and Other Poems* (1973). Unlike many of the other African American writers before and around her, she focused on the oppression and suffering of women within their own families and communities, themes that she also followed in her novels. Her early work "announced a new phase in African American literature in which male-female relationships, sexuality, and family conflict were just as significant as political protest and racial pride" (Jarrett 2014, 734).

Among her novels, *The Third Life of Grange Copeland* (1970) is an epic three-generation saga about a Southern family who try to lift themselves out of their condition as sharecroppers; *Meridian* (1976) is on African American motherhood; and *The Color Purple* (1982, adapted by Steven Spielberg into an Oscar winning film with Whoopi Goldberg in the title role) is a novel that depicts the life of Celie, a young woman living in rural Georgia with her father, Alphonso, who repeatedly rapes her, gives away her two infants as soon as they are born, and then forces her into an abusive marriage. The novel explores Celie's inner world through the letters she writes to God, even as it shows her gradual transcendence of the brutal conditions she is trapped in, through a number of empowering relationships with women, the most significant of which is that with Shug Avery, one time mistress of Celie's husband Albert, but who becomes Celie's friend and lover. Meanwhile, her sister Nettie's letters surface and through them Celie discovers that Alphonso is her stepfather and that her biological father had been lynched; she also learns of the life that Nettie has made for herself and of her travel to Liberia with the missionary Samuel and his wife and two adopted children who turn out to be Celie's lost infants. Celie leaves Albert and goes to Memphis with Shug where she begins a business selling tailored pants in vivid colours, and especially in purple. After Alphonso's death she inherits his house, develops a friendship with Albert who is regretful of his earlier ill treatment of Celie and is finally reunited with Nettie who has married Samuel after his wife's death. Walker went on to write two other novels that followed the lives of some of the characters from *The Color Purple*. *The Temple of My Familiar* (1989) has the characters of Celie and Shug Avery featuring in related stories. *Possessing the Secret of Joy* (1992), develops the missionary life of Celie's sister Nettie and the practice of female circumcision is criticised. Subsequent novels, essays and poetry continued to feature her favorite themes of women's oppression, empowerment and identity in the community and increasingly around the world. *By the Light of My Father's Smile* (1998) is about a family of anthropologists who present themselves as missionaries in pursuit of their research in Mexico.

Walker's critical position *In Search of Our Mother's Gardens* was ground defining. Essays collected in it illustrate the kind of criticism that she called "womanist", distinguishing it from traditional feminist criticism. The word and its sense runs through the short story "Coming Apart" where at one point the protagonist reads from Tracey A. Gardner's essay "Racism in Pornography and the Women's Movement", defining it as *"instinctively* pro-woman" and rooted in Black women's culture.

Walker's research and recovery of the work of Zora Neale Hurston, who had died in poverty and anonymity, is one of her most significant contributions to African American literary history. In an early essay "In Search of Zora Neale Hurston" (1975) that later appeared as "Looking for Zora" in *In Search of Our Mothers' Gardens,* she recounts the visit to Eatonville, Zora's hometown, posing as her niece and accompanied by a local graduate student who was writing a dissertation on Hurston. In a racy narrative that is equally ironic and outraged, she writes of the adventure of tracking down those who might remember her – the school classmate, eighty-two-year-old Mrs Moseley, and Mrs. Patterson whose father ran the funeral home when Zora died and was buried in the old cemetery, Garden of the Heavenly Rest, the knowledge that Zora had died of malnutrition, and finally setting out with scanty directions to find the grave with only one local resident, Rosalee, as guide. The discovery, through an uncanny calling out to Zora herself, of a sunken spot in the middle of the wild and unkempt cemetery that could be the grave, and the ordering of a headstone for it that would carry an epitaph containing Jean Toomer's line "A Genius of the South", is the beginning of a gradual discovery and bringing-to-light of this significant foremother. The essay goes on to descriptions of the place, the meeting with Hurston's friend, the handsome, elderly Dr. Benton who tells of her last years, the place itself, and the house she lived in, and the surprising knowledge of Hurston's enthusiasm for gardening (Wiley 2, 735–46). A tough, undaunted figure begins to appear and Walker takes up the task of retrieving and representing her to a new generation. In another essay, "Zora Neale Hurston: A Cautionary Tale and a Partisan View"(Wiley 2, 747–51), she offers her personal evaluation of Hurston's work and her place – as a cultural archivist for the practices that she documented in works like *Mules and Men*, and for what she identified as characteristically Hurston: "racial health: a sense of black people as complete, complex, *undiminished* human beings"; a quality that Walker says is only evident in one other black writer, Du Bois, who took "delight in the beauty and spirit of black people" (748, original emphasis).

The essay ends with a statement that might be representative of all such programmes of historical recovery and reinstatement: "*We are a people. A people do not throw their geniuses away.* And if they are thrown away, it is our duty *as artists and as witnesses for the future* to collect them again for the sake of our children, and, if necessary, bone by bone" (Wiley 2, 751; original emphases).

Walker is also the author of a memoir, *The Chicken Chronicles* (2011) where she reflects on her life while caring for chickens.

For **Gloria Naylor** (1950–2016) the examples set by older women authors were empowering. As she herself admitted, Morrison's work encouraged her to believe that "not only is your story worth telling but it can be told in words so painstakingly eloquent that it becomes a song" (quoted in Gates Jr. and McKay 2542–43). In an interview to Ethel Morgan Smith, Naylor says, "As an older student at Brooklyn College, I had discovered black women writers like

Nikki Giovanni, Paule Marshall, Toni Morrison and Alice Walker. Discovering all of their work led me to believe that I could also add my own voice" (1432).

Naylor was born in New York City to Roosevelt and Alberta McAlpin Naylor who had migrated from Mississippi to escape the life of sharecropping that was almost the only option available to African Americans in the rural South. Roosevelt Naylor found work on the New York subway while his wife worked as a telephone operator. Alberta Naylor's fondness for reading and efforts to improve herself by joining a local book club created an enabling atmosphere in the home that taught her children the value of education and opened up for them the joys of literature. After finishing school Gloria Naylor joined the Jehovah's Witnesses and served as a missionary in New York, North Carolina and Florida from 1968–75. She left the group in 1975 and joined Brooklyn College from where she received a BA degree in English literature, following it with an MA from Yale University.

Naylor's first novel, *The Women of Brewster Place* (1982) tells the story of Southern migrants who move into the housing at Brewster Place over a thirty-year period from the 1940s, through seven different narratives that feature women from diverse backgrounds and with very different character and experiences. Mattie, Etta, Ciel, Kiswana (the only one among the women who lives in the locality by choice), Cora, and Lorraine and Theresa (the lesbian couple whose coming causes friction in the community) are finely drawn, with each life evoked through their relationships with one another, and in one of the stories, "The Two", through their position with regard to the lesbian relationship that puzzles and worries them. Each woman's story shows her individual life and her relationship to the community. Naylor's distinctive style is already apparent in this early work. In "The Two", describing the way a rumour started and spread, she writes: "It had first spread through the block like a sour odor that's only faintly perceptible and easily ignored until it starts growing in strength from the dozen mouths it had been lying in, among clammy gums and scum-coated teeth" (Norton 2544) – a metaphor that emerges from the filth of the block and the mouths that carry it, but that centres on the old woman

Sophie with her "squinted eyes and drooping lips" who initiates and carries it around. Naylor's other novels are *Linden Hills* (1985), set in a middle class neighbourhood and featuring a couple of poets who meet the people living there; *Mama Day* (1988), which signifies on Shakespeare's play *The Tempest,* is set on an island off the southeastern coast of the United States and also uses African American folk materials; and *Bailey's Café* (1992) set in Brooklyn and showing the violence that is a part of life in the place, but that is also deeply immersed in jazz style and mood. Subsequently, she also wrote another novel, *The Men of Brewster Place,* where she traced the lives of men like Ben and Mattie's son who had appeared in the first novel.

The career of **Terry McMillan** (b. 1951) represents the emergence of popular fiction by black women. Coming from a working class background, McMillan studied at Berkeley and Columbia Universities and taught at Wyoming and Arizona. Her first novel was *Mama* (1987) about a single mother of five children. But it was with *Waiting to Exhale* (1992), about four black women and their quest for love that she emerged as one of the most popular writers of romances, entered *The New York Times* best seller list and received a six million dollar publishing contract for her next novel. This was *How Stella Got Her Groove Back*, a novel about a middle aged black woman falling in love with a younger Jamaican man that was based on her own love story with a much younger Jamaican, Jonathan Plummer who she married and later divorced. She went on to write several other novels, one of which, *Getting to Happy* (2010), was a sequel to *Waiting to Exhale.* Several of McMillan's novels were made into movies. She also edited *Breaking Ice: An Anthology of Contemporary African American Fiction* (1990).

McMillan's extraordinarily successful career is the outcome of significant changes that began in the publishing industry as well as among the reading public from the late 1970s that also saw the emergence of other writers of popular romances like Connie Briscoe, Tina McElroy Ansa, and Bebe Moore Campbell. McMillan's works are typical examples of popular fiction with references to aspects of popular culture known to readers like movies, fashion brands, television shows and consumer goods, and featuring mostly young, urban, middle class women who are very similar to the target readership. As Susanne Dietzel writes: "For popular fiction to work, to be successful and to attract a body of devoted readers, it has to embody elements of recognition and identification" (159). By representing romantic relationships as central to the lives of the black women she portrays, McMillan achieves another interesting result – a deflection from the usual privileging of racial conflict that goes against the expectations of critics. As Robin Smiles notes of her work and that of other popular romance writers, they defy expected critical paradigms, redefine domesticity, gender roles and black female sexuality, and create new friendships and communities, in the process offering a fresh look at society and social and cultural roles and assumptions (353). The emergence of influential black female intellectuals like Morrison, Walker, Bambara and Naylor and their revision of the representations of black women from earlier periods as just victims of racial and sexual exploitation enabled the shifts seen in works of popular fiction. At the same time there was a rising readership among black women as a result of book clubs and community reading groups (Smiles 349). Smiles notes a number of important aspects of the 1990s: publishers found that romance novels that presented stories of intimate relationships between black men and black women were likely to be commercially successful. In 1994, "Kensington Publishers launched Arabesque, the first imprint devoted to black romance novels". Probably the most significant change was "corporate consolidations within the publishing industry that focused on such bottom-line issues as profits and entertainment" and with large media conglomerates buying out small, independent publishing houses. New corporate owners looked to maximize profits by publishing books that "could be transferable to other entertainment media (such as movies and television)". Two examples of such corporations were Disney, owner of Hyperion Books and Viacom, owner of Simon and Schuster. And Terry McMillan's popular works were taken up for film adaptations: "Twentieth Century Fox paid $1 million for the film rights to *Waiting to Exhale*, and, just several years later, $2 million for *How Stella Got Her Groove Back*" (Smiles 349).

With its huge success this literature helped to bridge the gulf between the popular and the canonical and also gave a new dimension to the idea of community. Popular fiction created a legitimate space for the domestic and the romantic and the role it might have played in supporting the increasing emergence of such themes across all kinds of literature is an area that is worth more attention than this book is able to give it.

The next writer we discuss is **Ernest Gaines** (1933–2019) whose work presents themes that bring together love in the backdrop of slavery (in *Catherine Carmier* for instance), but also continues to show the sexual exploitation of black women and their hard lives as they struggled during enslavement and after freedom. Gaines was born on a plantation in Louisiana on which four generations of his family had lived, first as slaves and then after freedom, as sharecroppers. He attended the parish school and then went on to a segregated school for three years. When he turned 15, his mother and stepfather moved to Vallejo, California, with their children and here Gaines started spending time in the public library while attending junior college. He was attracted to the work of the Russian novelists and especially Ivan Turgenev, as well as the novels of William Faulkner. These early influences can be seen in his work, with Faulkner being especially important as a model for the use of Southern dialect and the creation of a fictional locale, Bayonne. He went on to graduate with a degree in English literature from San Francisco State College, served for two years in the Army and then studied creative writing at Stanford University. His first novel, *Catherine Carmier,* a love story set in a tense, multiracial location in Louisiana, was published in 1964. He went on to write *Of Love and Dust* (1967) about a young man Marcus who is sent from prison to work on a plantation, under a Cajun overseer, Sidney Bonbon, and who retaliates for ill treatment and overwork by seducing, first Bonbon's mistress and then his wife. This was followed by *Bloodline* (1968), a set of five stories – "A Long Day in November", "The Sky is Gray", "Three Men", "Bloodline" and "Just like a Tree" – that explores the suffering of poor African American sharecroppers in post-Civil War Louisiana, with its derelict plantations now standing as signs of a traumatic past, while the former slaves try to eke out a living from their cane fields. Gaines' next work was *The Autobiography of Miss Jane Pittman* (1971) set in the fictional region of Bayonne in rural Louisiana. It has a narrator recording the story of the 110-year-old Miss Jane who looks back and recounts her life as a young slave who escaped with an orphaned little boy, and brought him up as her own through continuous struggle and resistance. The unemotional tone with which the old woman narrates the horrors she saw and lived through is a remarkable feature of this work, framing a whole history of slavery with a stability and sharpness of vision that is both critique and condemnation. Gaines went on to write *A Long Day in November* (1971), *In My Father's House* (1978), *A Gathering of Old Men* (1993) *A Lesson Before Dying* (1993), and a collection, *Mozart and Leadbelly: Stories and Essays* (2005), all set in the rural South and representing lives lived under various kinds of racial and familial tensions and psychological distress.

The setting in plantations in the South, the invention of the fictional region of Bayonne, use of dialect, and narrators of varied complexity are some of the remarkable features of Gaines' writing.

As we examine the works of all these writers, it is a matter of wonder that so many of them have written new versions of the slave narrative, a form that emerges in the 1970s in the aftermath of the Civil Rights and Black Power movements. This fictional form, revisiting the past in order to examine and critique aspects of slavery that had been forgotten or perhaps not perceived, was part of the revisionist historiography of this time that is represented in historical studies, but that was given flesh by the neo-slave narrative. The new perspective reframed the Middle Passage, enslavement, slave-master relationships, escape, and the difficult remaking of lives after the Civil War, and it involved a recovery of the enslaved voice. Two terms have been used to describe these writings – the "neo-slave narratives" (Bell 1987) and "contemporary narratives of slavery" (Keizer 2004), and the first full-length study of the form is that of Rushdy (2001). The text that inaugurated this tradition was Margaret Walker's *Jubilee* (1966) that relied on her great-grandmother's oral tales of slavery.

3

In theatre the best known African American name is that of **August Wilson** (1945–2005) who "animated the cultural consequences" of the Great Migration (Jarrett 2014, 869) in plays set in the poor Hill District of Pittsburg, Pennsylvania, where he was born and spent his childhood. Considered among the greatest of twentieth century playwrights, he represented some of the significant periods of black history through the lives of individual characters, capturing desires and frustrations and exploring them through his own artistic and political interests. Ten such plays were written as "The Pittsburgh Cycle", with one play for each decade of the twentieth century, and characters who occasionally recur in different plays of the cycle and who are caught in the socio-historical situations of each decade.

Wilson was born to a German father who was a baker and an African American mother who worked as a domestic. Following his parents' divorce, his mother remarried an African American and the family moved to Hazelwood, a white suburb in Pittsburgh. The experience of being in hostile white environments was repeated in the schools he attended, forcing him to leave and educate himself through self-study at the Carnegie Library in Pittsburgh. There he read extensively in African American literature and also studied blues music, the work of Jorge Luis Borges, the African American painter Romare Bearden (whose collage, "Mill Hand's Lunch Bucket" showing a man sitting with a bowed head inspired Wilson's 1984 play *Joe Turner's Come and Gone*), and Amiri Baraka. An additional resource he garnered was from sitting in cigar stores and barber shops, listening to older men of the area talk and tell stories (in Jarrett 2014, 869). Following a brief stint in the army he decided to become a writer, initially seeing himself as a poet while he associated with the Black Power Movement and founded the Black Horizons Theater Company with a fellow Pittsburgan, Rob Penny. His interest in blues music resulted in the poem "Bessie" on the great blues singer, Bessie Smith. Art and music continued to influence his sensibility as he began his career as a dramatist with children's plays based on Native American folk tales. His first play, *The Homecoming* (first staged in 1976) was based on the life of blues singer and guitarist, Blind Lemon Jefferson, while the second, *Black Bart and the Sacred Hills* (1977) was a musical satire about an outlaw in the Old West (first staged in 1982). The next, *Jitney* (written in 1979, premiered on Broadway in 2017), a two-act play on the lives of unlicensed jitney or cab drivers in Pittsburgh, was the first of his "Pittsburgh Cycle". The next play in the cycle was *Ma Rainey's Black Bottom* (written in 1982, premiered in 1984), set in 1920s Chicago, that showed in its two acts the lives of black musicians and their struggles against racism in the music industry with its predominantly white producers. It was based on the life of blues singer, Gertrude "Ma" Rainey, also known as the mother of the blues, the first professional blues vocalist whose experience as a recording artist in white-run studios is the source of the play's setting and theme. Ma Rainey was famously played by Viola Davis (both on stage and in the film adaptation of the play by George C. Wolfe in 2019) who transformed herself into the famous singer, complete with gold teeth, kohl lined eyes, horsehair wig and a body weight of 300 pounds. In the play Ma Rainey says of the blues: "White folks don't understand about the blues. They hear it come out, but they don't know how it got there. They don't understand that's life's way of talking. You don't sing to feel better. You sing 'cause that's a way of understanding life" (Wilson 79). This play explores a crucial tension in the reception of jazz music – that between the live music with its improvisations that are quintessentially jazz and the recorded forms that freeze a version for listeners – through its setting in a recording studio (see Teague 2011). As Ma Rainey says in the play, recording meant to take her "voice and trap it in them fancy boxes with all them buttons and dials" (Wilson 92). The next play, *Joe Turner's Come and Gone* (premiered in 1984), features the character Harold Loomis who moves from one boarding house to another with his young daughter, looking for his wife who has left them. Set in 1911 at the start of the great migration, it is a play that has received considerable scholarly attention "with its assertion of the African presence in America, with its articulations of the power of the spirit, its representation of ritual observances and spiritual rebirth" (Elam Jr. 260). It was also part of what is called "a watershed moment in the development of Black theatre in

America" in June 2009, when President Barack Obama and his wife attended a production of the play directed by Bartlett Sher, a white director (Elam Jr. 259).

Other plays in the cycle are *The Piano Lesson* (written in 1987, staged in 1990), set in 1936 and featuring a dispute between siblings, Boy Willie and Berniece, over the selling of a piano, a family heirloom, to purchase land where their slave ancestors toiled. *Two Trains Running* (1990) set in a diner in 1969, during the Civil Rights and Black Power movements, has a bunch of Hill District residents discussing the various aspects of the times and considering the selling of the diner. *Seven Guitars* (written in 1995) set in 1948, moves back and forth in time, beginning after the funeral of Floyd 'Schoolboy' Barton, a blues singer, who after release from prison, tries to embark on a musical career with the help of a recording studio in Chicago. But having sold his guitar in straitened circumstances he is unable to get it back and the play tells of the events that finally ends in his death. *King Headley II* (written in 1999) set in 1985, during the Reagan era, features a character, Aunt Ester, a 285-year-old former slave and spiritual healer, from the earlier *Gem of the Ocean* (premiered in 2003, set in 1904), who also appears in *Two Trains Running* and *Radio Golf*. *Radio Golf* (premiered in 2005) is set in 1990 and shows real estate developers planning to raze the house where Aunt Ester lived in order to build an apartment complex in the area, presenting through this design the competing claims of history and progress facing the African American community.

The play by which Wilson is best known is *Fences,* also from the cycle. It is a two-act play set in 1957, just before the start of the Civil Rights Movement. It represents a phase in baseball history where the game has officially become integrated even as racism continues. In the story of the fifty-three-year-old Troy Maxson and his family, "Wilson uses both the history and mythology of baseball to challenge the authenticity of the American dream" (Koprince 349), and especially its inaccessibility for African Americans. Troy indignantly responds to a comment made by his friend Jim Bono that he had been born too early, and to his wife Rose's claim that things had changed with "lots of colored boys playing ball now":

"I'm talking about if you could play ball then they ought to have let you play. Don't care what color you were. Come telling me I come along too early. If you could play . . . then they ought to have let you play" (Wiley 2, 876).

The theatre has been an essential part of black consciousness-raising and empowerment. As Amiri Baraka, among the most influential theatre activists of his generation, had written of "Revolutionary theatre", it must bring about radical change, "must Accuse and Attack because it is a theatre of Victims", "must take dreams and give them a reality." Further he announced that "we will change the drawing rooms into places where real things can be said about a real world. . . Our theatre will show victims so that their brothers in the audience will be better able to understand that they are the brothers of victims" (Norton 1899–1901).

The theatre was a powerful forum for critiques of racism and inequalities, of the material and psychological effects resulting from one people being oppressed and discriminated against by another. It provided motivation and mobilised and urged Black people to take an active part in bringing about social change – especially adding to the raised awareness of the Civil Rights Movement. It is worth noting its transformative role. The showing on stage, visual representations and aural power – all of this would be much more effective for a community for whom the gains of education and literacy were inadequate, and this was exploited to the full by playwrights of this period even as growing sophistication in the craft meant that they were now drawing both white and black audiences and performing on Broadway.

4

Among poets one of the most brilliant and most consistent voices is that of **Rita Dove** (b. 1952), the first African American Poet Laureate of the US (1993–95) and winner of the Pulitzer Prize in 1987 for the collection *Thomas and Beulah*. Her career is often compared to that of Gwendolyn Brooks, especially for the way she eschewed radical themes and styles in favour of traditional poetic forms, seeking "to frame the quotidian in elegantly tight verse" and "gracefully interpolat[es]ing the political and historical into a personal register" (Jarrett 2014, 835).

Rita Dove was born in Akron, Ohio. Her parents, Elvira and Ray Dove, ensured that she received an excellent education at school and university. She was a Presidential Scholar, an honour given to the top 100 high school seniors in the nation, went on to Miami University from where she graduated *summa cum laude* and then won a Fulbright Scholarship to study for a year in Germany. On her return she joined the writer's programme at the University of Iowa from where she graduated with an MFA. While attending this programme she met her future husband, the German writer, Fred Viebahn who was visiting on a Fulbright fellowship, and also published *Ten Poems* (1977). The two collections, *The Yellow House on the Corner* (1980) and *Museum* (1983), followed. In these Dove can be seen expanding the scope of her work beyond the usually expected themes from African American history. In the first she draws on her time in Germany, setting images and cultural references from this site alongside African American cultural moments. She retrieves figures like Benjamin Banneker and David Walker and also has poems like "The Bird Frau", combining aspects from both her American and her international experiences. In *Museum* too she avoids the direct political statement and instead employs finely nuanced images to explore stories and spaces from African, European and Asian sites alongside the American. In an interview in 2008 Dove declared: "The wider world was ready for nuance" (Rowell 716), and her poetry certainly met the challenge of this range of subjects.

Thomas and Beulah, her third collection has a connected narrative built around the lives of her grandparents but also contains other characters who are portrayed with great sensitivity. The first poem, "The Event" is the story of Thomas and his close friend Lem who was accidentally killed and whose presence haunts Thomas throughout his life. Alternating perspectives shift between Thomas and Beulah. These are poems that speak about their life together and separately, about ordinary everyday experiences that are expressed with startling turns of phrase, and images that are unexpected and beautiful: "Sound quivered / Like a rope stretched clear to / To land, tensed and brimming" ("Variation on Pain"); or in "Courtship" the lover's gesture of wrapping the yellow silk scarf, "still warm from his throat / around her shoulders". The next collection, *Mother Love* (1995) is about the mother-daughter relationship and draws on the myth of Demeter and Persephone, while moulding the sonnet form to develop the linked series of poems. Dove's other works include *Grace Notes* (1989), *On the Bus with Rosa* (1999) based on the Civil Rights era, *American Smooth* (2006) that uses the rhythm of dance, a verse play, *The Darker Face of the Earth* (1994), a collection of short stories, *Fifth Sunday* (1985), a novel, *Through the Ivory Gaze* (1992), and *Sonata Mullatica* that features a black violinist, George Augustus Polgreen Bridgetower who, Dove discovered, had played for Beethoven. This is a sample of her effort to retrieve lost figures from history and frame them in her poetry. Another example is Claudette Colvin, who refused to give up her seat on a bus, long before Rosa Parks's historic moment of resistance, and who is portrayed by Dove in the poem "Claudette Colvin Goes to Work".

Among other writers who have made significant contributions in several genres are John Edgar Wideman (b. 1941), Edward P. Jones (b. 1950), Harryette Mullen (b. 1953), Percival Everett (b. 1956), and Edwidge Danticat (b. 1969).

Of these **Harryette Mullen,** poet, short story writer and professor of English at the University of California, follows Dove in rejecting expectations of what a black poet should write and how she should be read. In an interview to the journal *Contemporary Literature,* she acknowledges her influences: "Gertrude Stein to the Black Arts Movement, from Sappho to Bessie Smith, from Language poetry to rap" (in Frost 397). She wrote *Trimmings* (1991) as a conversation with and poetic critique of Gertrude Stein, noting her use of words as colours and melody, and referencing it in her own use of contemporary language drawn from several media and from material cultures from around the world, demonstrating "a kind of archeological interest in words, word patterns, word sounds" (Moore 521–22). Moore offers a close reading of her one-line poem from *Trimmings:* "Shades, cool dark lasses. Ghost of a smile", displaying an "archeological" aspect in the density and depth of each word:

"Reading down from 'shades' we can word associate to a familiar pejorative for black people, to a hip expression for sunglasses, to a synonym for ghosts, to the coolness of shade beneath a tree. If we read across and down, 'cool dark lasses' puns on 'dark lasses' i.e., dark girls, and dark glasses etc.," illustrating how Mullen's work is "allusive, suggestive, and open to multiple readings" (522).

Mullen uses African American folklore, jump rope rhymes, word play, jokes, and the blues, as well as issues of commodity and racial culture. Her interest in consumerism is especially seen in *S*PeRM**K*T* (1992) where she captures the frenetic pace of buying in the supermarket while rushing up and down aisles. Of *Muse and Drudge* (1995) Mullen says that it is a "book of echoes" and "a recycling of fragments of language" (Frost 412), and poems in this volume refer to the history of black women's lives as they laboured in house and field, and in odd jobs in the cities, and also became famous jazz and blues performers. Mullen's other works include *Sleeping with the Dictionary* (2002), where poems appear like verbal games, many of which were developed by the literary group OuLiPo, and that contains variations on earlier texts, including two, "Dim Lady" and "European Folk Variant", that rewrite Shakespeare's Sonnet 130, "My mistress' eyes are nothing like the sun"; *Recyclopedia* (2006), which is a collection of her three earlier books; and *Urban Tumbleweed: Notes from a Tanka Diary* (2012), containing poems that grew out of her daily walks through Los Angeles streets. Through all this Mullen is also concerned with understanding "what we believe about ourselves. . . When are we ourselves? Beyond being a credit or discredit to our race, who are we?" (Frost 416). In her introduction to the interview with Mullen, Elizabeth Frost, one of her most perceptive critics, writes that Mullen "has pioneered her own form of bluesy, disjunctive lyric poetry, combining a concern for the political issues raised by identity politics with a poststructuralist emphasis on language" (397). In this interview Mullen describes her own practice: "I am writing for the eye and the ear at once, at that intersection of orality and literacy, wanting to make sure that there is a troubled, disturbing aspect to the work so that it is never just a 'speakerly' or a 'writerly' text" (401).

John Edgar Wideman (b. 1941), another writer and academic, who resisted easy incorporation into black politics especially of the Black Power era, was influenced by the modernists – T. S. Eliot, James Joyce and William Faulkner – even as he struggled with how to use race in his work. He expressed this dual positioning when he said that African Americans "have become experts at living in at least two places simultaneously, cultivating a sensitivity to the distance – comic, ironic, tragic – between our outer and inner lives" (quoted in Jarrett 2014: 988). This struggle is seen in novels like *A Glance Away* (1967) on a drug addict and a gay English professor, and *Hurry Home* (1970) about an African American intellectual who is alienated from his community and his racial history. As Jarrett writes of such works, these and later novels represent a crucial tension between the African American intellectuals and professionals and the mostly working class communities from which they may have emerged (988). Wideman is also the author of the *Homewood Trilogy* made up of two novels, *Hiding Place* (1981) and *Sent for You Yesterday* (1983), and a short story collection, *Damballah* (1982), set in his old Homewood neighbourhood, *Philadelphia Fire* (1990), a fictionalised account of the 1985 attack on a black liberation group, the MOVE Organizers, and *The Cattle Killing* (1997), a novel based in plague-affected eighteenth century Philadelphia where African Americans are free but struggle against the plague that is killing mercilessly. This novel is built around a tale about the South African Xhosa people who kill their cattle in the belief that this will drive away their white oppressors. Wideman has also written essays (with his brother Robert, who was a convicted and imprisoned robber and murderer) on the psychological and emotional wounds left by slavery, especially the descent into a criminal existence, and collected as *Brothers and Keepers* (1984). A similar set of issues is explored in *Fatheralong: A Meditation on Fathers and Sons, Race and Society* (1994), that is made up of personal pieces about his relationship to his son, Jacob Wideman, serving a life sentence for killing a classmate in Arizona in 1986. He has also authored a memoir, *Hoop Roots: Basketball, Race, and Love* (2001).

5

Henry Louis Gates, in his essay on "Blackness" suggests that there is a trend where writers "simultaneously critique both the metaphysical presuppositions inherent in Western ideas and forms of writing and the metaphorical system in which the 'blackness' of a writer and his [or her] experiences as a writer have been valorized as a 'natural' absence" (297). The next author we discuss is someone who represents this dual impulse through deconstruction of form and of what has been an essentialized history of African American victimhood.

Ishmael Reed (b. 1938) author of plays, poetry, fiction, essays and song lyrics for many contemporary singers, is an important figure in this period. He represents the growing trend of black writers who question and critique contemporary life in the United States, using satire and irony and taking advantage of postmodern techniques of collage and parody. Born in Chattanooga, Tennessee, and raised in Buffalo, New York, he attended the State University of New York, Buffalo, before going on to join the local *Empire Star Weekly* for which he wrote pieces on current events relating to the black community. He taught at the University of California, Berkeley, for thirty-five years, besides holding visiting positions at Harvard and Yale Universities and at Dartmouth College and SUNY. His first novel was *The Free-Lance Pallbearers* (1967) where he lampooned politicians. This was followed by another satirical work, *Yellow Back Radio Broke Down* (1969) which is a comic take on the classic western novel and featured a black cowboy, Loop Garoo. He went on to write novels like *Mumbo Jumbo* (1972), *Flight to Canada* (1976) which is a parody of the slave narrative, *The Terrible Twos* (1982), *Reckless Eyeballing* (1986), *Japanese by Spring* (1993), *Juice* (2011) and *The Terrible Fours* (2021). In the novel *Conjugating Hindi* (2018), he has a protagonist, Peter Bowman, or Boa as he is called, who learns Hindi and reads South Asian literature, an interest that stems from his meeting with Shashi Paramara, a right wing Hindu intellectual with whom he is invited to debate by the Columbia Speakers Bureau for a fee. He is told of Indian racism by his chauffeur (incidents where African students are beaten up in India are mentioned as also the view that Indians are the most racist people in the world), and finds it endorsed by Kala, the dark skinned sister of Shashi, who is a misfit in her Brahmin family. Reed's poetry collections include *Chattanooga* (1973), *A Secretary to the Spirits* (1978), *New and Collected Poems* (1988), *New and Collected Poems 1964–2007* (2007), and *Why the Black Hole Sings the Blues, Poems 2007–2020* (2020).

He has several collections of essays commenting on contemporary life and prominent figures in black history. Among these are *The Complete Muhammad Ali* (2015), *Going Too Far: Essays about America's Nervous Breakdown* (2012), *Barack Obama and the Jim Crow Media, Or The Return of the 'Nigger Breakers'* (2010) and *Mixing It Up: Taking on the Media Bullies and Other Reflections* (2008). Reed is also an illustrator and cartoonist (many of his novels are illustrated) and his cartoons have appeared in the *San Francisco Chronicle, Black Renaissance Noire,* and the *New York Amsterdam News*. Among the several plays and librettos he has written and produced is *The Haunting of Lin-Manuel Miranda* (which premiered with a four-night reading at the Nuyorican Poets Café in May 2019, and was published by Archway Editions in 2020), the much acclaimed take on the 2015 historical musical *Hamilton* by Miranda, on Alexander Hamilton, founding father of the nation and interpreter of the Constitution. Reed's play uses critiques of Hamilton and has its creator Miranda haunted by figures from the past.

The deconstructionist aspect of his work is acknowledged by Reed himself and noted by his critics, as in the following:

> Ishmael Reed's self-conscious use of form is as noticeable as it is distinctive. His writing is pun-packed and moves to a variety of jazz and blues rhythms; the cinema informs his quick-splice scene changes; a metafictional impulse plays lightly through his tales; exuberant parody abounds; and purposeful anachronism penetrates his reader's defenses. Reed's literary canon is permeated by his unique blend of the verbal and visual, prosaic and poetic, old and new, fictive and factual, serious and satiric, African and American, traditional and popular. (Weixlmann 58)

His exuberant and richly suggestive style, creating a collage out of everything that catches the author's attention, is evident in *Mumbo Jumbo,* his novel of the ragtime era developed around ragtime, blues and jazz while also referring to the Harlem Renaissance, the Back to Africa movement and the American occupation of Haiti, and moving with abandon over several visual and literary genres. Reed picks up a term "jes grew" used by James Weldon Johnson in his preface to *The Book of American Negro Poetry* (1922), to label the plague, Jes Grew, that spreads from New Orleans and infects people, making them lose all inhibitions and hesitations and dance frenziedly. Jes Grew is most feared by the Atonists, a group who invent ways to infiltrate the black communities to arrest the infection. They are countered by PaPa LaBas who uses voodoo to keep the spirit of Jes Grew alive. The novel is also a search by its detective protagonist for a lost anthology of black literature. Reed continues to be creative with works in the several genres he is so adept in, with his latest being an audiobook, *Malcolm and Me* (2020), and a play.

Charles Johnson (b. 1948) in his landmark study of black writing, *Being and Race: Black Writing since 1970* (1988) placed an important challenge before African American writers, urging them to write "a fiction of increasing artistic and intellectual growth, one that enables us as a people – as a culture – to move from narrow complaint to broad celebration" (quoted in Jarrett 2014: 1021). As we have seen in the literature that has preceded, two broad movements are discernible – one that has persisted in seeing the darker aspects of black history and shown the African American as victimised and exploited by the economic, social and political processes of a growing nation; and another that has chosen to see the African American as a survivor who has triumphed against impossible obstacles and presented herself as beautiful, strong, and resurgent. But Johnson's articulation of these directions becomes especially relevant for the writing that emerged in the post 1970s period when historical experience and cultural material from the community came to be retrieved, read and represented in new ways and formal experimentation became the norm in poetry, fiction and the theatre. Johnson's own essay "The End of the Black American

Narrative" (published in the *American Scholar* in 2008) expresses his conviction that the time was ripe for a major shift, as "the old black American narrative of pervasive victimization" has become "an ideology" (Wiley 2, 1029), no longer able to say anything new but capable of trapping people within itself, making them reiterate the same old facts and impressions.

Johnson's career as a creative artist is an example of these times. He began as a cartoonist for the *Chicago Tribune* and other newspapers, collecting and publishing two volumes of his cartoons, *Black Humor* (1970) and *Half-Past Nation Time* (1972) while still a student at Southern Illinois University. His first published novel was *Faith and the Good Thing* (1974). His influences were Richard Wright, Jean Toomer, James Baldwin and Ralph Ellison but also as his writing reveals, Herman Melville, besides the novelist John Gardner, who was his mentor at Southern Illinois, and who encouraged him to move beyond protest novels and explore the philosophical possibilities of fiction. These ideas are expressed in his 1988 essay, "Where Philosophy and Fiction Meet." Johnson went on to do a PhD in phenomenology and literary aesthetics and began teaching English at the University of Washington, Seattle. While working here he also began writing screenplays for the PBS (Public Broadcasting Service) Network. *Charlie Smith and the Fritter Tree* (1978) had a 134-year-old nursing home resident who had been a train robber, bounty hunter and saloon keeper, telling stories from the long years he had lived through, while *Booker* (1984) was a biography of Booker T. Washington. *Oxherding Tale* (1982) is a take on the slave narrative that is by turns dark and funny. It begins with a slave owner and his African American butler drinking together and then switching beds resulting in the birth of the protagonist, Andrew Hawkins, from the union of the white woman and the African American man, and whose skin color enables his 'passing'. This common theme from the literature of an earlier era representing anxiety and desperation, is now not even worth considering, with Andrew's marriage to a white woman quietly succeeding. Andrew and his wife name their daughter after Andrew's white mother and the race question does not come up at all in the marriage (see for instance, Little [1991] for a reading of this novel and its radical thematic and stylistic innovations). The novel represents what Johnson himself believes is the aim of fiction, that is the opening up of perception, something that is in tune with his firm belief that the new African American literature needs to be liberated from its past obsessions. The novel, often descried as postmodern, refers freely to eastern myth (that of the god Shiva for instance), Zen Buddhism, and African American Soulcatcher, even as it signifies on Frederick Douglas's autobiographies (see Gleason 1991). Johnson's other works include a collection of stories, *The Sorcerer's Apprentice: Tales and Conjurations* (1986), *Dreamer* (1998), a novel based on the life and philosophy of Martin Luther King Jr., *Soulcatcher* (2001), a series of pieces on slavery, and *Africans in America: America's Journey Through Slavery* (1999) written as an accompaniment to the PBS series on the subject. But it was *Middle Passage* (1990), the novel that references the scandalous journeys that brought Africans to America where, after the *Oxherding Tale*, Johnson's virtuoso style is most evident as it cleverly blends the forms of epic, romance, sea story and slave narrative. The novel is set aboard one of the last of the nineteenth century slave ships, *The Republic*, features slave uprisings and has a stowaway as narrator, clearly echoing Melville's *Billy Budd* and *Moby Dick*. Rutherford Calhoun, a newly freed slave who stows away aboard the ship to avoid the Boston schoolteacher who wishes to marry him, once discovered, becomes a cabin boy to the captain. He is the only black American aboard and he helps the Africans who constitute the illegal cargo on the ship in their revolt against crew and captain.

6

Much of the literature written after the 1970s has been influenced by theoretical developments in postmodernism. Self-reflexivity, parody, intertextuality, and above all a revisionist approach to the past have been features of the literature produced in this period. Toni Cade Bambara, Toni Morrison, Ishmael Reed, Charles Johnson, the playwrights Adrienne Kennedy and Susan Lori Parks, and poets like Rita Dove and Harryette Mullen have drawn on a wide variety of cultural, historical and artistic resources to write innovative works that have enabled fresh assessments of many of the long sustained themes and concerns of African American literature. These developments, seen from the time of the Black Arts Movement, characterise what is often seen as a "self-consciously black postmodernism" (Dubey and Goldberg 569), that shows "two distinct trends: textual self-reflexivity and historical revision" and that has enabled questioning of the expectation that black writers must only present realistic accounts of the collective black experience. According to Dubey and Goldberg, "[P]ostmodern African American writers self-consciously revaluate dominant literary forms of racial representation by parodying these forms and revealing them to be textual constructs rather than authentic reflections of black life". Such revisionism and the "effort to render a post-1970s black 'polyconsciousness' in literature involves a range of innovative formal strategies, including textual fragmentation, linguistic bricolage, and the transgression of generic and cultural boundaries". These enable exploration and representation of multiple affiliations like "feminist, nationalist, ecological, and labor politics" and the many "differences within the category of blackness" as well as for "subverting monolithic conceptions of black culture" (Dubey and Goldberg 569). Some of this is seen in experimental performance texts like *Fierce Love* (1991) which dramatises the stories of a variety of queer black men in subverting the homogeneity of black male identity. Another depiction of hybrid identity is seen in the album *The Inevitable Rise and Liberation of Niggy Tardust!* (2008) where the title character is performed by the poet musician Saul Williams in feathers, face-paint and a black and white mohawk, drawing on multiple cultural identities to present a hybrid figure.

One writer who perhaps best represents these diverse and changing characteristics of contemporary black culture is **Colson Whitehead** (b. 1969). Considered to be among the finest of contemporary writers, Whitehead moves with assurance amongst several kinds of fictional forms. Born and brought up in Manhattan, he attended Trinity School and graduated from Harvard University with a degree in English and comparative literature, and began his writing career as a reviewer and critic of books, films and television for a weekly, *The Village Voice*. He left in the late 1990s to begin his career as a novelist. His first novel *The Intuitionist* (1999) shows evidence of his early reading in science fiction, blending fantasy and detection in the story of the elevator inspector Lila Mae Watson who uses her intuition in her job and especially when she is wrongly accused of involvement in an elevator accident. The coming of age novel *Sag Harbor* (2009) sits alongside the zombie novel *Zone One* (2011), and the Pulitzer Prize winning *The Underground Railroad* (2016), quiet, unemotional, "matter-of-fact", shows another way of retelling the past as it describes life on a plantation through chapters that each focus on a single person or place, but with the running thread of Cora's story. The narrator Cora, moving from one horrific episode to the next as slaves are whipped, roasted alive, sold or lynched, speaks without overt indictment or commentary, leaving it to the reader to feel shock and revulsion at the extent to which the white slaveholders dehumanised themselves while perpetrating unimaginable tortures on their slaves. At fifteen she escapes from the plantation in Georgia along the Underground Railroad – the famous institution comprised of safe houses, different forms of transport and individuals – that helped slaves to escape to the North. This is depicted as an actual railroad that literally runs underground – a childhood fantasy for the author that here translates into a form with exceptional aesthetic and critical potential. Jennifer Schuessler mentions Whitehead's keen interest in exploring the "metaphoric possibilities of mechanized modes of transport" – the elevator and the railroad being examples (n.p).

In an interview to Harsimran Gill, during the Jaipur Literary Festival (Feb 10, 2019) Colson Whitehead spoke about the brutalisation of slaves on the plantation, the special anguish of female slaves who could not claim the infants they routinely gave birth to, because they were merely the master's property, and his exploration of this psychology in the novel as well as the use of fantasy in a matter-of-fact manner. This particular style is said to have derived from his reading of *One Hundred Years of Solitude* (Schuessler n.p.).

On the fantastical element of the novel Whitehead said: "By having a fantastic structure to *The Underground Railroad* I could have my own reckoning with history, take something that happened in the nineteenth century, something from the twentieth century like the Holocaust or eugenics and move them around and put them in conversation." So the South Carolina of the nineteenth century has skyscrapers, government experiments on syphilis and eugenics, a museum where the former slaves become exhibits that depict Africa, a scene that can critically engage with the present, especially as it is written in the backdrop of the Black Lives Matter movement. One critic who has written of the novel uses the term "speculative satire" (Dischinger 2017) to describe this new kind of engagement with the past, where the familiar often has a throbbing undercurrent: "the novel's speculative premise works in conjunction with satire to create a narrative space in which fantasy can work in the service of understanding, rather than obscuring, peripheralized histories" (83). According to Dischinger the novel "uses speculative literary strategies in order to enact political satire of real histories that, of course, stretch into the present" showing "how the poetics of fantasy point[s] toward the possibility of justice without knowing whether justice is possible" (84). Whitehead in the interview to Gill also spoke of the language used by the slaves as the kind he has himself used when "stopped by police or handcuffed for being black in the wrong space at the wrong time". Of the general theme of slavery in the novel he has said elsewhere: "I wanted it to be like the slave narratives I read, where you get a very matter-of-fact contemplation of all these weird and horrible things that keep happening" (to Schuessler n.p.).

Paul Beatty (b. 1962), author of novels like *The White Boy Shuffle* (1996), *Tuff* (2000) and *Slumberland* (2008), won the Man Booker Prize in 2016 for *The Sellout* (2015), the first African American to do so. His novels are comic, knowing and stylistically complex. He has said, "I have these weird languages in my head . . . nonsense language my friends and I spoke growing up . . . academic language. . . . And it's the same with demographics a little bit. I'm just trying to weave all those into one thread, instead of talking 'us, them those.'" Of his humorous and often ironic take on African American life he says, "I'm evil. I think that everything's funny at some level, you know?" (n.p.).

Twenty-first Century

With the watershed event of 9/11, the wars in Iraq and Afghanistan, and the presidential election that brought Barack Obama to the White House as the first coloured President, the twenty-first century sees the emergence of writers like Ta Nehisi Coates, Claudia Rankin, Colson Whitehead, Yaa Gyasi, and Tayari Jones with works that mark shifts in experience, and new kinds of engagement. While many of the older writers continue to write well into this century, African-born writers like Chimamanda Ngozi Adichie bring in different influences into the literature with diasporic perspectives on race, and new understanding of blackness and experiences like slavery and escape. Of the many exciting authors and texts that have emerged or are emerging are Chris Abani with *GraceLand* (2004), NoViolet Bulawayo with *We Need New Names* (2013), and Dinaw Mengestu with *The Beautiful Things That Heaven Bears* (2007) – all diasporic works that modify notions of blackness, since these are writers who have neither the experience of slavery nor of the kind of racism prevalent in the US.

Stephanie Li in "What is 21st African American literature?", her Introduction to a special issue of the journal *American Literary History*, calls this period "an era defined by horror and anxiety if also by the hope of new possibilities" (632). To the events mentioned above she adds others – Hurricane Katrina and the Great Recession, one, that brought devastation and the second, that exposed the continuing inequalities of American society. But she also mentions changes like the Tea Party protests that began throughout the US in 2009 (calling for fiscal conservatism like lower taxes, reduction of national debt etc.) and the Occupy Wall Street movement (left wing movement in 2011 in New York to protest against corporate greed and economic inequality). Above all the most significant event for this century has been the Black Lives Matter movement that put the victimisation and murder of blacks by state forces in full view and inaugurated a sharper engagement with persistent racism. Another significant shift is that engendered by "the impact of a generation of African-born or -identified authors like Chimamanda Ngozi Adichie, Teju Cole, and Mfoniso Udofia, who all bring a contemporary diasporic perspective to US race relations" (632). Further Li notes:

> As these writers limn new understandings of blackness, others like James McBride and Colson Whitehead have reimagined familiar historical experiences of slavery and escape with inventive humor and sobering echoes of contemporary racial dynamics. The exciting new voices of Tyehimba Jess, Tarell Alvin McCraney, and Brit Bennett, among many others, echo the innovations of such well-established writers as Yusef Komunyakaa, Suzan-Lori Parks, and Toni Morrison. (632–33)

A recent novel, *Homegoing*, by an American writer of Ghanaian origin, Yaa Gyasi, tells the stories of African people who came to America but also of the families and clans left behind. As slavery flourished and oppressed those who came, their families back home fought battles, supplied captives from these battles as slaves to the British, loved and married and went on with their lives. *Homegoing* shows the intricate family lines that connected those who were taken away with those who were left even when they did not know each other anymore.

Commenting on the diasporic aspect of this literature, Yogita Goyal writes of "three key differences from earlier forms of migration: it is largely voluntary, rather than coerced; it is connected to globalization; and it results from the failure of the postcolonial state" (642). A term like Afropolita, implies the swerve from Atlantic world slavery as the only history for the African American to a global sense of African identity which is diasporic, but also acknowledges different and often more localized histories. These new writers of recent African origin have changed ideas about African American literature even as they have opened up numerous possibilities for the study of diaspora (Goyal 2017).

Candice Jenkins mentions four ideas that mark the contemporary or twenty-first century African American literature: "audience, form, region, and labor" (779): "Audience, then, is a question of not just simple consumption, but also of possibility; which audiences draw what from this body of work that we call twenty-first-century African American literature? How does this literature speak to particular audiences and either 'educate' them or sustain them and mirror their experiences?" (781). Of form, she cites an essay by Abdur Rahman who "provocatively claims that narrative itself fails to offer the expected redress to black subjects" and "argues that the black grotesque embraces this failure, and indeed that its aesthetic approach refuses and ruptures narrative form and 'resists both the narrativization of collective injury and the very notion of remediation'" (782). Of region, Jenkins says,

> [s]ituating twenty-first-century African American literature in a global context need not blind us to the nuances of the local, and – particularly in a moment both when African Americans are migrating south in massive numbers, called by some a reversal of the Great Migration, and when black media and popular culture are dominated by artists working out of Southern cities like Atlanta and New Orleans. (785)

And as her fourth point she urges that critics and readers of this literature "consider in more detail how class, labor, and capital circulate in . . . in African American literature of this century" (786).

The arrival of a new black diaspora from all over the globe has certainly given a fresh impetus to the exploration of black subjectivity. Stephanie Li's 2018 book studies the expansion of the African American literary canon by these diasporic writers and their rethinking of displacement not only as coercive as in the Middle Passage but as voluntary and ebullient. But the issues raised by Jenkins continue to be important and suggest a necessary attention to conditions within the nation that may get lost in the glamour of the transnational turn in African American Literature.

Works Cited

Beatty, Paul. "In Conversation with Oscar Villalon." *Literary Hub*. June 4, 2018. N.p. lithub.com.

Bell, Bernard. *The Afro-American Novel and its Tradition*. Amherst: U of Massachusetts P, 1987.

Bolden, Tony. "Cultural resistance and Avant-Garde Aesthetics: African American Poetry from 1970 to the Present." *The Cambridge History of African American Literature*. Eds. Maryemma Graham and Jerry Ward. Cambridge: Cambridge UP, 2011. 532–65. Kindle EBook (paginated).

Byerman, Keith E. "Anger in a Small Place: Jamaica Kincaid's Cultural Critique of Antigua." *College Literature*, Vol. 22, No. 1, Third World Women's Inscriptions (Feb. 1995). 91–102. https://www.jstor.org/stable/25112166. Accessed 12 April 2022.

Call, Lewis. "Structures of Desire: Erotic Power in the Speculative Fiction of Octavia Butler and Samuel Delany." *Rethinking History*, 9:2–3 (2005). 275–96. doi:10.1080/13642520500149194.

Dery, Mark. "Black to the Future: Interviews with Samuel Delany, Greg Tate and Tricia Rose." *Flame Wars: The Discourse of Cyberculture*. Ed. Mark Dery. Durham, NC: Duke UP, 1994. 179–222.

Dhairyam, Sagri. "'Artifacts for Survival': Remapping the Contours of Poetry with Audre Lorde." *Feminist Studies*, Vol. 18, No. 2 (Summer 1992). 229–56. https://www.jstor.org/stable/3178226. Accessed 23 March 2022.

Dietzel, Susanne B. "The African American Novel and popular Culture." *The Cambridge Companion to the African American Novel*. Ed. Maryemma Graham. Cambridge: Cambridge UP, 2004. 156–70.

Dischinger, Matthew. "States of Possibility in Colson Whitehead's *The Underground Railroad*." *The Global South*, Vol. 11, No. 1, Engaging with the Poetics of Peripheralization (Spring 2017). 82–99. https://www.jstor.org/stable/10.2979/globalsouth.11.1.05. Accessed 28 May 2022.

Dove, Rita and Charles H. Rowell. "Interview with Rita Dove, Part 2." *Callaloo*. Vol. 31, No. 3 (Summer 2008). 715–26. https://www.jstor.org/stable/27654886. Accessed 7 Sept. 2022.

Dubey, Madhu and Elizabeth Swanson Goldberg. "New Frontiers, Cross-Currents and Convergences: Emerging Cultural Paradigms." *The Cambridge History of African American Literature*. Eds. Maryemma Graham and Jerry Ward. Cambridge: Cambridge UP, 2011. 566–617. Kindle EBook (paginated).

Frost, Elizabeth A. "An Interview with Harryette Mullen." *Contemporary Literature*. Vol. 41, No. 3 (Autumn 2000). 397–421.

Gates Jr., Henry Louis and Nellie McKay. Eds. *The Norton Anthology of African American Literature*. New York and London: W.W. Norton & Company, 1997.

Gates Jr., Henry Louis. "The Blackness of Blackness: A Critique of the Sign and the Signifying Monkey." *Black Literature and*

Literary Theory. Ed. Henry Louis Gates. New York: Methuen, 1984. 285–321.

Gleason, William. "The Liberation of Perception: Charles Johnson's Oxherding Tale." *Black American Literature Forum*, Vol. 25, No. 4 (Winter 1991). 705–28. https://www.jstor.org/stable/3041718. Accessed 22 Aug. 2022.

Goyal, Yogita. "We Need New Diasporas." *American Literary History*, Vol. 29, No. 4. 640–63. doi:10.1093/alh/ajx030 Advance Access publication 10 October 2017.

Hampton, Gregory. "In Memoriam: Octavia E. Butler (1947–2006)." *Callaloo.* Vol. 29, No. 2 (Spring 2006). 245–48. https://www.jstor.org/stable/3805596. Accessed: 3 April 2022.

Jarrett, Gene Andrew. Ed. *The Wiley-Blackwell Anthology of African American Literature.* 2 Vols. Malden, Oxford, Chichester: Wiley–Blackwell, 2014.

Jenkins, Candice M. "Black Refusal, Black Magic: Reading African American Literature Now." *American Literary History*. Vol. 29, No. 4, 779–89. doi:10.1093/alh/ajx033. Advance Access publication 23 September, 2017.

Jordan, June. "Childhood Memories, Poetry and Palestine." Interview to David Barsamian. 2000. *Alternative Radio.* https://www.alternativeradio.org/products/jorj002/ cited in poetryfoundation.org. Accessed 12 Feb. 2022.

Keizer, Arlene. *Black Subjects: Identity Formation in the Contemporary Narrative of Slavery.* Ithaca, NY: Cornell UP, 2004.

Killens, John Oliver. "The Writer and Black Liberation." *Black America 1968: The Year of Awakening.* Ed. Patricia Romero. Washington DC, United Publications Corporation, 1969. 265–71.

Kincaid, Jamaica. "Girl." In *The New Yorker,* June 19, 1978. https://www.newyorker.com/magazine/1978/06/26/girl Accessed 13 April 2022.

———. *A Small Place.* New York: Penguin Books, 1989.

Koprince, Susan. "Baseball as History and Myth in August Wilson's Fences." *African American Review,* Vol. 40, No. 2 (Summer 2006). 349–58. https://www.jstor.org/stable/40033723o. Accessed 11 March 2022.

Li, Stephanie. "Introduction: What is Twenty-First Century African American Literature." *American Literary History*, Vol. 29, No. 4,

631–39. doi:10.1093/alh/ajx03.5 Advance Access publication 19 October, 2017.

———. *Pan African American Literature: Signifying in the Twenty-First Century*. New Brunswick, New Jersey: Rutgers UP, 2018.

Little, Jonathan. "Charles Johnson's Revolutionary *Oxherding Tale*." *Studies in American Fiction*, Vol 19, No. 2, (Autumn 1991). 141–51. https://doi.org/10.1353/saf.1991.0027.

Lorde, Audre. *Zami: A New Spelling of My Name*. London: Pandora, 1996 [1982].

Lordi, Emily. "Post-Soul Aesthetics." oxfordbiblographies.com. DOI: 10.1093/OBO/9780190221911-0012.

McMillan, Laurie. "Telling a Critical Story: Alice Walker's 'In Search of Our Mothers' Gardens'." *Journal of Modern Literature*. Vol. 28, No. 1, Autobiography and Memoir (Autumn 2004). 107–23. https://www.jstor.org/stable/3831781. Accessed 22 Aug. 2022.

Moore, Opal J. "Redefining the Art of Poetry." *The Cambridge History of African American Literature*. Eds. Maryemma Graham and Jerry Ward. Cambridge: Cambridge UP, 2011. 497–531. Kindle EBook (paginated).

Morrison, Toni. "Recitatif." In *The Wiley-Blackwell Anthology of African American Literature*. Vol 2: 1920 to the Present. Ed. Gene Andrew Jarrett. Malden, Oxford, Chichester: Wiley-Blackwell, 2014. 823–34.

Naylor, Gloria and Ethel Morgan Smith. "An Interview with Gloria Naylor." *Callaloo*, Vol. 23, No. 4 (Autumn 2000). 1430–39. https://www.jstor.org/stable/3300089. Accessed 21 March 2022.

Neubauer, Carol E. and Maya Angelou. "An Interview with Maya Angelou." *The Massachusetts Review*, Vol. 28, No. 2 (Summer 1987). 286–92. https://www.jstor.org/stable/25089856. Accessed 11 March 2022.

O'Brien, Susie. "The Garden and the World: Jamaica Kincaid and the Cultural Borders of Ecocriticism." *Mosaic: An Interdisciplinary Critical Journal*. Vol. 35, No. 2 (June 2002). 167–84. https://www.jstor.org/stable/44029988. Accessed 22 Aug, 2022.

Peach, Lynden. "Toni Morrison." *The Cambridge Companion to American Fiction after 1945*. Ed. John N. Duvall. Cambridge and New York: Cambridge UP, 2012. 233–43.

Pearl, Monica B. "'Sweet Home': Audre Lorde's *Zami* and the Legacies of American Writing." *Journal of American Studies*. Vol. 43, No. 2 (2009). 297–317. doi:10.1017/S0021875809990041.

Ramsey, William. "An End of Southern History: The Down-Home Quests of Toni Morrison and Colson Whitehead." *African American Review*, Vol. 41, No. 4, Post-Soul Aesthetic (Winter 2007). 769–85. https://www.jstor.org/stable/25426989. Accessed 23 May 2021.

Rushdy, Ashraf H.A. *Remembering Generations*. Chapel Hill: U of North Carolina P, 2001.

Sale, Maggie. "Call and Response as Critical Method: African-American Oral Traditions and Beloved." *African American Review*, Vol. 26, No. 1, Women Writers Issue (Spring 1992). 41–50 https://www.jstor.org/stable/3042075. Accessed 30 May 2020.

Schuessler, Jennifer. "Colson Whitehead on Slavery, Success and Writing the Novel that Really Scared Him." *The New York Times*. 2 Aug. 2016. www.nytimes.com.

Smiles, Robin V. "Popular Black Women's Fiction and the Novels of Terry McMillan." *A Companion to African American Literature*. Ed. Gene Andrew Jarrett. Malden, Oxford, Chichester: Wiley-Blackwell, 2013. 347–59.

Smith, Valerie. "Neo-Slave Narratives." *The Cambridge Companion to the African American Slave Narrative*. Ed. Audrey Fisch. Cambridge: Cambridge UP, 2007. 168–85.

Teague, Jessica E. "The Recording Studio on Stage: Liveness in *Ma Rainey's Black Bottom*." *American Quarterly*, Vol. 63, No. 3, Sound Clash: Listening to American Studies (September 2011). 555–71. https://www.jstor.org/stable/41237566. Accessed 21 Aug. 2022.

Tucker, Jeffrey Allen. "African American Science Fiction." *A Companion to African American Literature*. Ed. Gene Andrew Jarrett. Malden, Oxford, Chichester: Wiley-Blackwell, 2013. 360–75.

Walker, Alice. "Looking for Zora." *The Wiley Blackwell Anthology of African American Literature. Vol 2: 1920 to the Present*. Ed. Gene Andrew Jarrett. Malden, Oxford, Chichester: Wiley-Blackwell, 2014. 735–46.

———. "Zora Neale Hurston: A Cautionary Tale and a Partisan View." *The Wiley-Blackwell Anthology of African American Literature. Vol 2: 1920 to the Present*. Ed. Gene Andrew Jarrett. Malden, Oxford, Chichester: Wiley-Blackwell, 2014. 747–51.

Warner, Marina. "'Among Flowers': Jamaica Kincaid in Conversation." *European Journal of Cognitive Psychology*, Vol. 21, No. 2 (2006). 52–57. doi: 10.1080/02690050600694968.

Weixlmann, Joseph, Ishmael Reed and Clarence Major. "African American Deconstruction of the Novel in the Work of Ishmael Reed and Clarence Major." *MELUS*, Vol. 17, No. 4, Black Modernism and PostModernism (Winter 1991–Winter 1992). 57–79. https://www.jstor.org/stable/467268. Accessed 11 May 2022.

Whitehead, Colson. Interview to Harsimran Gill at Jaipur Literary Festival (Feb 10, 2019, 5.30 pm). https://scroll.in/article/912623/colson-whitehead-on-the-underground-railroad-theres-no-rule-about-what-i-can-write.

Wilson, August. "The Ground on Which I Stand." *Callaloo*, Vol. 20, No. 3 (Summer 1997). 493–503. https://www.jstor.org/stable/3299355. Accessed 20 Aug. 2022.

———. "Fences." *The Wiley-Blackwell Anthology of African American Literature. Vol 2: 1920 to the Present*. Ed. Gene Andrew Jarrett. Malden, Oxford, Chichester: Wiley-Blackwell, 2014. 871–914.

———. *Ma Rainey's Black Bottom*. New York: Penguin Books, 1985.

CHAPTER 8

Conclusion

MATERIAL, APPROACHES AND SOME QUESTIONS

A conclusion to the history of a literature is an uncomfortable admission of the amount of work that is left out. This book has examined and touched upon a fraction of the huge volume of writing that constitutes African American literature. As new books get added to the corpus and writers experiment with the representation of emerging issues, many of the older periods and works are likely to get a new look. As I write I have on my table two books. One, a young adult debut novel, *The Hate U Give* (*THUG*) by Angie Thomas published in 2017, was written against the Black Lives Matter Movement. The second is the latest book by NoViolet Bulawayo (pen name of the Zimbabwean author and Stanford fellow, Elizabeth Zandile Tshele), *Glory,* which was in the Booker longlist for 2022. *THUG* tells the story of the sixteen-year old Starr Carter who lives in a poor neighbourhood and goes to a posh school, and who becomes the only witness to the police shooting of her unarmed childhood friend, Khalil. The shooting, which is similar to so many others that have become a common experience for black people in the US, grabs headlines and inaugurates threats from cops and drug lords to Starr and her family, even as Khalil is painted as a thug and drug dealer. The novel was made into a movie with the same title (George Tillman Jr. 2018). The book and the movie capture the systemic racism that plagues the lives of people of colour as they come up against the state's institutions. Bulawayo's *Glory,* which has been compared to George Orwell's *Animal Farm,* is a modern fable set in a kingdom called Jidada, that represents Zimbabwe but that could be any of the authoritarian regimes of postcolonial Africa, with their dictators replaced by others who soon become the new dictators (in the novel *Old Horse* the dictator is overthrown after forty years of misrule but his replacement is no different). Animal characters take on human characteristics as power, oppression, class struggle and failed political promises are represented with exaggeration and humour. Themes then have become universal even as the oppressions faced by African Americans in the past have now been expanded to include other more transnational experiences. The travel of writers from the Caribbean, and several African countries to the US that began in the early years of the twentieth century is now much expanded and authors like Adichie and Bulawayo have lent a rich and creatively fertile layer to the thinking and representation of race relations, to black identity and to the possibilities of fiction.

The way themes and earlier emphases have changed and *need* to be changed is the point made by Charles Johnson in an essay published in the journal *American Scholar* in 2008 and now anthologised in the *Wiley-Blackwell Anthology* (Vol 2). Titled "The End of the Black American Narrative", this essay begins by giving due acknowledgement to the history of violence and dehumanisation that is the story of slavery and race discrimination in America and declares that the "unique black American narrative, which emphasizes the experience of victimization, is quietly in the background of every conversation we have about black people, even when it is not fully articulated or expressed" (Wiley 2, 1024). But as Johnson goes on to speak of the achievements of black people in all fields and the mix of peoples who now make up the category of the coloured, "a complex and multifaceted people who defy easy categorization" (1027), he sees a new way forward in the twenty-first century. The need is now for newer stories, new vocabularies, and most significantly, for "narratives that do not claim to be absolute truth" but must be "tested everyday" (1030). The shift marked by Johnson is a shift in the community theme as well as in the persistence of the victimisation story – both now modified by the multi-ethnic, transnational story of race.

The category, African American Literature, is now a multifaceted body of work, diverse in character, and addressing the notion of race in multiple ways. But the accompanying scholarly work that helped to reveal and give shape to the literature, showed its character and uniqueness, put together anthologies, produced essays and critiques, re-evaluated periodisations, reviewed the material contexts in which writing happened, and acknowledged the importance of reception, has been equally important. The idea of a distinct literature, not imitative of white writing and attuned to an African American/black sensibility had, of course, been recognised from the time the first anthologies were created. Many of these have been mentioned earlier as have the critical manifestos produced from the time a consciously black literature emerged.

A number of works have been responsible for the recuperative effort that is at the heart of African American literary history – works of criticism and theory without which the exercise of putting together the literary history of a people would have been difficult. Here we can only look at a few selected critical-historical works that have facilitated study of African American literature. By making this aspect of literary historicisation and reconstruction visible, this book tacitly aligns itself with an approach that is drawn from the work of Hayden White, especially his distinction between narrativisation – when historical events speak themselves, and narration – where an identifiable agent narrates the past.

The early years of the twentieth century saw the critical sensibility expressing itself in trenchant, unambiguously separate and oppositional tones, expressing the need for a criticism that would keep creative efforts clearly on track. The most prominent of the voices raised in favour of a distinctive creativity as a necessary counter to the stereotyping of the race in white works was that of Sterling Brown (1901–1989). In his essay "Negro Character as Seen by White Writers", Brown listed seven stereotypes that would become part of subsequent critical rhetoric. These were "contented slave, wretched freeman, comedian or buffoon, brute, tragic mulatto, 'local color' negro, and 'exotic primitive'" (198 cited in Jackson 707). Brown's significant critical work set the ground for many others. The first sweeping study of modern literature, *The Negro Author: His Development in America to 1900* (1931), was published by Vernon Loggins, a Columbia University professor, followed by *The Negro Novelist* (1936) by Nick Aaron Ford and *To Make a Poet Black* (1939) by J. Saunders Redding. Redding offered a sharp critique of Phillis Wheatley for never "utter[ing] a straightforward word for the freedom of the Negro" (10).

Alongside the critical evaluations and surveys, were the major anthologies. While anthology-making had been an ongoing aspect of black scholarship, it was with *The Negro Caravan* (1941), edited by Sterling Brown, Arthur P. Davis and Ulysses Lee, that a modern anthology was made available for academic use. Critical essays and books, and anthologies continued to be produced in the process of shaping and historicising African American literature throughout the twentieth century. Many of those who contributed to this process were among the most powerful figures of this literature and their work has already been referred to in different chapters of this book.

While black studies has been ongoing from the nineteenth century, the rise of critical 'whiteness studies' as a distinct field (with bases in the social sciences), has been important in the process of formalising the long-established practice of black observation and analysis of white attitudes and texts, and has enabled understanding of black texts that often feature white figures or symbols. The persistent use of blackface minstrelsy by whites is the historical occasion for the use of whiteface, and this kind of effort has been noted as a deliberate and systematic device in the plays of Kennedy, Douglas Turner-Ward (*Day of Absence*) and Suzan-Lori Parks (*Topdog/Underdog*). It has made available concepts and motifs, "offering scholars a number of tropes to reference, substantiate, modify, and/or contest" and identified "persistent tropes of whiteness" like "the (anti-)normativity of whiteness, (de)privileging of whiteness, the (im)purity of whiteness, the (in)visibility of whiteness, the interdependence of whiteness and blackness, whiteness as a social construct, and whiteness as paradoxical" (Carpenter 175).

One significant line of thinking stemmed from the debate ongoing during the middle years of the twentieth century that is represented by Mintz and Price's anthropological study of African American culture, over whether African Americans had retained any of the practices of their home cultures, or whether their culture had been formed only in the circumstances of their captivity. In response, a number of works emerged that suggested the links, through collective memories, with Africa. These included *Black Culture and Black Consciousness: Afro-American Folk Thought from Slavery to*

Freedom (1977) by Lawrence W. Levine, *The Slave Community: Plantation Life in the Antebellum South* (1979) by John W. Blassingame, *Flash of the Spirit: African and Afro-American Art and Philosophy* (1983) by Robert Farris Thompson and *Going Through the Storm: The Influence of African American Art in History* (1994) by Sterling Stuckey. A specific site for this kind of thinking was language – the fact that slaves probably never had the opportunity to form linguistically homogenous communities because of the way they were captured and separated from members of their original African tribes, the pressures of speaking the master's language at work, and often the compulsions to learn, speak, read and write in it in order to escape and change their enslaved identities. Zora Neale Hurston in the essay "Characteristics of Negro Expression" (1934) writes that "the Negro has introduced no African words to the language" and yet has also "made over a great part of the tongue to his liking" (Norton 1020–21). The mixing of cultures has been studied also by Shelley Fisher Fishkin who, in *Was Huck Black?* (1994), suggests that Mark Twain's Huckleberry Finn was modelled on a black boy who was portrayed by Twain in a short piece titled "Sociable Jimmy" (21).

The issue of periodisation, crucial to any form of literary history writing, was turned on its head by Kenneth Warren in *What Was African American Literature?* (2011), where he suggested that a consciously African American literature can be said to begin only during the legally segregationist era following the 'separate but equal' Supreme Court judgment in the Plessy vs Ferguson case of 1896.

What has been called the "archival turn" in African American studies has had significant influence in shaping the field in recent years. A 2016 review essay (Rusert) of this phenomenon examines four books that break new ground by returning to the archive and discovering new settings and conditions for texts. These are: *Black Print Unbound: The "Christian Recorder," African American Literature, and Periodical Culture* (2015) by Eric Gardner; *Early African American Print Culture* (2012) edited by Lara Langer Cohen and Jordan Alexander Stein; *Publishing Blackness: Textual Constructions of Race Since 1850* (2013), edited by George

Hutchinson and John K. Young; and *Word by Word: Emancipation and the Act of Writing* (2013) by Christopher Hager. These works variously look at the way print culture contributed to the cultural and intellectual aspirations of African Americans, unearthing new texts and books, many of which had significant presence in the periods during which they were produced but subsequently disappeared. Such texts include the broadsides and pamphlets, as well as visual illustrations that were closely connected to particular events. The place of periodicals and magazines in their time is examined, showing how they were not only platforms for the formation of literary identities but helped in social transformation. They also discover new contexts for well-known texts, reviewing both the books and their times.

While dealing with print history these books draw our attention to earlier archival work done by feminists, anthropologists, sociologists and literary historians in recovering lost texts and writers. Archive-based study of literature also meant the involvement of many disciplines and clearly showed the multi- and interdisciplinary effort that helped shape the now much expanded field of African American Studies, where literature took its place alongside other disciplines in studying the history and culture of the race. Digitisation of the archives has meant a much greater degree of access for scholars not only with regard to literary texts but with supplementary material from the background, newspaper, periodical and magazine archives, tracts, pamphlets, historical and political texts, and in the case of many writers (Du Bois for instance), complete papers and other kinds of resources. Besides the availability of e-resources of different kinds, the institutional access to scholarly journals is particularly enriching. Among these are *African American Review, Journal of African American Studies, Journal of Black Studies, Callaloo, Phylon,* and *MELUS.*

Some interesting new directions have emerged. African American Ecocriticism is one such where the use of postcolonial studies and transnational race studies come together to offer alternative perspectives on diasporic writing. Sonya Posmentier's *Cultivation and Catastrophe* (2017) is an example of this kind of work. She offers fascinating readings of Claude McKay's sonnets and Derek

Walcott's "The Star Apple Kingdom" through the cultivation trope. With McKay she uses the "provision ground" which was the plot at the edge of the plantation to suggest diasporic consciousness. With Walcott she presents an imagination of the Caribbean as "a space of dwelling rather than ownership" (cited in Klestil 193). Besides Postmentier's book, Klestil also reviews two others: *Race Matters, Animal Matters: Fugitive Humanism in African America, 1840–1930* (2018) by Lindgren Johnson and *Civil Rights and the Environment in African-American Literature, 1895–1941* (2017) by John Claborn. These books give a sense of the critical developments in the field.

A particularly engaging critique comes from Anissa J. Wardi's work on water and African American Literature which offers water as a central trope, examining the many ways in which water figures in the history and the literature. She uses it "as a framework for theorizing survival and trauma, diasporic and regional connections, and physical and psychological dislocations" and shows the "confluence of water, loss, and migration in African American culture" (Wardi 3). She writes of "blood and water memory", drawing on August Wilson and his conviction that "blood carries a collective memory" and on Toni Morrison's reading of the Mississippi river floods as a "remembering" by the river of those places where it used to flow before it was straightened out for human uses (5). And in furthering the connection between memory and water, she suggests that, "read through an African American historical prism, humans, who lost their lives in the currents, have, by their very materiality, changed the composition of the waters. Altering the bones that have lain on the ocean floor for centuries, the Atlantic is part of the ancestral past and thus inherent in the collective memory" (8).

Reflecting back on the material referred to in this book, a reader will find much of the older material on different websites and repositories. Texts are available at archive.org, as Gutenberg EBooks, in websites of different universities etc. (many of these are indicated in parentheses in the body of this history as well). Among the key anthologies that have also become popular textbooks are the single volume first edition and the two-volume second edition of *The Norton Anthology of African American Literature* edited by

Henry Louis Gates Jr. and Nellie Y. McKay, and *The Wiley-Blackwell Anthology of African American Literature* in two volumes edited by Gene Andrew Jarrett. These multi-genre works with introductions to periods and authors have been crucial in giving a sense of the development of the literature.

Given the constraints of a *short* history, especially of a literature that is as varied and full bodied as the African American, much has had to be left out. Many authors that readers might look for do not appear or are only briefly mentioned. The general approach has been to discuss at least one or two important figures in each chapter while others are briefly touched upon. Readers will get indications, areas that can be explored further, and sometimes brief discussions of authors who might not be too well known but who are significant for the period in which they appear for the roles they played in public life or the works they produced.

In order to study any national literature, or a branch of it, it is important to acquaint oneself with the history of the race, societies and social developments, relationships amongst people of different races, economic forces at work in the nation, large national goals and the place of a particular people within these, the already existing and development of literacies, education and the effects of many of these processes on the psyche of the community and its individual constituents. These general issues are expected to be enabling for a reader. They will account for aspects of the literature and show how both commonalities and uniqueness evolved. But perhaps most importantly they will help to show what has been made of the material of life, how language and style came to be forged, and what the temper of the people might have been at a given point in its history. Some of this information is provided in the timelines that preface each chapter. While these have been mostly African American specific, the reader would find it enriching to consult a general American history, and American literature timelines as well as a world history timeline in order to get a lateral and vertical sense of literary-cultural-political developments.

I have briefly touched upon the commonalities between African American and Dalit literatures in the Introduction. The similarities and differences in these two experiences of oppression and cultural and socio-economic revivalist projects should be enabling rather than obstructive for the Indian reader. Literatures of the oppressed – African American, Dalit, Holocaust, South Asian, Middle Eastern and East European – offer comparative reading experiences. One might for instance note a tenacious narrative of victimhood that makes for considerable self-absorption in the literature, an obsession that results in formal and stylistic innovations. The example of African American literature should open up newer areas of literary responses to oppression and inequalities across the world.

In an essay on the discipline of English, Patricia Waugh writes:
> Though arguments about English tend to revolve around texts, canons and content, we need more discussion of its singular styles of thinking and practical reason. English might even be thought of as a 'thoughtcraft', ministering to individual needs for the purposive and the contemplative, but having much to offer in providing, for the nonspecialist, a means to grasp the various human challenges thrown up by an ever more complex and globalised world. (25)

As we try to make sense of the literature of another nation, this idea of a "thoughtcraft", a means to make sense of our world through the material and the styles it offers, seems eminently attractive. The body of literature that this book presents has this quality – inherent in its representation of the historical experience of a race that gives us the language and the examples to make sense of our world where the violent, the destructive, the inimical is either a reality or is in the offing. This is one compelling reason for reading this literature – as a salutary lesson on the depths of human action and their transcendence, both lesson and joy.

Works Cited

Carpenter, Faedra Chatard. "Spectacles of Whiteness from Adrienne Kennedy to Suzan-Lori Parks." *The Cambridge Companion to African American Theatre*. Ed. Harvey Young. New York: Cambridge UP, 2013. 174–95.

Brown, Sterling. "Negro Character as Seen by White Authors." *Journal of Negro Education* Vol. 2 (1993). 179–203.

Jackson, Lawrence P. "African American Literature: Foundational Scholarship, Criticism, and Theory." *The Cambridge History of African American Literature.* Eds. Maryemma Graham and Jerry Ward. Cambridge: Cambridge UP, 2011. 703–29. Kindle EBook (paginated).

Wardi, Anissa J. *Water and African American Memory: An Ecocritical Perspective.* Gainesville: UP of Florida, 2011.

Redding, J. Saunders. *To Make a Poet Black.* Ithaca, NY: UP Cornell, 1988 (1939).

Fishkin, Shelley Fisher. *Was Huck Black? Mark Twain and African American Voices.* New York: Oxford UP, 1994.

Rusert, Britt. "From Black Lit to Black Print: The Return to the Archive in African American Literary Studies." *American Quarterly.* Vol. 68, No. 4 (December 2016). 993–1005. https://doi.org/10.1353/aq.2016.0076.

Klestil, Matthias. "New Directions in African American Ecocriticism." (Review article). *ECOZONA.* Vol. 2, No.1. (2020). 192–96. https://doi.org/10.37536/ECOZONA.2020.11.1.3262

Index

Abolition/abolitionists, xvi, 7, 27, 32, 44–46, 50, 54–56, 59–60, 62–64, 224
African American detective novel, 129
African Blood Brotherhood (ABB), 116
Afrofuturism, 221
Agency, xv, xxxv, 32, 40, 118, 136
amanuensis, 44
Angelou, Maya, 173, 185, 200, 204–07, 257
  I Know Why the Caged Bird Sings, 173, 199, 204–06
  "Still I Rise", 185, 205
Attaway, William, 153
autobiography, xiii, xxxvi, 44, 47, 54–55, 65, 77, 80, 84, 89, 99, 120, 126, 144, 154, 164, 173, 178, 196, 199, 204–207, 211, 216, 235, 257

Baldwin, James, 2, 13, 18, 142, 145, 147, 156, 171–72, 247
  "Everybody's Protest Novel", 156
  Go Tell it on the Mountain, 142, 156–57, 170, 172
ballads, 1, 2, 12, 110, 131, 164, 165
Banneker, Benjamin, 24, 43, 154, 240
Baraka, Amiri, xvii, 131, 143, 147, 168, 173, 175–78, 180–85, 188–93, 198, 226, 236, 239
  Dutchman, 143, 178, 191–92, 197–98
  "Myth of a Negro Literature, The", 176
  "Revolutionary Theater, The", 192
Bayonne, 234–35
Beatty, Paul, 251, 254
Black Arts Movement, xi, xviii, 170, 173, 176, 178–80, 183, 185, 190, 192, 197–98, 202, 241, 249
Black Aesthetic, The, 173, 180, 181, 187, 190, 193, 198, 200
Black Fire, 181
Black Lives Matter Movement, xxxv, 251–52, 260
Black Power, 138, 173, 174, 177–78, 180, 186, 192, 202, 210, 235–36, 238, 243
Black speech, xiii, xvi, xxxiv, 2, 6, 8, 125, 174–75, 182, 184
blues, xii, xvi, xxii, 1–3, 8, 14–18, 52, 71, 101, 107, 112, 119–20, 129, 131–32, 135–36, 146, 149, 159–160, 173, 176, 183–84, 186–87, 189, 191, 203, 223, 236–38, 242, 245–46
Bontemps, Arna Wendell, 134, 137
Brooks, Gwendolyn, 145–48, 160, 163–65, 174, 186, 239

Annie Allen, 142, 163
Maud Martha, 142, 163
Street in Bronzeville, A, 142, 163,
Brown, Sterling, 8, 14, 17, 21, 103, 107, 130–31, 134, 136, 138, 141, 262–64, 268
  "Negro Character as Seen by White Writers", 262
  Southern Road, 101, 131, 138
  "When de Saints Go Ma'ching Home", 131, 136
Brown, William Wells, 55–56, 86
  Clotel; or The President's Daughter, 57
  Escape or, A Leap to Freedom, 56
  Narrative of William Wells Brown, A fugitive slave, 56
Bulawayo, NoViolet, 252, 260
  Glory, 260
Butler, Octavia, 200, 204, 217, 222
  Fledgling, 219
  Kindred, 203, 218
  Parable of the Sower, 219
  Parable of the Talents, 219
  Patternmaster, 200, 218
  Wild Seed, 218
  Xenogenesis trilogy, 218

Caribbean, xi, xiv, xvii, 7, 16, 18, 102–03, 105, 113–16, 139, 145, 189, 202, 207, 209, 213–14, 222, 261, 266
Chesnutt, Charles, 90
  "Goophered Grapevine, The", 91, 92
  Colonel's Dream, The, 93, 97
  Conjure Woman, The, 90
  Marrow of Tradition, The, 92
Chicago Renaissance, 104

child/childhood, 39, 65, 93, 96, 121–23, 125, 148, 154, 186–87, 204, 209, 211–13, 215, 236, 250, 256, 260
Christian Recorder, 60, 65, 264
Christian/Christianity, xxii, 8, 24, 30, 47
Civil Rights Movement, 143, 156, 165, 167, 174–75, 178, 181, 225, 227, 238–39
Civil War, xv, xvii, xx, xxxv, 28, 44, 64, 74, 76, 82, 84–86, 92, 105, 127, 137, 164, 166, 225, 234–35
colonialism, xxx, 170, 175, 202–03, 216–17
Colored American Magazine, 71, 73–74, 82, 129
community, xiii–xvi, xviii–xix, xxi–xxii, xxviii, xxxiii, 1, 3, 6–7, 14, 19, 30–31, 34–35, 41, 50, 53, 55, 64, 69, 75, 78, 81, 83–84, 95–96, 103–05, 114, 116–18, 130, 132, 140, 146–47, 155, 157, 161, 169–70, 175, 183–84, 186, 190–91, 193, 195, 211, 214, 222, 224, 229, 231, 233–34, 238–39, 243–44, 246, 261, 264, 267
Cooper, Anna Julia, 82, 85
  Voice from the South by a Black Woman of the South, A, 85,
Cortez, Jayne, 189
  "How Long has Trane been Gone", 189
Countess of Huntingdon, 36–37
Crisis (magazine), xxiii, 80, 101, 106, 111, 115–16, 120–21, 134–35, 138, 156
Cullen, Countee, 102–03, 115, 119–20, 132

Delany, Martin Robison, 60–62
  Blake; or The Huts of America, 61

Condition, Elevation, Emigration, and Destiny of the Colored People of the United States, The, 61
Delany, Samuel, 218, 220
   Dhalgren, 221
   Nevèrÿon, 221–22
   Nova, 220
Douglass, Frederick, 2, 33, 44, 50, 54–55, 61, 75, 77, 88, 132, 158, 224
   Life and Times of Frederick Douglass, The, 50, 55
   My Bondage and My Freedom, 27, 50, 54
   Narrative of the Life of Frederick Douglass, an American Slave, Written by Himself, 50
Dove, Rita, 200, 239, 240, 248, 255
   Museum, 16, 21, 202, 210, 240, 251
   Ten Poems, 200, 240
   Thomas and Beulah, 239–40
   Yellow House on the Corner, The, 240
Du Bois, W. E. B., xxxvii, 71, 99, 106, 115–16, 120, 166, 176, 181, 190, 204, 230
   "Criteria for Negro Art", 81
   Souls of Black Folk, The, 1, 20, 68, 71, 76–77, 79
Dunbar, Paul Laurence, 71, 86

Ellison, Ralph, 2, 14, 15, 18, 130, 145–46, 157, 247
   Invisible Man, 18, 142, 146, 157–60, 171, 203
equality, 13, 34–36, 43, 69–70, 96–97, 130, 142, 153, 167, 175, 185
Equiano, Olaudah, xiv, xvii, 14, 34, 45–46

Interesting Narrative of the Life of Olaudah Equiano, The, 46
   essay, xiv, xxxvi, 15, 17, 39, 45, 59, 62–64, 71–74, 80–81, 84–85, 88, 93–94, 98, 102, 107–09, 113–14, 118–20, 123, 125, 129–30, 145, 147, 149, 152, 153, 156–58, 160, 165–66, 171, 173, 175, 177, 179–81, 185, 187, 191–93, 198, 203, 208–09, 212–14, 217, 226–27, 229–30, 235, 243–47, 254, 261–64, 268
Evans, Mari, xxvii, 179, 186
   "I Am a Black Woman", 187
   "Speak the Truth to the People", 187
exchange, xii, xxiii, xxix, xxxi, 18, 22, 152

Falconbridge, Alexander, xiv, 52
Fauset, Jessie Redmon, 120
   Chinaberry Tree, The: A Novel of American Life, 121
   Comedy, American Style, 121
   Plum Bun: A Novel Without a Moral, 121
   There is Confusion, 107, 120
Federal Writers' Project, 44, 151, 153, 160, 164
Fisher, Rudolph, 107, 129
   "Caucasian Storms Harlem, The", 107, 129
   Conjure Man Dies, The, 129
Freedmen's Bureau, 28, 70, 90
freedom, xv, xvii, xxix, xxxv, 4, 7, 11, 13, 16–17, 23–24, 26–28, 30, 35–36, 40–45, 50, 52, 54, 56, 57, 59, 61–62, 66, 69, 70, 73, 76, 79–80, 87, 106, 109, 118, 136, 143, 144, 161, 166, 170, 175, 188, 193, 205, 213, 224, 234, 262, 264

Fugitive Slave Law, 22, 25, 28, 33
Fuller, Hoyt, 178–79, 181,
  "Towards a Black
    Aesthetic", 179

Gaines, Ernest, 234
  *Autobiography of Miss Jane
    Pittman, The*, 235
  Catherine Carmier, 234
  Of Love and Dust, 234
garden/s, 8, 126, 216, 217, 226–27,
  229–30, 257
Garvey, Marcus, 72, 102, 106,109,
  116, 175–76, 190
Gayle, Addison, 180, 181
  "Introduction" to *The Black
    Aesthetic*, 181
Giovanni, Nikki, 173, 186,
  226, 231
  "Black Power", 173, 180, 186
  "Nikki Rosa", 186
Gospel music, xvi, 2, 14,
Great Awakening, 34, 38
Griggs, Sutton E., 94
  *Hindered Hand, The; or, The
    Reign of the Repressionist*, 96,
  Imperium in Imperio, 94, 99
  Overshadowed, 96
  Pointing the Way, 97, 99
  Unfettered, 96
Grimke, Angelina Weld, 102, 118,
  Rachel, 68, 118–19

Hammon, Briton, 34, 47
  *Narrative of the Uncommon
    Sufferings and Surprizing
    Deliverance of Briton
    Hammon, a Negro Man*, 47

Hammon, Jupiter, 34, 41–42
Hansberry, Lorraine, 145–46, 166
  Raisin in the Sun, 143, 146,
    167–69
Harlem, xi, xvii–xviii, 3, 8, 17,
  20, 74, 81, 99, 101–02, 104–07,
  109–14, 120, 122, 126–27,
  129–30, 132–35, 137–40, 142,
  143, 145–47, 149, 154–60, 173,
  175, 185, 190, 192–93, 195, 213,
  220, 225, 246
Harris, Joel Chandler, xxvi, 8, 73,
  85, 90, 92
Hayden, Robert, 102, 145–47,
  160–61
  "Frederick Douglass", 161–62
  "Letter from Phillis Wheatley
    London, 1773, A", 161
  "Middle Passage", 161–62
Himes, Chester, 130, 153
Hopkins, Pauline, 71, 85, 94, 98,
  100, 129
  magazine novels, 82
  *Of One Blood; or, The Hidden
    Self*, 82
Hopkinson, Nalo, 222
Horton, George Moses, 34, 42–43
Howells, William Dean, 86, 87
Hughes, Langston, xiii, xxii, 2, 9,
  13, 17, 102, 105, 107, 112, 114,
  119–20, 124–25, 134, 164, 168,
  181, 204
  "Jazzonia", 17, 136
Hurston, Zora Neale, xxxi, 9, 37,
  102, 107, 123, 137, 229–30,
  258, 264
  *Barracoon: The Story of the Last
    Slave*, xxxvii, 126
  Dust Tracks on a Road, 126,
    142, 145

Jonah's Gourd Vine, 124
Mule Bone: A Comedy of Negro Life in Three Acts, 125
Their Eyes Were Watching God, 102, 124–25, 138

identity/identities, xii, xiv–xv, xviii, xix, xxviii, xxxiv, xxxvii, 33–35, 56, 69, 72, 83, 85, 89, 102–03, 108, 117–19, 121, 123, 127, 130, 139, 141, 159, 162, 176, 185, 189–90, 193–96, 204, 211, 213–19, 226–27, 229, 242, 249, 253, 256, 261
interactions, xii, xxxi, 29, 162, 217

Jacobs, Harriet, 28, 48, 66
Incidents in the Life of a Slave Girl, 28, 48, 66
Jazz, xvi, 1–3, 8, 14–18, 20–21, 101, 106, 113, 116, 129, 135–38, 140, 146, 157–59, 174–76, 179, 183–85, 189, 191, 225, 232, 237, 242, 245–46
Jefferson, Thomas, 30, 41, 57, 65
Johnson, Charles, 246, 248, 256–57, 261
"End of the Black American Narrative, The", 261
Middle Passage, 200, 248
Oxherding Tale, 247–48
"Where Philosophy and Fiction Meet", 247
Johnson, Fenton, 98
Johnson, Georgia Douglas, 109, 117, 124
Johnson, James Weldon, 71, 88–89, 108, 120, 164, 246

Autobiography of an Ex-Colored Man, The, 89
Jordan, June, 189, 204, 213
Soldier: A Poet's Childhood, 213
Voice of the Children, The, 213
Who Look at Me, 173, 213
journey/s, xvii, xviii, 34, 39, 43, 47, 49, 57, 74, 111, 159, 161–62, 165, 179, 226, 248

Karenga, Maulana, 180
"Black Art: Mute Matter Given Force and Function", 180
Kennedy, Adrienne, 143, 193, 248
Funnyhouse of a Negro, 193
Owl Answers, The, 195–97
Kincaid, Jamaica, 200, 204, 214
Among Flowers: A Walk in the Himalaya, 216
Annie John, 215
Autobiography of My Mother, The, 216
"Girl", 215
Lucy, 216
My Brother, 216
My Garden, 216–17
Small Place, A, 216, 255–56
Knight, Etheridge, 179, 187
Belly Song and Other Poems, 174, 188

Larsen, Nella, xxii, 81, 101, 121, 141
Passing, 22, 121–22
Quicksand, 81, 121–23
Liberator, The (magazine), 63, 111, 128, 182, 222

Locke, Alain, 68, 81, 88, 101–02, 107–08, 120, 124, 137, 145, 171, 223
  New Negro, The, 101, 107–09, 124
Lorde, Audre, 209, 214, 227, 255, 257–58
  "Coal", 210
  "Now That I Am Forever with Child", 210
  "Poetry is not a Luxury", 209, 212
  Sister Outsider: Essays and Speeches, 212
  Soulscript: Afro-American Poetry, 214
  Zami: A New Spelling of My Name, 211, 257
lynching, xxv, 68, 71, 83–84, 96–97, 101, 117, 119, 139, 151, 167, 170, 192, 205, 224

Marrant, John, 34, 47–48
  Narrative of the Lord's Wonderful Dealings with John Marrant, a Black, A, 47
Marshall, Paule, 139, 143, 204, 207, 231
  Brown Girl, 143, 207
  Brownstones, 143, 207
  "Making of a Writer, The: From the Poets in the Kitchen", 208
masking, xx, 39–40, 49, 66
Mason, Charlotte Osgood, 108, 124, 137
McKay, Claude, 17, 81, 101–02, 105, 110, 120, 138–40, 265
  Harlem Shadows, 101, 111, 112

  Home to Harlem, 17, 81, 101, 112–13, 140
McMillan, Terry, 200, 232–33, 258
  How Stella Got her Groove Back, 232–33
  Waiting to Exhale, 200, 232–33
memory, xiv–xvi, xviii–xix, xxi, xxxvii–xxxviii, 4–6, 18, 32, 40, 131, 165, 188, 201, 206, 217, 223, 226, 266, 269
Middle Passage, xiv, xxvii, 3, 34, 38, 45, 46, 52, 126, 161–62, 187, 200, 225, 235, 248, 254
mobility, xiv, xvii, xix, xxxiv, xxxviii, 43, 103
Morrison, Toni, xiii, xvi, xxii, 2, 32, 45, 173, 201, 203–04, 222, 231, 248, 253, 257–58, 266
  Beloved, xv, xix, xxxix, 19, 21, 32, 45, 200, 203, 225, 258
  Black Book, The, 224–25
  Bluest Eye, The, 173, 199, 203, 223
  Desdemona, 225–26
  Dreaming of Emmett, 225
  God Help the Child, 225
  Home, 225
  Jazz, 225
  Love, 224,
  Mercy, A, 38, 42, 51, 225
  Paradise, 225
  "Recitatif", 226, 257
  Song of Solomon, 192, 224
  Sula, 217, 224
  Tar Baby, 224
Mullen, Harryette, 241, 248
  Muse and Drudge, 242
  S*PeRM**K*T, 242

Sleeping with the Dictionary, 242
Trimmings, 241

NAACP, xxiii, 68, 72, 80, 84, 89, 106, 116, 119, 153, 163
Nation, The (magazine), 115, 129
Naylor, Gloria, 200, 230–31, 257
  Women of Brewster Place, The, 231
Neal, Larry, 175, 178–79, 181, 185, 193
  "Black Arts Movement, The", 178–80, 183
Negro spirituals, 12, 42
Neo-slave narrative, xix, 203, 218, 235, 258
New Negro, 10, 68–69, 72, 86, 97–103, 106–09, 114, 120, 124, 138, 141
New Yorker, The (newspaper), 200, 214, 217
Niger River Valley Experiment, 60

Occom, Samson, 41
Opportunity (magazine), 101, 105–07, 111, 116, 124, 134–35, 138

Pan African Congress (PAC), 68, 116
Passing, xxii, 7, 70, 78, 82, 89, 92, 99, 101, 120–23, 141, 225, 247
Petry, Ann, 142, 145–46, 154–56
  Street, The, 142, 154–55
Prince, Lucy Terry, 34, 36
protest, xx–xxi, xxix, xxxv, 14, 23, 25, 46, 64, 73, 81, 101–02, 117, 142, 146, 150, 152, 156, 167–68, 170, 174–75, 181, 228, 247, 252

rap, 3, 15, 18, 185, 241
Reed, Ishmael, 173, 199, 244, 248, 259
  Conjugating Hindi, 244
  Flight to Canada, 244
  Haunting of Lin-Manuel Miranda, The, 245
  Mumbo Jumbo, 174, 199, 244, 246
revolutionary theatre, 192, 239
Rodgers, Carolyn, M., 186
Romances, xxxiv, 131, 204, 232

Sanchez, Sonia, 17, 173, 178, 182, 184–85, 197
  Blues Book for a Blue Black Magic Woman, A, 184
Schomburg, Arthur, 117,
  "Negro Digs Up His Past, The", 118
Schuyler, George Samuel, 129
sexuality, 17, 133, 136, 155, 172, 209, 221–22, 228, 233
signifying, xii, xxxvii, 3, 6, 12, 227, 254, 257
slave narrative, xiii, xvi–xvii, xix, xxxvi, 2, 16, 36, 44–45, 48–49, 56–57, 75, 89, 152, 203–05, 211, 218, 235, 244, 247–48, 258
slave revolt, 23, 25–27, 49
soul (music), 136, 184, 189
Stewart, Maria J., 63
  Productions of Mrs. Maria J. Stewart [speeches], 63
Survey Graphic (magazine), 107

Thomas, Angie, 260
  Hate U Give, The [THUG], 260

Toomer, Jean, 101, 102, 120, 126–29, 160, 230, 247
  Blue Meridian, 127
  Cane, 101, 126–28
transnational, xvii–xviii, xxviii, xxxiv, xxxvii–xxxviii, 3, 61, 103, 105, 115–16, 170, 202–03, 254, 261, 265
Trickster, xxi, xxvi, 2, 7, 125

Underground Railroad, xv, xvii, 13, 25, 27, 54–55, 82, 156, 250, 255, 259
Universal Negro Improvement Association (UNIA), 68, 72, 106, 110, 116, 190
uplift, xiv–xv, xxxv, 40, 69–70, 72–74, 76–78, 80, 83–85, 88, 90, 99–100, 120, 150

victim/victimhood, xix, 35, 37, 114, 244, 268

Walker, Alice, xxxvii, 126, 172, 179, 200, 204, 207, 213, 226, 231
  Color Purple, The, xxvii, 200, 203, 228–29
  In Search of Our Mothers' Gardens, 126, 229, 257
  Meridian, 127, 228
  Possessing the Secret of Joy, 200, 229
  Temple of My Familiar, The, 229
  Third Life of Grange Copeland, The, 228
Walker, David, xxix, 34, 59, 240
  Appeal in Four Articles,
  Together with a Preamble, to the Coloured Citizens of the World, 59
Walker, Margaret, 104, 130, 145–46, 160, 164–65
  For My People, 142, 164–65
  Jubilee, 164–66, 235
  Wall of Respect, The, 183
Walrond, Eric, 101, 114
  Tropic Death, 101, 114–15
Washington, Booker T., xx, 44, 68, 71, 74, 79, 84, 95, 247
  Up from Slavery, 75–77, 87, 109
water, xvii, 12–13, 32, 65, 173, 266, 269
Wells-Barnett, Ida B., 82–83, 84, 85–86
  Mob Rule in New Orleans, 84
  On Lynchings, 84
West, Dorothy, 105, 130, 142
  Living is Easy, The, xxii, 130, 142
Wheatley, Phillis, 34, 36, 126, 162, 262
  "On Being Brought from Africa to America", 38, 126
  Poems on Various Subjects, Religious and Moral, 36
Whitehead, Colson, 249–50, 252–53
  Intuitionist, The, 250
  Underground Railroad, The, 250
Wideman, John Edgar, 241, 243
  Cattle Killing, The, 243
  Glance Away, 243
  Homewood Trilogy, 243

Hurry Home, 243
Wilson, August, 2, 192, 204, 236, 266
  Fences, 192, 238, 256
  Homecoming, The, 173, 185, 236
  Joe Turner's Come and Gone, 236–37
  Ma Rainey's Black Bottom, 237
  Piano Lesson, The, 238
  "Pittsburgh Cycle, The", 236–37
  Seven Guitars, 238
  Two Trains Running, 238
Wilson, Harriet, 57–58
  Our Nig; or, Sketches from the Life of a Poor Black, 57

Wright, Richard, 2, 103–04, 130, 145, 148, 158, 166, 181, 247
  "Blueprint for Negro Writing", 104, 130, 149
  Black Boy, 15, 142, 152–53
  "Ethics of Living Jim Crow, The: An Autobiographical Sketch", 150
  Native Son, 102, 143, 146, 150–53, 165, 203
  Twelve Million Black Voices: A Folk History of the American Negro, 151
  Uncle Tom's Children, 102, 148, 151

Yaa Gyasi, 252, 253
  Homegoing, 253

Other books in the series

For more information, visit www.orientblackswan.com